Beyond Training

CAMBRIDGE LANGUAGE TEACHING LIBRARY

A series covering central issues in language teaching and learning, by authors who have expert knowledge in their field.

In this series:

Beyond Training

Perspectives on Language Teacher Education

Jack C. Richards

CAMBRIDGE
UNIVERSITY PRESS

PUBLISHED BY THE PRESS SYNDICATE OF THE UNIVERSITY OF CAMBRIDGE
The Pitt Building, Trumpington Street, Cambridge, CB2 1RP, United Kingdom

CAMBRIDGE UNIVERSITY PRESS
The Edinburgh Building, Cambridge CB2 2RU, United Kingdom
40 West 20th Street, New York, NY 10011-4211, USA
10 Stamford Road, Oakleigh, Melbourne 3166, Australia

First published 1998

Printed in the United States of America

Typeset in Sabon

Library of Congress Cataloging-in-Publication Data

Richards, Jack C.
Beyond training : perspectives on language teacher education /
Jack C. Richards.
p.   cm.
ISBN 0-521-62270-0 (hc). – ISBN 0-521-62680-3 (pbk.)
1. Language teachers–Training of.   I. Title.
P53.85.R53   1998
418'0071'1–dc21   97-35705
                                                        CIP

A catalog record for this book is available from the British Library

ISBN 0 521 62270 0 hardback
ISBN 0 521 62680 3 paperback

Contents

Contents

Foreword

We have operated for a long time, in the education of second language teachers, as if we knew what we were doing. Or, perhaps more accurately, as if we knew how what we were doing would serve those who were learning to teach. The assumption was that the delivery of teacher education programs and activities was the key to success, and that learning to teach was a by-product of good raw material – capable trainees and skilled trainers – solid designs in short- and long-term training programs, and well-structured teacher-training materials. Delivery was thus synonymous with training, and *training* meant teaching people how to do the work of teaching. Underlying the various surface aspects of delivery, however, lay a rich and complex learning process, the process of learning to teach. Focusing on this learning process, as distinct from the delivery mechanisms, changed our perspectives in important ways. Principally, the shift in focus moved second language teacher education from concern over what content to deliver, and how to deliver it, to the broader and more ambiguous questions of how the content of language teaching is learned and therefore how it can be taught most effectively. The change is as fundamental as it is disorienting, for some, and energizing, for others. But basically, once we recast the focus of teacher education, to move it beyond training to core questions of learning to teach, the landscape of our work is changed permanently.

In this book, Jack C. Richards presides over the change. He brings together, in one volume, papers and talks that he has given over the past several years which open up this landscape. The work is noteworthy for two reasons: the conceptual tools and schemes that he assembles and the overall structure into which he sets these concepts. Just as furniture from a showroom looks better when it is integrated into the space and existing material of a particular room, Richards brings together ideas that have been in recent circulation in second language teacher education but have yet to be clearly set down in relation to one another. In so doing, he performs an invaluable service to our field by recognizing this change in direction in our thinking, and by drawing together useful tools to chart its development.

In the first chapter, Richards begins this mapping process by defining the scope of second language teacher education as he sees it. Defining the scope, or what has been called the *knowledge base,* of second language teaching is not a new undertaking. Beginning two decades ago, Strevens (1976), Spolsky (1978), and Kaplan (1980), among others, proposed various frameworks or models for the relationship between language teaching and the various academic disciplines that inform it, such as psychology, sociology, and linguistics. In fact, Stern's book, *Fundamental Concepts of Language Teaching* (1983), presents a comprehensive summary of the work to date that bears on a general model of language teaching. These antecedents differ significantly from the current work, however. Although they ranged in scale from the specificity of what Larsen-Freeman (1990) called a *theory of second language teaching*, which includes knowledge of language learners, learning, and pedagogy, to the breadth of Stern's (1983) T^1 type theory, which positions language teaching within the larger social and disciplinary milieu, they all took the enterprise of language teaching as their point of departure. The second language teacher is viewed as a dimension of the activity, not the primary focus. But to understand how to educate second language teachers, one must examine and ultimately understand not only the processes of teaching but also the thinking of the teacher (Freeman 1995). And one must examine how that thinking is learned. It is this focus on learning to teach that has pushed professional thinking beyond training to an examination of the full complexity of second language teacher education.

The concept of *second language teacher education* is central to Richards' work in this volume. It has always been an awkward, and at times undefined, hybrid, however. The ways in which we have grouped these four words have shifted over the past ten to fifteen years, implicitly reflecting the shifting conceptual emphasis in our work. In the idea of teacher training, on which the field has been based, we emphasized *second language teacher* education. The focus was, as I said earlier, on how to educate people to teach second languages, and *education* was largely synonymous with *training*. The distinction was thus drawn between the content, that is, the second language, and person of the teacher, on the one hand, and the process, that is, education, on the other. We tended to pay far more attention to the former than to the latter. In fact, until the second half of the 1980s, education was essentially defined as training or delivery of whatever we knew or thought was important about teaching second languages. The complexities of how that knowledge of teaching might be learned or taught were not a central concern. Although some writers in the field had begun to conceive of a hierarchy of functions among teacher training, development, and education (e.g., Freeman 1982; Larsen-Freeman 1983), interest in delineating how people learned to teach was hardly widespread. By 1990 the emphasis in the phrase had begun to shift in earnest to *second language* teacher education. Now the distinction was drawn between second language, as the content or subject matter, and the processes of teacher education, and within teacher education were housed the allied processes of teacher training and teacher development.

In a sense, the publication of Jack Richards and David Nunan's book *Second Language Teacher Education* (1990) marked a major opening in teacher education in the field, as the authors wrote in their preface: "The field of teacher education is a relatively underexplored one in both second and foreign language teaching. The literature on teacher education in language teaching is slight compared with the literature on issues such as methods and techniques for classroom teaching" (p. xi). However, although this work marked a clear move toward examining teacher education in its own right, the notion that learning to teach might itself be a process worth examining and theorizing about had not yet fully taken hold. Thus the relationship between the teaching of teaching and the learning of teaching was still to be examined. Understanding teacher education presented one set of issues; understanding teacher learning presents another. And linking the two is, indeed, a third area of work. In the past ten years, the work on understanding teacher education, its conditions, designs, and processes, has grown and indeed has flourished; this book provides some good examples, as in Chapters 6 and 10. Work on understanding teacher learning, although more recent (e.g., Freeman and Richards 1996), is evolving.

Work remains to be done, however. As a process, teacher learning suggests many questions and directions that have heretofore been ignored or not considered. These include notions of adult learning and development, as in the study of professional life spans, teaching as a career, stages in professional development and so on, the role of socioinstitutional contexts in learning, for example in teacher socialization, and the contingent nature of teachers' knowledge, as Richards discusses in Chapters 5 and 6. Because of its complexity, this terrain of learning to teach is largely uncharted; and there are, as yet, few agreed-upon constructs with which to map it. To do so involves conceptualizing the teacher's inner world and his or her interactions – both in actions and in thought – with the multiple and embedded teaching contexts of institution, students, curriculum, and materials. In terms of the phrase *second language teacher education,* charting the terrain of learning to teach has to encompass an examination of the person of the second language *teacher,* and how he or she thinks, and the process of *education,* and how he or she learns.

In the structure of this volume, Richards outlines one map of this terrain. He begins, in Chapters 2 and 3, by describing teachers' thinking and cognitive activity as the focus of this work. This point of entry moves us beyond training, as his title suggests, to examine how "to engage teachers not merely in the mastery of rules of practice but in an exploration of the knowledge, beliefs, attitudes, and thinking that inform such practice" (p. xiv). This domain, which Walberg (1977) first called teachers' mental lives, is a complicated one, primarily because it is not directly accessible, and so it requires the investigator to make assertions about how it might be organized (see, e.g., Freeman 1996: 736–44). This is what Richards does in Chapters 4 and 5 when he discusses teachers' decision making and pedagogical reasoning as constructs for examining teachers' thought processes. Then, from this inner, private world of teachers' thinking, Richards' discussions move outward, in Chapters 6 and 7, to the public world of teaching. He examines how teachers' decisions and reasoning are enacted through planning and conducting lessons (Chapter 6) and through using teaching materials and texts (Chapter 7). Here the move beyond training is quite clear. From the standpoint of delivery, one would be concerned with how best to train teachers to plan lessons or use textbooks; from the perspective of learning to teach, one wants to study, as Richards does, how lesson planning or the use of texts actually operates, and how thinking guides these public enactments of teaching.

In the last three chapters, Richards turns to the process of educating second language teachers. In Chapters 8 and 9, he discusses two popular means of accessing and working with teachers' thought processes: observing and talking about teaching (Chapter 8) and writing about teaching (Chapter 9). Both procedures serve, in Richards' view, the development of reflective practice because they engage teachers in reviewing and rethinking what they are doing. This technical view of reflection is quite useful in again illuminating how this approach differs from the emphasis in teacher training on carrying out teaching activities "correctly." Here the emphasis is on the teacher examining his or her own reasoning and responses to see how these achieve – or do not achieve – the intended ends. Other writers will point out that this technical focus marks one end of the reflective practice continuum that, at the other end, extends to critical reexamination of the teacher's role, the structure of curricula and materials, and the function of schools in establishing and maintaining social values and order (e.g., Zeichner and Liston 1996). Chapter 10 ends the book with a case study of a teacher education program that advances this cognitive view of learning to teach.

In *Beyond Training*, Jack Richards continues to establish the ground of second language teacher education. He does so by reviewing and compiling recent work in a fashion that creates a feasible map of this territory. In laying out a view of the principal elements and directions of how teachers think about their work, he helps to refocus the attention of the teacher education community in our field from an exclusive concern for how teaching gets done to a more comprehensive view of how teachers think in doing that work, and how they may learn to do it. The ultimate test of this redirection lies with students in the classroom, however. Our aim must not be simply to complicate second language teaching, and what goes into it. Rather, it should be to strengthen both the practice and the professionalism of second language teaching by better understanding the work that second language teachers do and how professional preparation can best serve them in that work.

Donald Freeman

Credits

Chapter 1: From G. M. Jacobs (ed.), *Language Classrooms of Tomorrow: Issues and Responses,* Anthology Series 38, RELC, Singapore, 1966. Chapter 3: From "Teachers' Maxims in Language Teaching," by Jack C. Richards, 1996, in *TESOL Quarterly, 30,* 281–296. Copyright 1996 by Teachers of English to Speakers of Other Languages, Inc. Adapted with permission. Chapter 4: From J. C. Richards, *The Sources of Teachers' Instructional Decisions,* in J. E. Alatis (ed.), *Educational Linguistics, Cross Cultural Communication, and Global Interdependence,* Georgetown University Round Table on Languages and Linguistics, 1994. Chapter 5: From J. C. Richards, "A Comparison of Pedagogical Reasoning Skills in Novice and Experienced ESL Teachers," *RELC Journal* 26(2), Singapore, 1995. Chapter 7: From J. C. Richards, "Beyond the Textbook," *RELC Journal* 24(1), 1993. Chapter 8: From "Teacher Development Through Peer Observation," by Jack C. Richards and Charles Lockhart, in *TESOL Journal,* pp. 7–10. Copyright 1992 by Teachers of English to Speakers of Other Languages, Inc. Adapted with permission. Chapter 9: From J. C. Richards and B. Ho, *Reflective Thinking through Journal Writing,* National Centre for English Language Teaching and Research, Macquarie University, NSW, Australia, May 1993. Chapter 10: From J. C. Richards and M. Pennington, "The First Year of Teaching," *Language Teaching Research* 1(2), 1997, Arnold Publishers, Hodder Headline Group, London.

Preface

This book concerns the beliefs, theories, knowledge, and practices of second language teachers and how these can become the focus of teacher education. The chapters examine a range of interconnected questions confronting anyone involved in the preservice or in-service education of language teachers or the design and evaluation of teacher development programs:

- How is the field of second language teacher education (SLTE) defined, and what does it encompass?
- On what theories, research, and practices is SLTE built?
- What knowledge base is appropriate for preservice and in-service teachers?
- What beliefs and principles do teachers hold, and how do these influence their practice?
- What constitutes skill and expertise in second language teaching?
- What role does experience play in the development of language teachers?
- What kinds of activities can facilitate the professional development of teachers?
- What is the relationship between the content of a teacher education program and the practices of its graduates?

These are the kinds of questions I have had to reflect on in my most recent experience in teacher education and program development. From 1989 to 1996 I served as head of a new Department of English at the City University of Hong Kong and, together with a group of exceptional colleagues, was responsible for developing both preservice (BA TESL) and in-service (MA TESL) degrees for teachers and teachers in training. At the same time, the university itself was implementing a variety of programs and initiatives designed to ensure the quality of its programs, teaching, and research as well as the long-term professional development of its academic staff. This book results from this experience, which took place in a city that provided a fascinating context for exploring the dynamics of language teaching and teacher education in a bicultural environment.

The book reflects changes in how I have come to understand my own work as a teacher educator over the years, as well as changes in the philosophy informing the field of SLTE. The title of the book – *Beyond*

Training – reflects this reorientation away from *training* as the primary focus of teacher preparation toward one that seeks a more holistic approach to teacher development, built on the notion of the teacher as *critical and reflective thinker.* By a *training perspective,* I am referring to a technical view of teaching which assumes that teaching can be defined in terms of a specified set of effective teaching practices and competencies, that these can be taught and tested, and that their application is sufficient to produce good second language teaching. Such competencies, or skills, are often identified with procedural and managerial aspects of teaching, such as lesson planning, rules and routines for classroom management, strategies for setting up grouping and seating arrangements, ways of opening and closing lessons, techniques for effective questioning, eliciting, and giving feedback.

Without discounting the importance of basic teaching skills in teacher preparation, the orientation to teaching discussed in this book is an attempt to look beyond these dimensions of teaching to the beliefs, knowledge, and thinking that underlie their successful use. The argument pursued throughout the book therefore is that teacher education needs to engage teachers not merely in the mastery of rules of practice but in an exploration of the knowledge, beliefs, attitudes, and thinking that inform such practice. This is a long-term process for which teacher education programs can establish only the starting point.

The opening chapter presents a framework for the book as a whole and identifies six domains of content and knowledge which I see as constituting the knowledge base of SLTE, namely, general theories of teaching, teaching skills, communication skills, subject matter knowledge, pedagogical reasoning and decision making, and contextual knowledge. The role of these dimensions of teacher knowledge and expertise is explored from different perspectives throughout the book.

Part I examines two different types of teaching theories that influence the beliefs and practices of teachers. Chapter 2 examines theories of teaching derived from research, theory, or practice and how these lead to different assumptions about the role of teachers and the nature of teaching skills. A number of theories of teaching are discussed, including science-research conceptions, theory- and values-based conceptions, and art-craft models of teaching. This chapter emphasizes the importance of reflecting on the theories, assumptions, and values underlying our teacher education practices, and the need to clearly articulate the teaching principles that a second language teacher education program seeks to impart to its graduates. Chapter 3 examines teachers' implicit theories of teaching and introduces the notion of teaching maxims, or personal working principles that teachers develop and that account not only for their interpretation of good practice but also provide the source for many of the interactive decisions teachers make while they teach.

Part II presents several perspectives on the nature of teacher thinking. Chapter 4 draws on research into teacher cognition and examines the effect of teachers' belief systems on their understanding of good teaching practice, as well as the effects of interactive decision making on classroom processes. The importance of focusing on teachers' cognitive and interpretative skills in teacher development activities is emphasized. Chapter 5 addresses the nature of teachers' pedagogical reasoning skills and the different kinds of thinking employed by novice and experienced teachers in planning lesson content. It also looks at the contributions to pedagogical reasoning of subject matter knowledge and experience. Chapter 6 examines teachers' use of lesson plans. The comparison of less experienced and experienced teachers' use of lesson plans demonstrates that a central dimension of teaching is "improvisational performance," or the ability to teach interactively and creatively while drawing on lesson content, plans, and student feedback to negotiate instruction on a moment-to-moment basis.

Practices in teacher education are the focus of Part III. Chapter 7 examines the role of textbooks in teaching, and considers the extent to which textbooks enhance or hinder creative teaching. The notion of deskilling is examined, and activities that attempt to develop teachers' ability to use textbooks critically and creatively are illustrated. Chapter 8 looks at how classroom observation activities can be used to move beyond a focus on teaching behaviors to assist teachers in developing a critically reflective approach to their own teaching. Chapter 9 looks at the use of teaching journals and the extent to which journal writing facilitates the development of critically reflective thinking.

The final section of the book describes a study of five novice teachers and the experiences they faced in their first year of teaching. Chapter 10 focuses on the ways in which the teachers were expected to teach upon completing their initial training, the extent to which teachers can employ the practices and thinking they were exposed to in their preservice program, and the restrictive factors they encounter in their initial teaching experiences.

I hope that the book as a whole will help in articulating a theoretical framework for the field of second language teaching education, clarifying some of the issues that are involved in developing a pedagogy of SLTE, and help identify an appropriate research agenda for the field. While I do not claim to offer many definitive answers to the foregoing questions, I hope that readers find that the explorations of the questions my colleagues and I have engaged in will stimulate their own research, theorizing, and professional practice.

My understanding of the field of second language teacher education has benefited greatly from ongoing dialogue with a number of colleagues over the years, in particular Kathleen Bailey, Donald Freeman, Karen Johnson, Dino Mahoney, David Nunan, and Martha Pennington, whose advice and encouragement are gratefully acknowledged. Thanks also to Sandra Graham for skillful editing of the manuscript.

Jack C. Richards

1 The scope of second language teacher education

This chapter presents an overview of the field of second language teacher education (SLTE) by considering its constituent domains of knowledge, skill, understanding, and awareness, as well as the different types of teaching activities that can be used in SLTE programs. The former are described as content and the latter as process issues. The field of SLTE is concerned with determining appropriate curricular content and effective instructional processes in language teacher education programs.

Content issues in SLTE

The content of the field of SLTE is a fundamental issue, though it has generated relatively little discussion in the considerable literature on language teaching. There is no general consensus on what the essential knowledge base or conceptual foundation of the field consists of. Perhaps this is inevitable with a field that draws on a variety of disciplinary sources, including linguistics, psycholinguistics, sociolinguistics, and education. Freeman (1989: 27) observed:

Language teacher education has become increasingly fragmented and unfocused. Based on a kaleidoscope of elements from many different disciplines, efforts to educate individuals as language teachers often lack a coherent, commonly accepted foundation. In its place, teacher educators and teacher education programs substitute their own individual rationales, based on pedagogical assumptions or research, or function in a vacuum, assuming – yet never articulating – the bases from which they work.

In this chapter, six domains of content are proposed as constituting the core knowledge base of SLTE – theories of teaching, teaching skills, communication skills, subject matter knowledge, pedagogical reasoning and decision making, and contextual knowledge. The first part of the chapter describes these domains, and the second part discusses the instructional processes that address each domain. In attempting to conceptualize language teaching in this way, however, it must be acknowledged that I am isolating points of reference in what is essentially a multifaceted yet integrated activity. Each of the domains discussed here overlaps and

1

intersects with others, yet each raises distinct issues in teacher education and hence merits independent consideration.

Theories of teaching

At the core of SLTE is a theory of teaching that provides the theoretical basis for the program as well as the justification both for the approach to teaching as well as the instructional practices students are expected to develop in the program. Teachers also teach within the context of a framework of beliefs that shapes their planning and interactive decisions. Theories of teaching are therefore central to how we understand the nature and importance of classroom practices. There are numerous conceptions of teaching in education. Teachers have been compared to scientists, to managers, to laborers, and to crafts persons (Darling-Hammond, Wise, and Pease 1983), and each of these conceptions embodies a different understanding of the essential knowledge and skills teachers need. As Posner (1985) observes, different theories of teaching lead to a different understanding of classroom life. For example, a *didactic view* of teaching is based on the belief that teaching is primarily concerned with transmitting knowledge through providing clear explanations, demonstrations, or discussions. A *discovery view* of teaching, by contrast, is based on the belief that students can develop knowledge themselves through active investigation and discovery, with a minimum of teacher structure and explanation and with provision of opportunities to learn inductively from direct observation. An *interactionist view,* on the other hand, holds that students arrive with well-formed ideas, so that there is a necessary interaction between the students' own ideas, their empirical observations, and the curriculum content.

Theories and frameworks such as these are generally formulated by educational researchers and theorists, and there is no shortage of such theories in the educational literature. The *International Encyclopedia of Teaching and Teacher Education* (L.W. Anderson 1995), for example, has chapters on nine different theories of teaching, including behaviorist, cognitive-developmental, information-processing, and social-psychological theories. While general teaching theories such as these have informed approaches to mainstream teaching since the 1960s, theories specific to the nature of second language teaching and learning have been developed and have often formed the basis for specific methodologies of language teaching, such as audiolingualism, the communicative approach, or the Natural Approach (see Richards and Rodgers 1986). Theories of teaching and how they reflect different views of the essential skills of teaching are the focus of Chapter 2.

While SLTE programs often reflect a particular theory of teaching, teaching is also a highly personal and individual activity. Teacher development involves teachers in creating an approach that draws on their experience and understanding as well as their personal principles and beliefs about good teaching. These are known as teachers' *implicit theories of teaching:*

The explanations given by teachers for what they do are typically not derived from what they were taught in teacher education programs. . . . Rather, the classroom actions of teachers are guided by internal frames of reference which are deeply rooted in personal experiences, especially in-school ones, and are based on interpretations of those experiences. (Marland 1995: 131)

The role of teachers' principles and beliefs and how these shape their approaches to teaching has become an issue of increasing significance in our understanding of teaching (e.g., Breen 1991; Woods 1996); teachers' implicit theories of teaching are the focus of Chapters 3 and 4 in this volume. Research on these issues suggests that teachers filter much of the content of SLTE programs through their own belief systems, and that this process needs to be understood in developing effective approaches to SLTE (see Almarza 1996). As teachers develop in their skills, awareness, and knowledge, they move from a level of what has been termed *technical rationality* (Putorak 1993), where the focus is on mastery of basic teaching techniques and skills (i.e., classroom competency), to a level that has been called *critical reflection,* where teaching is guided by the teacher's personal theory and philosophy of teaching, and is constantly renewed by critical reflection and self-assessment. Reflective approaches to teacher education programs often seek to engage teachers in articulating and examining the assumptions that underlie their teaching, and in developing personal principles of best practice that can support their approach to teaching (see Chapter 9).

Reflective approaches to teacher development start from the assumption that teachers, rather than methods, make a difference; that teachers are engaged in a complex process of planning, decision making, hypothesis testing, experimentation, and reflection; that these processes are often personal and situation-specific; and that they should form the focus of teacher education and teacher professional development. This approach involves teachers developing their own individual theories of teaching, exploring the nature of their own decision-making and classroom practices, and developing strategies for critical reflection and change.

Teaching skills

Skill in teaching a language would appear to be the core competency of a language teacher. But what does such skill consist of? This question can be approached by examining to what extent a language teacher is different from the teacher of other subjects. If we were to compare a language teacher with, say, a teacher of geography, we might conclude, first, that both need to be good teachers, but that they differ in their knowledge of the subject of their specialization and how to teach it. A language teacher might not normally be expected to be able to teach a good geography lesson, and vice versa, without special training. But what is there about being "a good teacher" that is common to both kinds of teachers?

The literature on education has traditionally identified a core of generic teaching skills that underlie competence in teaching any type of subject matter. L. S. Shulman (1987) refers to these as constituting the domain of *instruction:*

[Instruction] involves the observable performance of the variety of teaching acts. It includes many of the most crucial aspects of pedagogy: organizing and managing the classroom; presenting clear explanations and vivid descriptions; assigning and checking work; and interacting effectively with students through questions and probes, answers and reactions, and praise and criticism. It thus includes management, explanation, discussion, and all the observable features of effective direct and heuristic instruction already well-documented in the research literature on effective teaching. (1987: 17)

Teaching skills, or what Shulman terms *instruction,* refer to those dimensions of teaching regarded as essential to the repertoire of any teacher, regardless of subject. No matter what the content of a lesson might be, teaching typically involves:

- selecting learning activities
- preparing students for new learning
- presenting learning activities
- asking questions
- checking students' understanding
- providing opportunities for practice of new items
- monitoring students' learning
- giving feedback on student learning
- reviewing and reteaching when necessary

In addition to skills of this kind, which are part of the basic competency of all teachers, language teachers presumably need to acquire additional teaching skills that are specific to language teaching. Teacher-training schemes for language teachers, such as the RSA Diploma – a widely recognized ESL/EFL teaching qualification (Cambridge University 1991) describe such skills in detail as a basis for the assessment of language teachers, and include the following second language teaching skills:

- preparation of communicative interaction activities (e.g., group work, games, role plays, simulations)

- organization and facilitation of communicative interaction
- judgment of proper balance between fluency and accuracy
- awareness of learners' errors
- appropriate treatment of errors

Gower and Walters (1983) include skills such as:

- presenting language
- controlled practice
- checking
- eliciting dialogues and narratives
- using dialogues
- using texts
- setting up communication activities

The description of teaching in terms of skills is only one dimension of a theory of teaching, however, since there are a number of problems in describing teaching in this way. As we see in Chapter 2, different theories of teaching assume a priority for different teaching skills. The audiolingual method, for example, emphasizes a different set of skills from the communicative approach. In addition, the idea that good teaching can be reduced to a list of discrete behaviors or competencies ignores the fact that many of the skills so identified are linked to higher-level cognitive processing and decision making, as is shown in Chapters 4, 5, and 6. For example, even a traditional teaching technique such as choral repetition, if it is to be used at all, involves selecting from different types of repetition drills and knowing when a particular type of drill might be appropriate. While the ability to perform a choral drill might be a technical skill based on mastering certain rules of presentation, knowing when to use such a drill is not and involves a higher level of thinking and decision making.

Notwithstanding the limitations of the notion of skills, at the practical level the design of any teacher education program has to confront how basic teaching competency will be addressed and which skills will be the focus of the program at different levels. In an important article, Tetenbaum and Mulkeen (1986) hypothesize characteristics of the technological society of the twenty-first century and how teacher education would be affected. One of their conclusions is that teacher education will become increasingly competency based, a prediction that has been borne out by trends in TESOL teacher education throughout the 1990s. The current move toward performance-based and competency-based certification and assessment in SLTE in many parts of the world suggests that examination of the nature of basic skills in language teaching is a matter of some urgency.

Communication skills

GENERAL COMMUNICATION SKILLS

Since the medium for the teaching of any subject matter is normally speech, it is not surprising that the ability to communicate effectively is often considered one of the essential skills of a good teacher. When people say that someone is "a born teacher," they are often referring to the fact that people differ in their capacity to express themselves clearly and effectively, and that some people are more successful communicators than others. Cooper comments:

Although many variables affect classroom learning, it is generally agreed that the paramount variable is communication. The essence of the teaching-learning process is effective communication for without communication, teaching and learning would be impossible. Thus, one of the core components of teacher education should be speech communication. (1993: 473)

The importance of communication skills is recognized in the assessment scheme for the RSA Diploma, which includes a number of general communication skills on which to assess candidates, such as:

– personality, presence, general style
– voice – audibility, ability to project, modulation
– voice – speed, clarity, diction
– ability to establish/maintain rapport

There is a large literature on speech and communication, generally intended for native speakers, that addresses skills of this type, and recognition of the link between communication skills and teaching skills is seen in the fact that a number of SLTE programs are located within departments of speech and communication. Few SLTE programs, however, include general communication skills in their curriculum.

One of the practical questions that arises in training language teachers is whether there should be specific activities in the curriculum, not necessarily linked to the content of language teaching per se, that address general communication skills. There are various approaches to addressing communication skills in an SLTE program. For example, student teachers can be required to do their practice teaching initially in a subject area other than language. They might demonstrate a craft to their peers, discuss a style in art, or carry out a science demonstration to enable communication skills to be discussed and practiced. Afterward they go on to do practice teaching with second language classes. In some programs, activities such as public speaking and oral presentations are included for similar reasons.

LANGUAGE PROFICIENCY

There is an additional dimension to the issue of communication skills in SLTE, since many language teachers are nonnative speakers (NNS) of the languages they teach. Presumably one needs to attain a certain threshold level of proficiency in a language to be able to teach effectively in it, and activities addressing language proficiency are often a core component of many SLTE programs (see Chapter 10). Two key questions arise from a consideration of the significance of language proficiency for second language teachers: namely, what components of language proficiency are most crucial for language teachers, and how language proficiency interacts with other aspects of teaching skill.

The first question raises the issue of the nature of instructional discourse, and in particular the discourse used by second language teachers. Heaton (1981), in one of the first books to address this issue, argues that classroom discourse for language teaching contains a specific set of speech acts and functions, and fluency in these is essential for NNS language teachers. Among the functions he identifies as essential are:

– requesting, ordering, and giving rules
– establishing attention
– questioning
– repeating and reporting what has been said
– giving instructions
– giving and refusing permission
– warning and giving advice
– giving reasons and explaining

Inability to perform these functions fluently in English can lead to lack of clarity in giving directions and instructions, as well as the need to resort to the mother tongue if the teacher is teaching a linguistically homogeneous class (see Chapter 10). Willis (1981: 2) systematically reviews and practices the language needed by teachers "for the effective use of classroom English and to extend their language teaching skills and techniques," and provides extensive examples of linguistic expressions and routines that NNS teachers can use in teaching the different stages of a lesson. Spratt describes her book *English for the Teacher* (1994: 1) as "a language improvement course for [NNS] teachers" and addresses both classroom language and the English teacher's need for taking part in in-service training and professional development.

The relationships between the teacher's proficiency in the teaching language and general teaching skills is explored by Heaton (1981), who proposes the interdependence of the two:

One of the basic assumptions underlying the approach here is that language cannot be divorced from content and practice. It is considered impossible, for instance, to teach English appropriate to the needs of the practicing teacher without teaching basic classroom skills at the same time. By improving the language skills of the teacher, the course deliberately seeks to improve the particular teaching skills which involve the use of those skills. (1981: 14)

Therefore, for NNS language teachers, language proficiency can be seen as a factor that affects many aspects of teaching expertise, including teaching skills and subject matter knowledge.

Subject matter knowledge

Subject matter knowledge refers to what second language teachers need to know about their subject – the specialized concepts, theories, and disciplinary knowledge that constitute the theoretical basis for the field of second language teaching. Courses in areas such as the following are typical in both preservice and in-service SLTE programs, and reflect views as to what constitutes appropriate subject matter for second language teachers:

– phonetics and phonology
– English syntax
– second language acquisition
– curriculum and syllabus design
– discourse analysis
– sociolinguistics
– analysis of TESOL methods
– testing and evaluation

An examination of the course requirements in a sample of fifty MA TESOL programs listed in the TESOL directory reveals the following required courses (Richards 1991):

Type of required course in MA TESOL programs	*Number of programs that require each course*
TESOL methods and materials	47
English grammar/syntax	36
linguistics	36
practice teaching	33
phonology	32
second language acquisition	29
syllabus/curriculum design	24
testing	24
research in TESOL	16
language and culture	12
teaching reading	11
contrastive error analysis	11

sociolinguistics	11
bilingual education	10
teaching writing	10
history of English	7
psycholinguistics	5

Subject matter knowledge refers to what teachers need to know about what they teach (rather than what they know about teaching itself – see Cochran, DeRuiter, and King 1993) and constitutes knowledge that would not be shared with teachers of other subject areas, or indeed with nonteachers. (The role of subject matter knowledge and how it interacts with pedagogical reasoning skill is discussed in Chapter 5.) Ideas as to what constitutes the essential subject matter knowledge of the field of second language teaching clearly differs according to the theoretical orientation specialists have toward their subject matter.

Freeman (1989) argues that SLTE is confused about its subject matter base because the profession has failed to appreciate the distinction between language teaching and the areas of inquiry on which it is based (e.g., linguistics, applied linguistics, second language acquisition). He points out that *applied linguistics* and *methodology,* often assumed to be the core subject matter of language teaching, should not be confused with teaching itself, and "should not be the primary subject matter of language teacher education" (1989: 29). An alternative and more traditional view of the appropriate subject matter knowledge of SLTE is given in Diller:

The professional teacher of English as a Second Language needs pedagogical training to be a teacher, and academic training in English language and linguistics to be a professional in our field. But of the two, there is a certain priority for English language and linguistics, for a decision on the nature of language and on the psycholinguistic mechanisms of language acquisition will determine to a large extent our decision on the principles and methods of teaching. (Diller, cited in Richards and Hino 1983: 318)

An additional dimension of subject matter knowledge is the specialized discourse or register that language teachers use to talk about their discipline. Freeman and Cazden (1991: 7) point out that this professional discourse serves two important purposes: "One is a social/referential function which allows the teachers to make themselves part of the discourse community as they use it. The other is a cognitive function, which enables them to identify aspects of their experience and thus to organize and to develop their conceptions of teaching."

In a study of teachers completing a basic preservice short training course, the UCLES/RSA Certificate, Richards, Ho, and Giblin (1996) noted that the participants were introduced to a particular discourse for talking about teaching. Key terms in this discourse were *accuracy, concept checking, eliciting, feedback, fluency, intonation, modeling, monitoring, orchestration, practice, presentation, production, sequencing, stress, structure, skills, syllable,* and *target language.* Terms such as these belong to the metalanguage of the UCLES/RSA Certificate approach to teaching and would not be familiar to specialists outside of language teaching.

Pedagogical reasoning skills and decision making

The concepts of pedagogical reasoning and decision making focus on the complex cognitive skills that underlie teaching skills and techniques. While competence in a teaching methodology and the mastery of teaching skills and techniques may be thought of as the starting point in teacher development, they need to go hand in hand with an examination of the specialized thinking and problem-solving skills that teachers call upon when they teach. L. S. Shulman (1987: 15) sees pedagogical reasoning as constituting the essence of teaching:

The key to understanding the knowledge base of teaching lies at the intersection of content and pedagogy, in the capacity of a teacher to transform the content knowledge he or she possesses into forms that are pedagogically powerful and yet adaptive to the variations in ability and background presented by the students.

Shulman (1987: 15) describes the transformation phase of this process as consisting of:

Preparation: critical interpretation and analysis of texts, structuring and segmenting, development of a curricular repertoire, and clarification of purposes

Representation: use of a representational repertoire that includes analogies, metaphors, examples, demonstrations, explanations, and so forth

Selection: choice from among an instructional repertoire that includes modes of teaching, organizing, managing, and arranging

Adapting and tailoring to student characteristics: consideration of conceptions, preconceptions, misconceptions, and difficulties; language, culture, and motivations; and social class, gender, age ability, aptitude, interests, self-concepts, and attention

Understanding the nature of pedagogical knowledge and reasoning and how it is developed is critical for the development of SLTE programs. (See also Chapter 5 on the pedagogical reasoning skills of ESL teachers.)

A related dimension of teaching is the nature of the pedagogical knowledge and decisions that teachers employ while they teach. Teaching is a dynamic process characterized by constant change. Teachers therefore have to make decisions that are appropriate to the specific dynamics of the lesson they are teaching. These kinds of decisions are called *interactive decisions*. As Parker (1984: 220) observes, "Teaching-learning contexts change, and teachers' behaviors must change accordingly. The basic problem for teachers is, therefore, to acknowledge that there is no one best way to behave, and then to learn to make decisions in such ways that their behaviors are continually appropriate to the dynamic, moment-to-moment complexity of the classroom." There are a number of components to an interactive decision:

– monitoring one's teaching and evaluating what is happening at a particular point in the lesson
– recognizing that a number of different courses of action are possible
– selecting a particular course of action
– evaluating the consequences of the choice

The ability to monitor one's own instruction and evaluate it in terms of its appropriateness within a specific and immediate context is central to interactive decision making. It involves observing a lesson as it proceeds and asking questions of the following kind:

– Do the students understand this? Are my instructions clear and understood?
– Do I need to increase student involvement in this activity?
– Is this too difficult for the students?
– Should I try teaching this a different way?
– Is this taking too much time?
– Is this activity going as planned?
– How can I get the students' attention?
– Do students need more information?
– Do I need to improve accuracy on this task?
– Is this relevant to the aims of the lesson?
– Do students have the vocabulary they need in order to do this task?
– Is this teaching students something that they really need to know?
– Am I teaching too much rather than letting the learners work it out for themselves?

(Richards and Lockhart 1994: 84)

The comparison of interactive decision making among teachers with differing levels of teaching experience (see Chapter 6) enables the nature of teaching expertise to be more fully understood and can generate useful information for SLTE programs. The ability to make appropriate interactive decisions is clearly an essential teaching skill, since interactive decisions enable teachers to assess students' responses to teaching and to modify their instruction in order to provide optimal support for learning. K. E. Johnson (1992b) examined the interactive decision making of preservice ESL teachers, and found that they tended to rely on a limited range of instructional thoughts and actions in response to student performance cues.

Contextual knowledge

An important component of a language teacher's knowledge is an understanding of how the practice of language teaching is shaped by the contexts in which it takes place, and the role of societal, community, and institutional factors in language teaching. Posner (1985) points out that a key factor in understanding any teaching situation is the social and physical context – the "rules, facilities, values, expectations, and personal backgrounds, which act as resources, constraints, and direct influences on teaching and learning" (Posner 1985: 2). Among the contextual factors that need to be considered in language teaching are:

– language policies (e.g., status of the target language in the community)
– language teaching policies (e.g., required or optional subject, intensity of delivery)
– community factors (e.g., parents' expectations, community support)
– sociocultural factors (e.g., status of learners' native language, cultural values)
– type of school or institution (e.g., state, private, tertiary)
– administrative practices (e.g., line management, teachers' duties, work load)
– school culture (e.g., established beliefs and practices)
– school program (e.g., reception class, pullout class, transitional class)
– level of class (e.g., elementary, intermediate, advanced)
– age of learners (e.g., children, teenagers, adults)
– learning factors (e.g., learners' motivations, learning styles)
– teaching resources (e.g., syllabus, textbooks, other resources)
– testing factors (e.g., role of school and national tests)

Ashworth (1985: 1) is one of the first books to address these issues and considers "the relationship between language teaching and the community, and the ways in which teachers are both affected by broader social, political and economic policies and can also have an effect on those policies." Holliday (1994), in a book entitled *Appropriate Methodology and Social Context,* reflects a similar concern to examine the wider social contexts of second language teaching and employs an ethnographic framework to examine the relations between the cultures of language classrooms, student groups, and teachers. Both books emphasize that teaching methodologies that are not responsive to contextual issues are likely to be irrelevant and ineffective, and that SLTE programs need to equip student teachers with the ability to identify and understand relevant contextual factors in their own teaching situations.

For example, a teacher may believe in a particular philosophy of teaching but find, upon taking up a teaching position in a school, that this philosophy does not match with students' or parents' expectations. Potential areas of mismatch are many, such as differences in expectations about the role of grammar, the importance of examinations, the function of textbooks, the value of homework, and so on. The teacher may discover that despite believing in the importance of making classrooms communicative and learner centered, students' overriding concern is the extent to which teaching prepares them for an examination. Developing strategies for understanding the importance of contextual factors in language teaching is hence crucial in the design of SLTE programs. Such strategies need to be built into many components of the program, providing a framework for the delivery and interpretation of subject matter knowledge.

Posner (1985) prepares student teachers for practice teaching and other field experiences by engaging them in situation analysis. This consists of observations and conversations that focus on (1) the community or neighborhood in which the field experiences will take place; (2) the particular school agency or institution, including the physical, social, and personal setting; (3) the room or space in which the student teacher works; and (4) the cooperating teacher.

Interrelationships between the six dimensions of teaching

The foregoing analysis describes six dimensions of expertise, knowledge, and skill in language teaching in order to help map out the content domain of second language teaching. A key issue that arises from this discussion is the interrelationship of these different dimensions of teaching. Are they all equally important? Do they develop simultaneously, or are some the foundation for the development of others? For example, communication skills and proficiency in the teaching language would seem to be prerequisites to the development of basic teaching skills. Inadequate target language proficiency may lead to inadequate access to basic teaching skills, such as the ability to use questions effectively, or an inability to provide comprehensible explanations in the teaching language. Mastery of basic teaching skills would seem to be a prerequisite to acquiring a reflective and personal philosophy of teaching. Acquisition of subject matter knowledge as well as contextual knowledge provides a foundation for the development of pedagogical reasoning skills

13

and decision making, and the type of subject matter content and practical skills training student teachers receive will shape their pedagogical reasoning skills and decision making in different ways. A teacher with a firm training in phonetics and phonology, for example, might be expected to incorporate a focus on pronunciation into oral tasks, and to respond to various students' pronunciation errors differently from a teacher without such training.

Teachers' personal theories of teaching may provide either a positive or negative filter to acceptance of subject matter knowledge or general teaching skills. Almarza's study (1996) shows how teachers in a teacher education program respond differently to the theoretical model of teaching that underlies the program, some rejecting it because it is not in alignment with their personal theory of teaching. Personal theories of teaching may therefore be the key to the development of a teacher's overall understanding and approach to teaching.

Research on teacher cognition (e.g., Almarza 1996; Woods 1995) suggests that teachers' personal theories of teaching are central to teacher development and to our understanding of teachers' practices, and may act as a filter to the development of many other aspects of teaching. Teachers' beliefs and principles

act as an interpretative framework, through which teachers make sense of general teaching skills, make pedagogical decisions, and understand and translate subject matter knowledge (pedagogical content knowledge) into practice. . . . It may be that teachers' personal theories of teaching shape how they make sense of, and take up as their own, the general teaching skills, pedagogical reasoning and decision making, and the subject matter content. (Karen Johnson, personal communication).

Instructional processes in SLTE

The first stage in developing an SLTE program involves conceptualizing the model of teaching that will provide the theoretical foundation for the program, as illustrated previously. The next step involves selecting teaching and learning approaches that are compatible with the theory of teaching. The rest of this chapter concerns instructional options that seek to address the six core dimensions of SLTE.

Developing curricular goals

The discussion in the first part of this paper attempted to broaden our understanding of the traditional content base of SLTE to encompass domains of knowledge, skill, and awareness relevant to the preparation of second language teachers. Developing goals for teacher development is the first step in designing programs for second language teachers. The following are examples of goals that address the six content domains discussed in the first part of this chapter:

Theories of teaching
- to develop a critical understanding of major theories of second language teaching and their implications for language teaching practice
- to develop a personal theory of teaching and a reflective approach to one's own teaching
- to recognize the assumptions, beliefs, and values underlying one's own teaching practices
- to acquire skills needed for classroom-based inquiry
- to know how to initiate change in one's own classroom and monitor the effects of change

Teaching skills
- to master basic teaching skills (e.g., questioning skills, classroom management, lesson planning)
- to develop competence in using one or more language teaching methods (e.g., communicative language teaching)
- to be able to adapt teaching skills and approaches to new situations

Communication skills and language proficiency
- to develop effective communication skills as a basis for teaching
- to acquire an advanced level of proficiency in the language to be taught
- to be able to use the target language effectively as a medium of instruction

Subject matter knowledge
- to understand the nature of language and language use, particularly pedagogically based descriptions of the systems of phonology, syntax, and discourse
- to understand the nature of second language learning
- to be familiar with principal approaches to language teaching, curriculum development, testing and evaluation, and materials development

Pedagogical reasoning skills and decision making
- to be able to analyze pedagogical problems and develop alternative strategies for teaching
- to be able to relate theories of language, teaching, and learning to language teaching in actual situations
- to recognize the kinds of decision making employed in teaching and to utilize decision making effectively in one's own teaching

Contextual knowledge
- to understand the role of context in language teaching
- to be able to adapt one's teaching style according to contextual factors

How can goals such as these be addressed in SLTE programs? First, it needs to be recognized that these goals are of very different types, some short term and some long term. Some can be addressed with quite specific instructional strategies, while others require the use of a variety of approaches over time. Changing teachers' attitudes is very different from changing teachers' instructional techniques, and learning about a particular theory of pedagogical grammar and how to apply it in teaching is very different from learning how to design and implement a language curriculum. Table 1.1 shows some of the principal teaching and learning options available in SLTE programs. These learning-teaching options will now be briefly discussed and illustrated with examples from SLTE programs.

Learning and teaching options in SLTE programs

INFORMATION-ORIENTED APPROACHES

As with other areas of tertiary education, lectures and large group teaching constitute a major delivery mode for instruction in SLTE courses around the world, particularly where the primary focus is on subject matter knowledge. Tedick and Walker (1994: 304) observe: "The focus is on transmission of knowledge about methods and foundation courses followed by a student teacher experience during which students are expected to put into practice what they have learned in the preceding semesters." While within language teaching and second language acquisition there has been a considerable amount of research into and theorizing about the values of alternative modes of instruction (such as group work and pair work), there has been little attempt to apply these same teaching strategies to the teaching of content in SLTE courses or to research ways of presenting content. An exception is a study by F. Bailey (1996), which describes an ESL methods course for ESL/bilingual teachers built around collaborative peer learning involving both small group learning and peer teaching.

The course was organized around a "task-based" approach to the course content in which over half the course topics are presented by students. Students were divided into six small groups (four to six students each) and given the task of researching a particular topic in second language teaching (e.g. Freire's Problem Posing approach, Reading and Writing, Content based instruction, etc.) and planning and executing a ninety minute presentation in which they teach their classmates about their group's topic. The small groups met for the first hour of each class in order to collaboratively discuss ideas and topic readings and plan for their presentations. Each small group was assigned a "facilitator" who supported the group in their efforts to work collaboratively.

TABLE 1.1   LEARNING-TEACHING OPTIONS IN SLTE PROGRAMS

Information-oriented approaches
Lectures and large group teaching
Discussions and small group learning
Peer teaching
Learner-directed approaches

Communication activities
Student oral presentations
Public speaking
Skills training

Proficiency-focused activities
Analysis of classroom language and discourse
Practice of classroom functional language

Observing teaching in different settings
Observation of experienced teachers
Peer observation
Use of video protocols of lessons

Experiencing teaching in different settings
Practice teaching
Internships
Microteaching

Reflecting on teaching and learning
Journals and other written activities
Language learning experience
Audio or video recordings

Investigating teaching and learning
Analyzing classroom processes
Establishing databases

Focusing on critical events in teaching
Analysis of case studies
Role plays and simulations

Carrying out project work
Action research
Curriculum and materials development
Preparation of case studies

The instructor's design of this course focuses on two interrelated goals:
1) Create a rich learning environment in which a diverse set of students can
communally explore central pedagogical issues in second language teaching
within a Whole language perspective (e.g. learner-centered education, content-
based instruction, cooperative learning); 2) Create opportunities for students
to experience authentic issues in teaching and learning by making students
responsible for teaching (and learning) course content within the particular
context of the Methods course. (F. Bailey: 1996: 261–2)

T. Woodward (1992) likewise discusses a number of ways of structuring lectures to provide alternative teaching/learning modes for both lecturer and students. These include (a) *buzz-group lecture* (students listen in groups and at assigned times, then present orally the main points from the lecture); (b) *lecture key words* (the lecturer prepares a list of key words or phrases central to the lecture, which students receive beforehand, and students predict what the words mean and then note down for later discussion how the words were used during the lecture; (c) *Socratic questioning* (groups receive a list of carefully sequenced questions that explore assumptions and issues that will be covered in a lecture); (d) *Curran-style lecture* (two students sit behind the lecturer and, at times during the lecture, present and compare main points raised in the lecture); and (e) *instant questionnaire feedback* (after a lecture, students compare a list of sentences such as "I could now list . . . ," "I now know . . . ," "I'm still not sure about . . . ," based on the content of the lecture, to be discussed in class or collected by the lecturer).

COMMUNICATION ACTIVITIES

Cooper (1993) describes a curriculum for a course intended to develop effective communication skills for teachers in training, focusing both on an understanding of communication principles and practice in applying them. Teaching methods include lectures, small group activities, discussion, structured experiences, and course readings. Course units consist of:

- classroom communication
- interpersonal communication in the classroom
- listening
- nonverbal communication in the classroom
- sharing information
- leading classroom discussions
- small group communication in the classroom
- communicative reading in the classroom
- storytelling in the classroom
- teacher influence in the classroom
- communication barriers in the classroom
- systematic observation in the classroom

The course is designed for teachers of any subject.

PROFICIENCY-FOCUSED ACTIVITIES

The development of proficiency courses for prospective language teachers raises issues that are distinct from those involved in developing general language courses. This is a special case of LSP (language for specific purposes), though one that does not feature prominently in the literature.

R. K. Johnson (1990) describes the design of a unit on classroom language within a basic professional training program for Hong Kong Chinese secondary school teachers in all subject areas, which aims to make students aware of the role language plays in the classroom. The course employs both classroom sessions and language laboratory work, and involves tasks that engage teachers in exploring the nature and effectiveness of their classroom language. Each task has three stages – development, practice, and application:

1. *Development.* Particular teaching acts are identified and communication tasks are prepared which depend crucially for their success upon the effective performance of those teaching acts.
2. *Practice.* Teachers complete the communication tasks and evaluate their performances.
3. *Application.* Teachers identify general principles governing the effective completion of such tasks and discuss ways of applying those principles to their own teaching subjects.

(Johnson 1990: 272)

OBSERVING TEACHING IN DIFFERENT SETTINGS

Observation of teaching is a standard component of most teacher education programs. In both pre- and in-service courses it can serve to help develop concepts that can be used to describe and analyze the nature of classroom events. In preservice programs, observation (both of live teachers and of videotaped lessons) can be used to help teachers develop a terminology to describe and discuss teaching, and to provide data with which to examine central concepts in their own teaching. With in-service programs, teachers can first be taught techniques of ethnographic observation in order to dissociate observation from the notion of evaluation, to develop the ability to focus on the objective description of classroom events, and to develop a language to describe classroom processes. In preservice programs, observation can have a related focus. Since with preservice education participants have no teaching experience, observations of different kinds of second language classes can be used to orient student teachers to the nature of the second language classroom (its organization, practices, and norms) and to enable student teachers to develop an awareness of the kinds and levels of interaction that happen in language classrooms. Peer observation can provide opportunities for teachers to view each other's teaching in order to expose them to different teaching styles and to provide opportunities for critical reflection on their own teaching (see Chapter 8).

EXPERIENCING TEACHING IN DIFFERENT SETTINGS

Practice teaching. Practice teaching is a required component of most undergraduate or graduate SLTE courses and normally consists of a supervised period of teaching in a real language class, generally in a school or language program with which arrangements have been made for practice teaching placements. The regular classroom teacher becomes the collaborating teacher, whose responsibility (in conjunction with the campus-based supervisor) is to administer teaching assignments and give the service teacher performance feedback.

Internship. An internship differs from teaching practice only in the nature of the student teacher's responsibilities. Generally, the internship experience precedes practice teaching, and during the internship the student teacher assists the teacher but does not take full responsibility for teaching a class. In practice teaching, the novice teacher may carry a full teaching load for up to a semester.

Since the practice teaching experience is the crucial element in the design of many SLTE programs, it is surprising that the elements crucial to its success are often given little serious attention, such as orientation and preparation of cooperating teachers, and integration of the practice teaching experience with the campus program.

Microteaching. Microteaching is traditionally associated with a training-based view of teaching. This view is built on the assumption that teaching can be broken down into individual skills that can be isolated and practiced individually, such as drilling, correcting errors, and presenting new vocabulary or grammar. While this skills-based view of teaching has been criticized as offering a limited view of teaching, microteaching activities can be used to provide different kinds of teaching experiences, which can then be used as a basis for reflection and analysis. "The emphasis is placed not on mastering a specific isolated skill, for example, but on identifying and reacting to the total teaching act. The task given to the students is accordingly more holistic and the expectations from the feedback sessions are both broader and less precise" (Komblueth and Schoenberg 1990: 17).

Cruickshank et al. (1981) have developed an approach that has some of the features of microteaching but has a more reflective orientation:

- Student teachers are divided into small groups of four to six.
- Each teacher is given an identical lesson to teach and has a few days to prepare for teaching to the small group.
- Content is not drawn from their academic subject (e.g., future English teachers might present a geography lesson). This is intended to encourage focus on the process of teaching rather than the content.

- Lessons are taught within a 15-minute time frame.
- A reflection process follows, within each group and then with the class as a whole.

REFLECTING ON TEACHING AND LEARNING

Reflection and inquiry are key components of teacher development. The skills of self-inquiry and critical thinking are seen as central for continued professional growth, and can help teachers move beyond a level where they are guided largely by impulse, intuition, or routine (Boud, Keogh, and Walker 1985). Reflection, or *critical reflection*, refers to an activity or process in which an experience is recalled, considered, and evaluated, usually in relation to a broader purpose. It is a response to past experience and involves conscious recall and examination of the experience as a basis for evaluation and decision making, and as a source for planning and action (Bartlett 1990).

Reflection is seen as a process that can facilitate both learning and understanding, and plays a central role in several recent models of teacher development. Zeichner and Liston (1987: 4) suggest that a teacher education program that seeks to develop a reflective view of teaching seeks to develop student teachers who

are willing and able to reflect on the origins and consequences of their actions, as well as the material and ideological constraints and encouragements embedded in the classroom, school, and societal contexts in which they live. These goals are directed towards enabling teachers to develop pedagogical habits and skills necessary for self-directed growth and towards preparing them, individually and collectively, to participate as full partners in their making of educational policies.

Many different approaches are available to engage teachers and student teachers in critical reflection. Central to any approach, however, is a three-part process that involves:

1. *The event itself.* The starting point is an actual teaching or learning episode, such as a lesson in a foreign language (for preservice students, where a goal might be the study of language learning strategies) or a lesson taught by a student teacher or a practicing teacher. While the focus of critical reflection is usually the student's own learning or teaching, reflection can also be stimulated by observation of another person's teaching, hence both peer observation and team teaching can also be employed.
2. *Recollection of the event.* The next stage is to produce an account of what happened, without adding explanation or evaluation. This might be through the written description of an event, through the use

of a video or audio recording, or through the use of checklists or other procedures.

3. *Review and response to the event.* The student or teacher reviews and questions the event. The goal is to process it at a deeper level.

Procedures commonly used to promote critical reflection include the following.

Autobiographies.   Groups of up to ten students meet regularly with the teacher. Throughout the course each person creates a written account of experiences and expectations in teaching. These are read aloud and discussed during the weekly sessions.

Reaction sheets.   Reaction sheets are short responses written after particular learning activities have been completed. The students are encouraged to "stand back from what they had been doing and think about what it meant for their own learning and what it entailed for their work as teachers of others" (Powell 1985: 46). In a teaching practicum, for example, students work in pairs with a cooperating teacher and take turns teaching lessons. One serves as observer while the other teaches, and both complete a reaction sheet after each lesson. They then compare their responses in a follow-up session.

Journals.   Journals or diaries are another experience that can help develop a reflective orientation toward teaching. With the journal experience, the student or teacher regularly enters information about lessons he or she taught (or learning activities of other kinds) and regularly reviews these, with the help of classmates (if journals are shared with peers) or the teacher. Journal-writing experiences provide a record of significant learning experiences, help the participants understand their own self-development process, and foster a creative interaction between the student and other classmates or the instructor (see Chapter 8).

Language learning experience.   In many programs, language teachers in particular are required to take a formal course in a foreign language, in order to provide a basis for them to reflect on and analyze their language learning strategies and to experience firsthand some of the problems faced by their own students. For example, Birch (1992) describes a foreign language learning experience that is part of a postgraduate diploma for language teachers:

The Language Learning Case Study required teachers to begin the study of a language, to keep a diary in which they recorded their reflections on their language learning, and to use this diary to produce a case study which brought together themes which the learner considered particularly significant. They were free to focus on any aspect of the experience which they considered to be particularly important to their development as a second language teacher. This could include insights into the nature of language, the nature of language learning, or aspects of language teaching which had emerged from the learning experience. It therefore became largely a vehicle through which teachers were able to test the validity of theoretical issues which had been raised elsewhere in the programme. In addition, however, teachers reported that the experience of reflecting on their own language learning enabled them to understand better the language learning experience of their second language students and that consequently they had modified their teaching. (Birch 1992: 285)

Audio or video recordings. For many aspects of teaching, audio or video recording of lessons can also provide a basis for reflection. With a microphone placed in a central location like the teacher's table, for example, much of the teacher's language can be recorded as well as the exchanges of many of the students in the class. Pak (1986) recommends recording for a one- or two-week period and then randomly selecting a cassette for closer analysis. This recording could be used as the basis for an initial assessment. If video facilities are available, the teacher can request to have a lesson recorded, or students themselves can be assigned this responsibility. A 30-minute recording usually provides more than sufficient data for analysis. The goal is to capture as much of the interaction of the class as possible, both teacher-to-class and student-to-student. Once the initial novelty wears off, both students and teacher accept the presence of the technician with the camera, and the class proceeds with minimum disruption.

The recording is then used as a basis for critical self-analysis, by having the teacher review it and respond to such questions as:

– What kind of teaching does the recording illustrate?
– How are your values as a teacher reflected in the data?
– What aspect of your teaching (as seen in the recording) do you most value?
– Is there anything you would want to change?
– How should this change come about?

INVESTIGATING TEACHING AND LEARNING

A primary goal of in-service programs is to provide teachers with ways of looking at their own classrooms from a different perspective. Activities that promote self-inquiry and critical thinking are central for continued professional growth, and are designed to help teachers move from a level where their classroom actions are guided by routine to a level where their practices are guided by reflection and critical thinking. In a course I designed on reflective teaching for in-service teachers at the master's level, the focus was on exploring different dimensions of teaching. Each week one aspect of classroom life was examined. Topics covered included structuring, learner roles and strategies, teacher roles, teacher decision making, tasks, grouping, teacher-student interaction, and classroom language. Initially in seminar sessions, video protocols of actual lessons were used to identify different dimensions of classroom behavior. Each week the teachers audiotaped one of their own lessons and then wrote a reflective response to it, focusing on the topic under discussion that week. An assignment during a week in which the topic of teacher decision making was being discussed consisted of the following activity:

1. *Planning decisions.* As you plan a lesson for the coming week, make notes of the planning decisions you made:
   (a) What alternatives did you consider?
   (b) How did your belief system influence your decisions?
   (c) What final decisions did you make? Why?

2. *Interactive decisions.* Audiotape the lesson you planned. Later that day, review the lesson by listening to the recording and comparing the actual lesson to your plan. Write a commentary on your lesson focusing on the interactive decisions that you made during the lesson:
   (a) What happened during the lesson that you did not plan for?
   (b) What kinds of interactive decisions did you make? Why?
   (c) On reflection, do you think an alternative decision would have been better? Why?

Investigation of different aspects of language teaching, language learning, and language use is common among teacher education courses. In a course on pedagogical grammar, for example, as part of a unit on aspect and tense in English, students might build up a database of native-speaker usage (based on occurrences in newspapers or other sources) as well as of learner usage (based on a written corpus either collected by teachers themselves or provided by the course instructor). This is then used to test particular theories of tense and aspect or of second language acquisition. Or in a course on second language acquisition, teachers might administer a language-attitude questionnaire to their students, to compare published findings on language attitudes with data from their own students. In preservice programs, small-scale investigative projects help students develop an awareness of the significance of issues they study in their theory courses, as well as give them a familiarity with collecting and analyzing different kinds of language data. This is also true at the in-service level, but here such activities help teachers develop a research orientation to their own classrooms and to appreciate their potential roles as classroom researchers.

FOCUSING ON CRITICAL EVENTS IN TEACHING

Analysis of case studies.   Case materials, including both written and videotaped cases, also provide another rich vehicle for helping student teachers develop the capacity to analyze situations, to explore how teachers in different settings arrive at lesson goals and teaching strategies, and to understand how expert teachers draw on pedagogical schemas and routines in the process of teaching. Case-based approaches are widely used in other professions, such as business, law, and medicine, but have only recently begun to be used more generally in teacher education (J. H. Shulman 1992). Case reports can reveal ways of thinking about a significant teaching incident and, when accompanied by "deconstruction" through questioning and critical interpretation, can help reveal how teachers' beliefs, knowledge, personality, and pedagogical reasoning shape a particular event.

A number of advantages have been suggested for using case studies in this way in teacher education (Kleinfeld 1992):

– Students are provided with vicarious teaching problems that present real issues in context.
– Students can learn how to identify issues and frame problems.
– Cases can be used to model the processes of analysis and inquiry in teaching.
– Students can acquire an enlarged repertoire and understanding of educational strategies.
– Cases help stimulate the habit of reflective inquiry.

A collection of case reports for use in this way is a priority in SLTE, since case methods offer a potentially useful complement to other procedures used in the program, such as journal writing and other forms of reflective inquiry. An example of a case study designed to be used in this way is given in Chapter 4.

Role plays and simulations.   An important dimension of teaching is interactive decision making – that is, the ability to analyze a classroom problem, determine what range of options is available, and decide on the best course of action. Decision making for some educationists is the most crucial dimension of the teacher's work. In teacher education, decision making can be approached in a number of different ways, including problem solving and role play.

Pennington (1990) gives examples of problem-solving activities involving a sequence of activities that begin with individual or small group discussion of a problem and then move to whole-class discussion. For example:

STUDENT CASE

You are a teacher in a large second language program whose administration includes a director of courses or department chair, several student advisors, and a clerical assistant. In speaking informally with you, a student from your class suddenly states that she is very much dissatisfied with her situation in the United States, so much so that she wishes to return immediately to her home country.

Questions:
1. What is the immediate problem?
2. What might the direct and indirect causes of the immediate problem be?
3. What other potential or actual problems do you see?
4. What else do you need to know (e.g., about the student or about the situation relating to the problem)?
5. How do you obtain the information that you need?
6. What should you say or do (a) when meeting with the student and (b) after meeting with the student?
7. What other people (if any) need to become involved?
8. What are some of the things to watch out for or to be particularly sensitive to?

(1990: 145)

Pennington points out that such an activity can easily lead to a discussion of such things as the difficulty of determining the source of student problems, the appropriate role of the teacher, and the extent to which teachers should become involved in students' personal problems.

Role play is another useful activity that can help develop an awareness of the kinds of beliefs and values implicit in teaching and how these can lead to different kinds of decisions and classroom actions. Pennington (1990) illustrates how role-play activities can be used in conjunction with video viewing to explore different perspectives of the same classroom event. In the example she gives, student or in-service teachers first view a short video segment of a class several times, completing viewing tasks from three different perspectives. On first viewing, an objective viewpoint is taken, and details about the lesson are recorded. On second viewing, the viewpoint of someone who has a positive view of the teacher/lesson is taken, and positive behaviors are noted. On the third viewing, a negative viewpoint is taken, and negative aspects of the lesson are noted. The following role-play activity is then enacted:

As a follow-up to the video that you just observed, two or more role plays will take place. You will take the role of either the person just observed or the teacher's new supervisor. Both positive and negative roles are provided so that you may try out different combinations of these. Assume that you are having a conference soon after the observation has taken place, as part of the normal teaching evaluation process. The aim of the meeting is to review performance in the class observed and to reach agreement on two potential areas for professional growth/improvement and to develop concrete action steps that both parties can agree on to accomplish the goals.

Teacher: Positive role
You have basic confidence in yourself and your teaching, yet you realize that there is always room for growth and improvement. In the conference, your primary objective is to establish a good working relationship with your new supervisor. Secondarily, you would like to get some constructive advice about your classes from the supervisor, whom you know to have considerable experience and expertise in language teaching.

Teacher: Negative role
You lack basic confidence in yourself and your teaching, and you are not comfortable accepting feedback on your teaching unless it is 100% positive. Because of negative experiences with a previous supervisor, you feel threatened by this conference. Your primary objective is to convince your new supervisor that you are doing a good job and that no one needs to worry about you. Secondarily, you want to establish the fact that you have job security and do not have to listen to any advice.

Supervisor: Positive role
You are a confident and supportive person, with positive attitudes about teachers and teaching. You strongly believe that a "carrot" rather than a "stick" is more effective in changing behavior. Your primary objective is to establish a good working relationship with the teacher. Secondarily, you would like to discuss areas of common ground based on your observation of the teacher's class.

Supervisor: Negative role
You lack confidence in your abilities as both teacher and supervisor. As a consequence, you tend to take a defensive, condescending stance toward those you supervise. Your primary objective is to establish that you are an experienced expert, and know how the teacher can improve teaching performance. Secondarily, you want to establish that you have control over the teacher's job.

(Pennington 1990: 149)

CARRYING OUT PROJECT WORK

The use of classroom-based or school-based project work is another strategy available in in-service programs, and it often provides a valuable link between campus-based program input and the contexts in which teachers work or in which student teachers do practice teaching or internships. Action research takes its name from two processes that are central to it: a data-gathering component (the research element) and a focus on bringing about change (the action component). Action research typically involves a four-part sequence of activities:

1. *Identify a problem.* Through observation of their own classrooms, teachers identify some aspect of their teaching that they would like to change. For example a teacher may decide that the class is too teacher dominated, that students do not have many opportunities to speak, and that the teacher would consequently like to increase the amount of student participation in lessons.
2. *Develop a strategy for change.* The next step, developed in consultation with peers or with the instructor, is to work out an action plan that will address the problem. For example, the teacher may decide to change the classroom seating arrangement, or keep a record of how often students initiate talk during lessons. The teacher might use a simple coding instrument for this purpose.
3. *Implement the strategy.* The teacher decides to put his or her plan into operation for a fixed period of time, say, two weeks. During this time the teacher monitors students' classroom participation by audiotaping lessons and by inviting a colleague into the class to complete an observation form that records how often students participated in the lesson and for what purpose.
4. *Evaluate the results.* The teacher decides if the action plan has brought about the intended changes in style of teaching, and reflects on the goals, procedures, and outcomes of the project.

In carrying out small-scale research of this kind, teachers also learn skills involved in conducting classroom-based research, such as how to frame a problem, how to select a research question, what kind of data to collect, and how to analyze data. Project work can be linked to many of the issues teachers study in their subject matter courses, and it often enables teachers to develop a pedagogically grounded understanding of the subject. For example, when students take a course on syllabus design and curriculum development, a central focus of the course might be the development of a syllabus and curriculum for a real class. This enables teachers to test applications of theory in a real context and better understand the reasons underlying alternative models and theories. A course on materials adaptation and evaluation likewise can more fully engage teachers in some of the complex decisions involved in materials development, if at the same time teachers are working on a materials development project and are trying to solve some of the problems that arise in such projects (see Chapter 5).

Case studies of individual language teaching contexts also provide a valuable opportunity for teachers in training to gain an in-depth understanding of teaching. For example, pairs or groups of teachers might conduct case studies of:

- how a school handles non-English-speaking students in their first few months of schooling
- how an ESL learner copes with school assignments during a semester
- the kinds of out-of-school uses of English an adult ESL learner encounters during a week or month
- how a teacher uses a textbook during a two-week teaching period

Conclusion

Six domains of content have been identified as forming the core knowledge base of second language teacher education: theories of teaching, teaching skills, communication skills, subject matter knowledge, pedagogical reasoning and decision making, and contextual knowledge. The focus on these dimensions of teaching as the foundation of SLTE is an attempt to give priority to teaching itself and to acknowledge the complexity of what we understand about the nature of effective second language teaching.

The taxonomy of SLTE instructional approaches likewise reflects an attempt to examine teaching from multiple dimensions, and illustrates some of the trends of SLTE practice discussed in Richards and Nunan:

- a movement away from a "training" perspective to an "education" perspective, and recognition that effective teaching involves higher-level cognitive processes, which cannot be taught directly
- the need for teachers and student teachers to adopt a research orientation to their own classrooms and their own teaching
- less emphasis on prescriptions and top-down directives and more emphasis on an inquiry-based and discovery-oriented approach to learning (bottom-up)
- a focus on devising experiences that require the student teacher to generate theories and hypotheses and to reflect critically on teaching
- less dependence on linguistics and language theory as a source discipline for second language teacher education and more of an attempt to integrate sound, educationally based approaches
- use of procedures that involve teachers in gathering and analyzing data about teaching

(1990: xii)

In order for this to happen, it is suggested that practitioners of SLTE need to reach consensus on what the fundamental nature of the field is and how its pedagogical content knowledge should be defined. In many situations, SLTE still reflects the history of its development as a branch of applied linguistics. A consistent approach or philosophy of SLTE has not yet emerged to serve as a basis for sound instructional practice. If the movement away from language-based to more teaching-based approaches gains momentum in the future, however, both pedagogical content knowledge and accompanying instructional practices will need to be evaluated to ensure that the process of teaching assumes a more prominent role within the field of second language teacher education.

Part I *Theories of second language teaching*

2 Theories of teaching in language teacher education

Underlying any approach to the preservice or in-service development of second language teachers is a conception of what good teaching is and what the essential knowledge and skills of teachers are. Fundamental questions in the design of SLTE programs include consideration of what type of teacher the program is intended to graduate and what attitudes toward research, conventional wisdom, experiential knowledge, and self-development the graduate of the program is expected to have. Therefore, in planning SLTE programs, decisions need to be made concerning what philosophy of teaching and of teachers the program will embody (see Chapter 1). Perhaps the commonest conception of teaching in SLTE in the seventies and eighties was a method-based model of teaching. Lange comments:

Foreign language teacher development ... has a basic orientation to methods of teaching. Unfortunately, the latest bandwagon "methodologies" come into prominence without much study or understanding, particularly those that appear easiest to immediately apply in the classroom or those that are supported by a particular "guru." Although concern for method is certainly not a new issue, the current attraction to "method" stems from the late 1950s, when foreign language teachers were falsely led to believe that there was a method to remedy the "language teaching and learning problems." Audiolingualism is no longer the reigning theory of language learning, but it has been deeply ingrained in foreign language teachers' routines as basic practice. The obsession with methods makes the connection between university teacher development programs difficult, particularly in clinical experiences aspects, because the practice in schools is different from the more theoretical "up-to-date" approach of college/university teacher development programs. (1990: 253)

Alternative paradigms have also been proposed, such as that of Fanselow in his book *Breaking Rules* (1987), which might be described as an "anti-methods" perspective. In Fanselow's approach, teachers are encouraged to develop their own methods of teaching through exploring alternatives to conventional prescriptions for good teaching.

Judgements and prescriptions based on preconceived notions of good teaching given by outsiders, general in nature, and with no means to explore congruence between practices and prescriptions, obviously serve a critical function in teacher preparation and development. These practices are

33

widespread, and almost all teachers have experienced them. It is partly because of the fact that most teachers are aware of the normal rules in teacher preparation and development that I provide a different set of practices. The practices I invite you to experience are basically the exact opposite of those most followed. Thus, I invite you not to judge, or if you do, to withhold your judgement, to substitute specific descriptions for general prescriptions, and as a result to be free to generate alternatives unrelated to your preconceived notions of good and bad teaching, to serve as your own expert rather to depend on those in authority, and to explore congruence between what you think you do, what you want to do, and what you actually do. (1987: 2)

Other conceptions of teaching in SLTE include the teacher as classroom researcher (Nunan 1989) and the teacher as reflective practitioner (Richards and Lockhart 1994). Each model of teaching makes specific assumptions about what the essential knowledge base, skills, and attitudes of teachers are. This chapter examines a number of conceptions of teaching that have affected the field of second and foreign language teaching, explores the assumptions they make about the nature of teaching skills, and considers the implications of each view of teaching for approaches to second language teacher development. The framework for this discussion is based on Zahorik (1986). In a paper on the relationship between theories of teaching and teaching skills, Zahorik divides conceptions of teaching into three main categories: *science-research conceptions, theory-philosophy conceptions,* and *art-craft conceptions.* These categories will be used to illustrate the implications of different conceptions of teaching in language teaching and their implications for SLTE.

Science-research conceptions

Science-research conceptions of language teaching view teaching as a type of scientific activity, or at least one that is informed and validated by scientific research and supported by experimentation and empirical investigation. Zahorik (1986) includes *operationalizing learning principles, following a tested model,* and *doing what effective teachers do* as examples of science-research conceptions. How have these conceptions influenced the field of second and foreign language teaching?

Operationalizing learning principles

Operationalizing learning principles involves developing teaching principles from research on the psychology of learning, specifically memory, transfer, motivation, and other factors believed to be important in learning. Mastery learning and programmed learning are examples of science-research conceptions of teaching that have been developed in general education. In second language teaching, audiolingualism, task-based language teaching, and learner training represent applications of learning research to language teaching.

Audiolingualism was the language teaching method in vogue in the 1960s and early 1970s, particularly for the teaching of foreign languages, and was firmly grounded in the learning theory of the day associated with the school of psychology known as behaviorism (Richards and Rodgers 1984). A second language could be learned through a process of habit formation and overlearning. Mimicry, memorization of set phrases, and repetitive drills were the primary teaching techniques, which were justified according to the Skinnerian concept of conditioning (Rivers 1964). Rivers (1964) offers a critique of the audiolingual method and its attempts to apply learning principles to language teaching. Her criticism is not that such an application is misplaced, but rather that the wrong learning principles were applied, leading to the excesses of the audiolingual method that led to its decline. Rivers' belief was that the method could be improved through the application of other learning principles. Her influential book concludes:

What can the practical teacher take from this intensive study of psychological learning theory and apply to specific problems of foreign-language teaching? Scattered throughout the preceding chapters have been a number of suggestions and recommendations for the modification or improvement of audiolingual techniques – recommendations which have emerged from consideration of the experimental work of several schools of psychological thought. (Rivers 1964: 149)

Thus the way forward in language teaching depends upon applying the results of experimental studies of human learning.

A more recent example of attempts to develop a theory of teaching from learning research is referred to as task-based language teaching (TBLT). Like the audiolingual method, it too is said to derive from the application of principles derived from studies of learning. Long and Crookes (1992: 27) point out that task-based approaches to language teaching are distinguishable from earlier approaches because "part of their rationale derives from what is known about human learning in general and/or second language learning in particular." While rejecting linguistic units of analysis, syllabus design, and presentation in language teaching, task-based approaches "opt instead for some conception of task" (p. 27). "The basic rationale for TBLT derives from SLA research, particularly descriptive and experimental studies comparing tutored and naturalistic learning" (p. 42). Proponents of task-based language teaching argue that second language acquisition research shows that successful language learning involves learners in negotiation of meaning. In the process of negotiating with a speaker of the target language, the learner receives the kind of input needed to facilitate learning. It is proposed that classroom tasks that involve negotiation of meaning should therefore form the basis of the language teaching curriculum, and that tasks can be used to facilitate practice of both language forms and communicative functions. Research is intended to enable curriculum and materials designers to know what kinds of tasks can best facilitate acquisition of specific target language structures and functions and in what ways fluency and accuracy can be achieved within a task-based approach (Skehan 1996). Prabhu (1984) initiated a large-scale application of this approach in schools in India, developing a syllabus and associated teaching materials around three major types of tasks: information-gap tasks, opinion-gap tasks, and reasoning-gap tasks.

A different type of science-research conception is the approach known as learner training. This draws on research on the cognitive styles and learning strategies used by successful learners in second language learning and in completing different types of classroom learning tasks. An early example of research on learner strategies (the *Good Language Learner* studies) sought to identify the strategies employed by successful second language learners. The assumption was that people with above-average success in learning languages should be studied to determine what it is they do that makes their efforts more successful. Naiman et al. (1978) identified six broad strategies employed by people who were good language learners:

- Find a learning style that suits you.
- Involve yourself in the language learning process.
- Develop an awareness of language both as system and as communication.
- Pay constant attention to expanding your language knowledge.
- Develop the second language as a separate system.
- Take into account the demands that second language learning imposes.

The motivation behind learner strategy research was that such principles could provide the basis for training less successful language learners, hence the notion of learner training: "It is a fundamental tenet of learner training that learning strategies of successful learners can be codified and taught to poor language learners with a resulting increase in their learning efficiency" (Rees-Miller 1993: 680). Hosenfeld (1984) investigated the strategies employed by successful and unsuccessful readers when reading foreign language texts, and argues that the strategies employed by the successful readers (e.g., keeping the meaning of the passage in mind, reading in broad phrases, skipping inessential words, having a good self-concept as a reader) should be taught to unsuccessful readers. O'Malley and Chamot (1990) demonstrated that training students to use particular learning strategies can improve their language learning performance. Not all approaches to learner training seek to teach students specific strategies, however; some merely seek to develop awareness of the nature and role of strategies in successful language learning (see Oxford 1990).

Following a tested model of teaching

Following a tested model of teaching involves applying the results of empirical or experimental research on teaching to classroom teaching. In this approach, "a view of good teaching is developed through logical reasoning and previous research; good teaching is defined in terms of specific acts" (Zahorik 1986: 21). While not a common paradigm in language teaching, it has at times been advocated as a way to advance the scientific basis of second language teaching. An example of an approach of this kind is work done by Long in the 1980s on teachers' question patterns and *wait-time* (the amount of time teachers wait before answering a question). Long (1984) argued that research had established the contribution of questioning patterns and wait-time to the quality of interaction in second language classrooms, particularly the need for teachers to use more *referential questions* (genuine questions in which the answer is not known in advance) than *display questions* (questions asked to elicit a structure or sentence pattern and for which no genuine information exchange is involved). In applying this research to teacher preparation, a simple training model was developed in which teachers were taught the differences between display questions and referential questions, and the advantages of providing longer wait-time after questions. Teachers' question use and wait-time before and after training were measured, and "it was found that the training modules affected teaching behaviors, and that the new behaviors affected student participation patterns in ways believed to be significant for these students' language acquisition" (Long 1984: vi). Thus, by identifying specific teaching behaviors, such as question patterns and wait-time, that are more effective in facilitating second language acquisition than other types of classroom discourse, a conception of good teaching was identified and validated.

Doing what effective teachers do

Another approach to developing a research-based theory of teaching is to derive teaching principles from studies of the practices of "effective" teachers. This involves identifying teachers who are regarded as exemplary (based on supervisors' reports, the results their students achieve in school or on standardized tests, or on other criteria of effectiveness) and studying their teaching practices through classroom observation and interviews.

In a study of effective teachers in bilingual education programs in California and Hawaii, for example, Tikunoff (1985) observed a group of teachers who had been identified as achieving exemplary results in their classes to find out how they organized instruction, structured teaching activities, and enhanced student performance on tasks. Teachers were interviewed to determine their instructional philosophies and goals, and the demands they structured into class tasks. Then they were observed while teaching their classes. An analysis of the classroom data revealed that there was a clear linkage between:

1. teachers' ability to clearly specify the intent of instruction, and a belief that students could achieve accuracy in instructional tasks
2. the organization and delivery of instruction such that tasks and institutional demands reflected this intent, requiring intended student responses
3. the fidelity of student consequences with intended outcomes

In a summary of research of this kind (Blum 1984: 3–6), twelve characteristics of effective teaching were identified:

1. Instruction is guided by a preplanned curriculum.
2. There are high expectations for student learning.
3. Students are carefully oriented to lessons.
4. Instruction is clear and focused.
5. Learning progress is monitored closely.
6. When students do not understand, they are retaught.
7. Class time is used for learning.
8. There are smooth and efficient classroom routines.
9. Instructional groups formed in the classroom fit instructional needs.
10. Standards for classroom behavior are high.
11. Personal interactions between teachers and students are positive.
12. Incentives and rewards for students are used to promote excellence.

Research on effective teaching thus leads to the identification of principles that, in theory, can be used as the basis for teacher training and teacher assessment. In general education, an approach to teaching that reflects this approach has been labeled *direct instruction* or *active teaching*.

Theory-philosophy conceptions

Theory-philosophy conceptions of teaching are built not on empirical research but on generally data-free theories and principles that are justified on logical, philosophical, political, moral, or other grounds. "Their truth is not based on a posteriori conditions or on what works. Rather, their truth is based on what ought to work or what is morally right" (Zahorik 1986: 22). Such conceptions of teaching are much more common in language teaching than science-research conceptions, which as Lange (1990) notes, abounds with examples of methodologies that have been developed by inspired linguists, educationists, or teacher educators, adopted as the received truth of the day by teaching organizations, and promoted, often uncritically, as the answer to "the language teaching problem." Teaching conceptions derived from beliefs about what ought to work are essentially rationalist in approach, while those derived from beliefs about what is viewed as morally right will be referred to here as *values-based approaches*.

Rational approaches

Rational conceptions of teaching generally result from attempts to apply particular theories of language or of language learning to teaching. *Communicative language teaching* is an example of a teaching conception based primarily on a theory of language, while *the proficiency movement* in foreign language teaching in the United States is based on a nonempirical model of foreign language proficiency development. In neither case is research or empirical investigation the starting point for the development of the teaching conception.

Communicative language teaching, today still one of the major language teaching movements worldwide, arose in the 1970s as a reaction to grammar-based approaches to teaching, which had been dominant since the 1950s. Communicative language teaching was an attempt to build language teaching around the theory of communicative competence. The consequence of a paradigm shift within applied linguistics as well as a response to changes in the practical circumstances of language teaching within Europe and the British EFL network at that time, the proponents of communicative language teaching often described it as a "principled approach," based on a "proper" view of the nature of language. As R. Allwright pointed out in 1979, summarizing the mood of the time in British ELT circles, "It has been accepted for many years that 'communication' is the proper aim for language teaching." Allwright goes on to describe the background to the adoption of a communicative approach in a British University English for applied purposes program:

In retrospect it seems possible to see a rational thread through the thinking that preceded the change of strategy, but at the time we felt we were taking quick decisions on little more than very strong feelings of distrust concerning past experience, and strong, almost euphoric, self-confidence and optimism concerning the possibilities offered by a radical break with the past. (1979: 172)

Communicative language teaching was not propelled by a body of research evidence or research studies that sought to demonstrate that communicative language teaching programs were more effective than the grammar-based programs abandoned with the enthusiasm Allwright describes. Rather, it quickly became the new orthodoxy, supported in high places and rapidly implemented worldwide (see Richards 1984). It is a classic example of an innovation being accepted because of the compelling nature of its underlying principles and the status and influence of its proponents. The literature on communicative language teaching in the seventies is hence not linked to empirical questions or research findings. Rather, it is largely devoted to persuasive articulation of its underlying principles and their implications for language teaching, and to foster debate on such matters as the appropriateness of different syllabus types and the roles of accuracy versus fluency. The major principles of the communicative approach are summarized by Finocchiaro and Brumfit (1983: 91–3) and include:

- Meaning is paramount.
- Contextualization is a basic premise.
- Language learning is learning to communicate.
- Effective communication is sought.
- Attempts to communicate may be encouraged from the very beginning.
- Communicative competence is the desired goal.
- Linguistic variation is a central concept in materials and methodology.
- Sequencing is determined by any consideration of content, function, or meaning that maintains interest.
- Language is created by the individual through trial and error.
- Fluency and acceptable language are the primary goals; accuracy is judged not in the abstract but in context.
- Intrinsic motivation will spring from an interest in what is being communicated by the language.

The Proficiency Movement represents another rationally based conception of teaching that has had a significant impact on approaches to foreign language teaching in the United States. Its origins lie in dissatisfaction with the quest for best methods of language teaching, which had dominated approaches to language teaching in the 1960s and 1970s. In 1982 the American Council on the Teaching of Foreign Languages published the *ACTFL Proficiency Guidelines,* which were intended to provide a frame of reference for the design of language teaching programs and to establish language proficiency achievement goals for foreign language teaching.

The shift from methodology to measurement questions marks a significant change in direction for the profession. After many years of fruitless searching for the "one true way," we may be realizing at last that the controversy has been raging on the wrong battlefield. Instead of searching for one definitive approach to teaching, we have begun looking for some "organizing principle" that can facilitate communication about the nature of language proficiency, and thus about the development of goals and objectives for language teaching. (Omaggio-Hadley 1993: 75)

Like the specifications for notional, functional, and communicative syllabuses that generated such interest in relation to communicative language teaching in the seventies, the *ACTFL Proficiency Guidelines* were not research based (despite claims to the contrary, e.g., Liskin-Gasparro 1984) but the product of a working group drawing on conviction, experience, intuition, and oral proficiency scales that had been developed for the purposes of assessing oral language proficiency (e.g., the Foreign Service Institute Oral Interview). Omaggio-Hadley (1993), in a major book on the methodology of foreign language teaching, uses the proficiency guidelines as a framework for developing "guiding principles for organizing and planning instruction in a second language" (p. 76) The five guiding principles she identifies are:

1. Opportunities must be provided for students to practice using language in a range of contexts likely to be encountered in the target culture.
2. Opportunities should be provided for students to practice carrying out a range of functions (tasks) likely to be necessary in dealing with others in the target culture.
3. The development of accuracy should be encouraged in proficiency-oriented instruction. As learners produce language, various forms of instruction and evaluative feedback can be useful in facilitating the progression of their skills towards more precise and coherent language use.
4. Instruction should be more responsive to the affective as well as the cognitive needs of students, and their different personalities, preferences, and learning styles should be taken into account.
5. Cultural understanding must be promoted in various ways so that students are sensitive to other cultures and prepared to live more harmoniously in the target-language community.

(Omaggio-Hadley 1993: 77)

Values-based approaches

A different approach to a conception of teaching is to develop a teaching approach from the values one holds about teachers, learners, classrooms, and the role of education in society. Certain ways of going about teaching and learning are then seen to be educationally or ideologically desirable and others as morally, ethically, ideologically, or politically unsupportable. Teaching is seen to always encompass a moral or ideological dimension. What has been acknowledged as true for literacy

41

could also be said of teaching English as a second or foreign language, namely, that it "always serves social purposes in creating and exchanging meaning, needs to be understood in its context of use, is ideological, is linked to social power, and should be taught with a critical dimension that calls into question such ideological and social relations" (Pennycook 1996: 163).

Values or ideologically based approaches in education are not hard to identify. For example, advocates of "literature in the language curriculum," "school-based curriculum development," or "the teacher as action researcher" essentially appeal to cultural, educational, or social value systems in justifying their proposals. The Marxist ideology underlying Kemmis and McTaggart's approach to action research, for example, is relatively transparent, as seen in their insistence that action research must be a collaborative rather than an individualistic activity:

The importance of the group in action research cannot be overemphasised. Activities where an individual goes through cycles of planning, action, observation and reflection, cannot be regarded as action research. Action research is not individualistic. To lapse into individualism is to destroy the critical dynamic of the group and to risk falling victim to the fallacious liberal notion that all educational practices and the values which they purport to realise are equally defensible. (1981: 15)

Other examples of values-based approaches in language teaching include team teaching, humanistic approaches, the learner-centered curriculum movement, and reflective teaching. Team teaching is based on a view that teachers work best when they work in collaboration with a peer, and that the interaction with a colleague in all phases of teaching is beneficial to both teachers and learners. Humanistic approaches in language teaching refer to approaches that emphasize the development of human values, growth in self-awareness and in the understanding of others, sensitivity to human feelings and emotions, and active student involvement in learning and in the way human learning takes place. Community Language Learning is sometimes cited as an example of a humanistic approach, as is the work of Earl Stevick and Gertrude Moskowitz.

The *learner-centered curriculum* is one of a number of terms used to refer to approaches to language teaching that are based on the belief that learners are self-directed, responsible decision makers. Learners are seen to learn in different ways and to have different needs and interests. Language programs and the teachers who work in them should therefore set out to provide learners with efficient learning strategies, to assist learners to identify their own preferred ways of learning, to develop skills needed to negotiate the curriculum, to encourage learners to set their own objectives, to encourage learners to adopt realistic goals and time frames, and to develop learners' skills in self-evaluation.

Reflective teaching is an approach to teaching based on a belief that teachers can improve their understanding of teaching and the quality of their own teaching by reflecting critically on their teaching experiences. In teacher education, activities that seek to develop a reflective approach to teaching aim to develop the skills of considering the teaching process thoughtfully, analytically, and objectively, as a way of improving classroom practices (Richards and Lockhart 1994). This is brought about through using procedures that require teachers to collect data on their own teaching practices (e.g., through audio or video recordings), to reflect on their own decision making (e.g., through journal writing), and to examine their own values and assumptions about teaching (e.g., through peer or group discussion, or observation of videos). Some link reflective teaching to broader and more fundamental goals:

Becoming a critically reflective teacher is intended to allow us to develop ourselves individually and collectively; to deal with contemporary events and structures (for example, the attitudes of others or the bureaucratic thinking of administrators) and not to take these structures for granted. Reflective teaching as a form of critical inquiry is located in a socially critical orientation to teaching. (Bartlett 1990: 205)

Art-craft conceptions

A third way of conceptualizing teaching is to view it as an art or a craft, and as something that depends upon the teacher's individual skill and personality. Zahorik (1986: 22) characterizes the approach in these terms: "The essence of this view of good teaching is invention and personalization. A good teacher is a person who assesses the needs and possibilities of a situation and creates and uses practices that have promise for that situation."

The artist metaphor has appeared in different forms in the literature on teaching in the last fifty years (see Delamont 1995), one of the earliest articulations being a book on EFL teaching methodology called *The Art of Teaching English as a Living Language* (Morris 1954). While researchers rarely use such a description, the invocation of teaching as artistry is intended to highlight a nontechnical view of teaching that focuses on some of the tacit, implicit, and unexamined sides of teaching. Pennington (1990: 132–3)) provides a clear description of the art-craft conception of teaching as it applies to second language teaching, pointing out that it underlies the philosophy seen in Stevick's work, who viewed teaching as a "kind of mystical experience that is "hard to explain or describe." He referred to teaching as "the mystery-behind-mystery" and the "simple, daily miracle" (Stevick 1990: 295). "From this perspective," writes Pennington,

43

individual acts of teaching are essentially irreplicable and noncomparable, and the inherent characteristics of individual teachers are the strongest predictor of classroom outcomes. Under this abstract view of teaching, in which the teaching act cannot be analyzed and described in rational, consistent terms, teacher development or evaluation cannot be justified. . . . In a less radical conception, teaching viewed as a kind of "artistic" performance depends in large measure on the characteristics of the particular teacher and so cannot be reliably predicted from teacher preparation. (1990: 133)

The craft metaphor of teaching emphasizes that teachers have to acquire a personal repertoire of specialized skills and techniques, and that these may be unique to each teacher and hence in some sense unpredictable. According to Gage (1978), teaching involves "a process that calls for intuition, creativity, improvisation, and expressiveness – a process that leaves room for departures from what is implied by rules, formulas, and algorithims" (p. 15). Art-craft approaches to teaching seek to develop teaching as a unique set of personal skills that teachers apply in different ways according to the demands of specific situations. There are no general methods of teaching; rather, teachers should develop an approach to teaching that allows them to be themselves and do what they feel is best. Teacher decision making is an essential competency in this approach, because a good teacher is seen as one who analyzes a situation, realizes that a range of options is available based on the particular class circumstances, and then selects an alternative that is likely to be the most effective for the circumstances.

In this view, the teacher must draw upon not only a body of professional knowledge and skill, but also a set of personal resources that are uniquely defined and expressed by the personality of the teacher and his or her individual and collective interactions with students. (Darling-Hammond, Wise, and Pease 1983: 292)

This does not deny the value of knowing about different methods of teaching and how to use them, but it suggests that commitment to a single method of teaching may impede the teacher's full potential. Fanselow (1987) advocates an art-craft conception of teaching and urges teachers to break conventional rules (the ones that emanate from research, theory, or other external models of teaching) in order to discover the teacher's inner rules:

For too long, we have sought suggestions, insights, and information only from psychologists, linguists, researchers who did comparison of methods studies, advocates of particular schools of language teaching, authors of texts, or tests or other experts. Of course, these sources have been helpful and should not be discarded. But they can be supplemented by self-generated alternative suggestions, insights, and information. Initially, we may not trust our own self-generated alternatives as much as those provided by experts. But confidence comes as we remember the Socratic idea of teaching: aiding each other to remember what we already know, helping us each see what is within each of us. (1987: 7)

Implications for teacher education

Although none of the conceptions of teaching discussed in this chapter can be viewed as an ideal type that exists in pure form in the real world, different philosophies or conceptions of teaching embody quite different assumptions about what the essential skills of teaching are, and hence raise different issues in teacher preparation and teacher evaluation (Darling-Hammond et al. 1983).

Science-research conceptions can be seen as essentially top-down approaches to teaching. Teaching is viewed as the application of knowledge and theories that have been developed by researchers, typically academics. Learning theory, research on second language learning, and research on effective teaching practices are regarded as the basis for the development of teaching strategies and principles. Theoretical models of teaching then become "entrenched as a methodological cornerstone of classroom teaching" (Rees-Miller 1993: 681). The essential knowledge and skills of teaching from this perspective are an understanding of the theory or research principles that form the basis of the teaching strategy or methodology, and the ability to apply research-based principles in one's own teaching. The role of teacher research is to provide further validation of the theory and research findings. Teachers need to constantly update their knowledge of current research findings and seek ways of applying such knowledge to their teaching. They should make their teaching conform to the research principles as far as possible. They are part of the process by which research findings get turned into practice.

Teacher education programs built around science-research conceptions of teaching will consequently give a primary emphasis to the importance of research and theory in teaching and the "validity" of particular theoretical perspectives on second language teaching and learning. Typically they will focus on a particular research paradigm, such as "second language acquisition research," and prospective teachers or in-service teachers will be trained in the research techniques associated with that approach. Good teaching, according to this conception, is teaching that is in conformity with the findings of research.

Theory-philosophy conceptions of teaching require teachers first to understand the theory underlying the approach and then to teach in such a way that the theory is realized in classroom practice. With communicative language teaching, for example, lessons, syllabuses, materials, and teaching techniques can be judged as more or less "communicative." Specifications as to what constitutes communicative teaching have been proposed, and a teacher's performance can be assessed according to the degree of "communicativeness" found in his or her lessons. Other methodologies that derive from theory-philosophy conceptions, such as the Silent Way, lead to prescriptions as to what teachers should and should not do in the classroom. The essential skills the teacher needs to acquire are those that reflect the theory and spirit of the Silent Way approach. There is little room for personal interpretation of the method.

Philosophical or values-based approaches are prescriptive in a different kind of way, since the choice of instructional means is not based on educational criteria (e.g., on effectiveness or learning criteria) but on a wider set of values that are not subject to accountability (e.g., ideological, political, social, or personal beliefs). Applying the teaching conception to classroom practice begins with a change in ideas, values, principles, or beliefs. In preparing teachers for reflective teaching, for example, Bartlett observes:

A teacher's actions are influenced by intentions in the social settings and by the beliefs and chains of reasoning that are held before and after the occurrence of the action. The point in all this is that if we want to improve our teaching through reflective inquiry, we must accept that it does not involve some modification of behavior by externally imposed directions or requirements, but that it requires deliberation and analysis of our ideas about teaching as a form of action based on our changed understandings. (1990: 203)

The role of teacher education in an art-craft conception of teaching is very different from that appropriate in science-research or theory-philosophy conceptions of teaching. Whereas the latter can be seen as top-down conceptions, which require teachers to modify their teaching in the direction of an externally based model of teaching, art-craft conceptions are essentially bottom-up. Teachers should not set out to look for a general method of teaching or to master a particular set of teaching skills but should constantly try to discover things that work for them, discarding old practices and taking on new ones. The role of teacher education is to help teachers discover their own personal style of teaching through focused teacher education activities and teaching practice. While generic teaching skills, principles, and techniques might be appropriate starting points in teaching, the teacher will select, adapt, and extend these, creating a unique personal style of teaching in the process. Teacher education is a process of constantly discovering and creating new alternatives (Fanselow 1987).

The different principles underlying the three conceptions of teaching can thus be summarized in the following statements of essential teaching skills:

Science-research conceptions
– Understand the learning principles.
– Develop tasks and activities based on the learning principles.

– Monitor students' performance on tasks to see that desired performance is being achieved.

Theory-philosophy conceptions
– Understand the theory and the principles.
– Select syllabuses, materials, and tasks based on the theory.
– Monitor your teaching to see that it conforms to the theory.

In the case of values-based approaches, the essential skills in teaching are:

– Understand the values behind the approach.
– Select only those educational means that conform to these values.
– Monitor the implementation process to ensure that the value system is being maintained.

Art-craft conceptions
– Treat each teaching situation as unique.
– Identify the particular characteristics of each situation.
– Try out different teaching strategies.
– Develop personal approaches to teaching.

In planning teacher education programs, decisions therefore have to be made concerning which conception of teaching is considered an appropriate basis for the program. Pennington (1990: 132) notes:

Whether implicitly or explicitly, every teacher preparation program embodies a philosophy of teaching that connects performance goals to training methods and course content. In the ideal case, each program requirement is covered by an explicit rationale that relates course content to specific outcomes for program graduates. Such a rationale incorporates (1) an articulated philosophy or theory of teaching and (2) statements relating that philosophy or theory to one or more specializations for which preparation is offered in the program.

How is the issue of an appropriate philosophy of teaching typically addressed in SLTE programs? One approach is to opt for *eclecticism*. In many programs, different courses reflect different assumptions about the nature of teaching. In a course on second language acquisition, for example, a science-research position may be advoocated, whereas in the same program a course on methodology might be built around a theory-philosophy approach, such as communicative language teaching or the Natural Approach. The instructor in charge of the teaching practicum course, however, might promote yet a third position, such as an art-craft approach. But as Zahorik (1986) pointed out, since these three conceptions of teaching offer quite different perspectives on what the essential skills of teaching are, it is not the case that they can simply be regarded as alternatives that can be exchanged according to the whims of the moment. Eclecticism is not an option, since the different conceptions of teaching represent fundamentally different representations of what teaching is and how teachers should approach their work.

A second approach is the *noncompatible view,* which is based on the belief that a particular teaching conception is valid and others are unacceptable and should be discouraged. This approach underlies teacher education programs that are articulated around a specific teaching methodology, such as the RSA Certificate and RSA Diploma, for which teachers are assessed according to how closely their performance during teaching practice matches the "presentation-practice-production" model of teaching. Many teacher education programs are similarly structured around a "received methodology," which teacher trainees are expected to assimilate and be able to replicate in their own teaching. Almarza (1996) documents the role such a methodology played in the foreign language teaching component of a postgraduate certificate in education course and the interaction between the teachers' own theories of teaching and the theory embodied in the program.

An alternative approach is to regard the different conceptions of teaching as forming a *developmental continuum.* From this perspective, teachers entering the teaching profession need technical competence in teaching and the confidence to teach according to proven principles. Science-research conceptions of teaching might well provide a good starting point for inexperienced teachers. As they gain experience, they can then modify and adapt these initial theories of teaching, moving toward the more interpretative views of teaching implicit in theory-philosophy conceptions. Eventually, as they develop their own personal theories of teaching, they can teach more from an art-craft approach, creating teaching approaches according to the particular constraints and dynamics of the situations in which they work. In this way, teacher development can be seen as a process of ongoing self-discovery and self-renewal, as top-down approaches to teaching are replaced by more bottom-up approaches, or approaches that blend the two.

3　Teachers' maxims

> The final source of the knowledge base
> [of teaching] is the least codified of all. It
> is the wisdom of practice itself, the
> maxims that guide (or provide reflective
> rationalization for) the practice of able
> teachers. (Shulman 1987: 11)

In recent years, research on teaching has attempted to understand teaching from the "inside" rather than from the "outside in" (Cochran-Smith and Lytle 1990). In both general research on teaching (e.g., Cortazzi 1991) as well as research on second language teaching (e.g., Bailey and Nunan 1995), the need to listen to teachers' voices in understanding classroom practice has been emphasized: "What is missing from the knowledge base for teaching, therefore, are the voices of the teachers themselves, the questions teachers ask, the way teachers use writing and intentional talk in their work lives, and the interpretive frames teachers use to understand and improve their own classroom practices" (Cochran-Smith and Lytle 1990: 2). Such an approach seeks to understand teaching in its own terms and in ways in which it is understood by teachers. This approach is in contrast to earlier research traditions, which presented an outsider's perspective on teaching and sought to identify quantifiable classroom behaviors and their effects on learning outcomes (Chaudron 1988; Dunkin and Biddle 1974). This chapter further explores an insider's perspective by examining teachers' understanding of teaching and the motivations for language teachers' interactive decisions and actions. The focus is hence on teachers' *implicit theories of teaching* (see Chapter 1). The basis for interactive decisions during lessons will be discussed in terms of working principles, or maxims, that teachers consciously or unconsciously refer to as they teach. The nature of these maxims and the ways in which they shape teachers' interpretation and management of teaching will be explored.

Two dimensions of teacher knowledge

Teachers employ different types of conceptual organization and meaning. One level of meaning relates to subject matter knowledge and how curricular and content aspects of teaching are conceptualized (Shulman 1987). Woods (1996) describes teachers' conceptions of lessons as made

49

up of conceptual units at different levels of abstraction. He distinguishes between the following: *overall conceptual goals* – the overall purposes teachers identify for a course; *global conceptual units* – the individual subcomponents of the curriculum (e.g., the grammar, reading, writing, and listening components of an integrated skills course); *intermediate conceptual units* – activities or clusters of activities framed in terms of accomplishing one of the higher-level conceptual goals; and *local conceptual units* – the specific things teachers do to achieve particular instructional effects. Other constructs that have been proposed to account for how teachers realize the curricular agendas they set for lessons and the kinds of cognitive processes they employ include *lesson formats* (Wong-Fillmore 1985), *tasks* (Doyle 1983), *scripts*, and *routines* (Shavelson and Stern 1981). Constructs such as these seek to describe how teachers approach the subject matter of teaching and how they transform content into learning. Much of this research draws on a framework of cognitive psychology and has provided evidence of the kinds of pedagogical content knowledge, reasoning, and problem solving teachers make use of as they teach (Clift 1991).

In addition to the curricular goals and content, teachers have other more personal views of teaching (Johnston 1990). Zeichner, Tabachnick, and Densmore (1987) try to capture this with the notion of *perspective,* which they define as the ways in which teachers understand, interpret, and define their environment and use such interpretation to guide their actions. They followed teachers through their year-long professional training and their first year in the classroom, and found that their personal perspectives served as powerful influences on how they taught. In describing the basis for teachers' conceptualizations of good practice, Clandinin (1985, 1986) introduced the concept of *image,* which she describes as "a central construct for understanding teachers' knowledge" (1985: 362). An image is a metaphor, such as "the classroom as home," "setting up a relationship with children," or "meeting the needs of students," that teachers may have in mind when they teach. Johnston (1992) suggests that images such as these are not always conscious, that they reflect how teachers view themselves in their teaching contexts, and that they form the subconscious assumptions on which their teaching practices are based. In a study of what second language teachers perceive to be good classes, Senior (1995) found that experienced ESL teachers in an Australian educational setting attempting to implement a communicative methodology appeared to have arrived at the tacit assumption that, to promote successful language learning, it is necessary to develop a bonded class – that is, one in which there is a positive, mutually supportive group atmosphere. The teachers appeared to employ a range of both conscious and unconscious strategies in order to develop a spirit of cohesion within their class groups.

Halkes and Deijkers (1984) refer to *teachers' teaching criteria,* which are defined as "personal subjective values a person tries to pursue or keep constant while teaching." Teachers hold personal views of themselves, their learners, their goals, and their role in the classroom, and they presumably try to reflect these in their practice. Marland (1987) examined the principles used to guide and interpret teaching, and identified five such working principles that were derived from stimulated recall interviews with teachers. For example, the "principle of progressive checking" involved checking students' progress periodically, identifying problems, and providing individual encouragement for low-ability students. Conners (1978) studied elementary teachers and found that all of those in her study used three overarching principles of practice to guide and explain their interactive teaching behavior: "suppressing emotions," "teacher authenticity," and "self-monitoring." The "principle of teacher authenticity" involved the teacher presenting herself in such a way that good personal relationships with students and a socially supportive classroom atmosphere would be achieved. This principle required the teacher to attempt to be open, sincere, and honest, as well as fallible.

In summary, two different kinds of knowledge influence teachers' understanding and practice of teaching. One relates to subject matter and curricular issues, and how the content of a lesson can be presented in an effective and coherent way. This is the aspect of teaching that has to do with curricular goals, lesson plans, instructional activities, materials, tasks, and teaching techniques. The other kind of knowledge relates to teachers' implicit theories of teaching – that is, their personal and subjective philosophy and their understanding of what constitutes good teaching. It is this dimension that forms the focus of this chapter.

Teachers' accounts of what they set out to achieve in lessons

When teachers talk about their teaching, they generally present a rational view of the kind of learning environment they try to create in their classes. They often describe their approach to lessons in terms of beliefs or principles that they try to put into practice in their teaching, reflecting their individual belief systems. Teachers' belief systems are founded on the goals, values, and beliefs they hold in relation to the content and process of teaching, and their understanding of the systems in which they work and their roles within it. These beliefs and values serve as the background to much of their decision making and action, and hence constitute what has been termed the "culture of teaching" (Richards and Lockhart 1994). Teachers' belief systems are stable sources of reference, are built up gradually over time, and relate to such dimensions of teaching as the teachers' theory of language, the nature of language teaching, the role of the teacher, effective teaching practices, and teacher-student relations (K. E. Johnson 1992a; see also Chapter 4 this volume).

Teachers are generally articulate in describing their belief systems, as the following extracts from conversations with teachers illustrate.[1] Carol, a British Council ESL teacher in Hong Kong, completed her education degree in the sixties and taught elementary school children for a number of years, then stopped and only recently returned to second language teaching. Both her earlier experience as a primary teacher and her more recent experience as a teacher of adults have influenced her approach to teaching.

"I think it's important to be positive as a personality. I think the teacher has to be a positive person. I think you have to show a tremendous amount of patience. And I think that if you have a good attitude you can project this to the students and hopefully establish a relaxed atmosphere in your classroom so that they will not dread to come to class but have a good class. I feel that it's important to have a lesson plan. Even though I did teach many years ago, at this stage coming back into the classroom, I think it's important to have a lesson plan of some sort. Because you need to know what you want to teach and how you are going to go from the beginning to the end. And also taking into consideration the students, where their ability is, what their background is. I have been in situations where I did not understand what was being taught or what was being said, and how frustrating it is and so when I try to approach it I say: how can I make it the easiest way for them to understand what they need to learn?"

Carol's philosophy emphasizes the teacher's attitude and the need to create a supportive environment for learning in the classroom. She stresses the need for lesson planning, but her justification for lesson plans is based on helping the students rather than helping the teacher.

Sally, who also teaches for the British Council in Hong Kong, has over ten years of teaching experience in a wide variety of situations, and is a certified TESL teacher and teacher trainer. Over the years her view of her role as a teacher has changed, moving from a teacher-led, tightly planned and executed approach to teaching to her current approach, in which she sees herself more as a guide or facilitator and consequently "takes a back seat." She tries to create lessons that enhance communication and cooperation between learners. Sally tries to implement this philosophy in every lesson, including a business English class she is currently teaching. Prior to one of her lessons, she described the approach she planned to take:

---

1 The teachers' narratives cited in this chapter are part of a corpus of teacher narratives, teacher interviews, and lesson observations collected at the British Council in Hong Kong in 1995.

"I know it's a business lesson but I really like to activate their knowledge. My beliefs are very much humanitarian in that they will learn if they feel a warm cooperative atmosphere in the classroom, so I'm very concerned that they build up a trust amongst themselves, and with me, so I like them to do activities that are more student-centered rather than relying on the teacher all the time. I'd like to be more a guide, a motivator rather than the one-and-all person who knows it all. A lot of students here are reluctant to accept that. They are reluctant to take on that responsibility. So sometimes it's like teaching them how to learn, and I find it a bit frustrating sometimes. I feel that perhaps they come in with expectations which aren't met. Some students receive those ideas very well and other students have barriers. So that's me as a teacher, and I like to vary things very much especially in three hours and twenty minutes. It's just very tiring. So I love to have variety of activities and that you could only do standing on your feet, in a way."

Here Sally articulates a student-based approach to teaching that is dependent on establishing trust between the students and the teacher. In order to achieve a student-centered lesson, Sally conducts most of the lesson as small group activities, with students working on tasks in pairs or groups and carrying out many of the functions that the teacher might perform in a more teacher-fronted class. The teacher's role is limited to setting up and monitoring activities, occasionally correcting errors, and maintaining variety and pace throughout the lesson. To enable her to achieve variety and timing, she uses a brief written lesson plan and monitors students' interest level throughout the lesson to decide when to move from one activity to the next. She explains that the final judge of whether to keep to the lesson plan or not "is the atmosphere in the class and the looks on my students' faces."

As these examples illustrate, teachers are generally concerned with more than simply issues of curriculum content. When they teach, they also attempt to implement a personal philosophy of teaching that reflects their understanding and beliefs about what good teaching is and how it is achieved.

The nature of teachers' maxims

maxim: a rule for good or sensible behavior, especially one which is in the form of a proverb or short saying. (*Cobuild English Language Dictionary*)

Conversations with teachers and observations of how teachers conduct their lessons suggest that teachers' belief systems lead to the development of rational principles that serve as a source of how teachers interpret their responsibilities and implement their plans, and that motivate their interactive decisions during a lesson. These principles function like rules for best behavior in that they guide the teachers' selection of choices from among a range of alternatives. Hence they function as maxims that guide the teachers' actions. These maxims are reflected both in how they conduct their teaching as well as in the language they use to talk about it.

Some interesting examples of the role of teachers' maxims in native language teaching are given in Cortazzi (1991). He examined 1,000 narratives (accounts of personal experiences) from elementary schoolteachers discussing their beliefs, perceptions, and values; their perspectives on teaching; and accounts of classroom incidents. Although the people in his sample were not teaching L2 students, a number of general working principles recurred in the narratives, including, "treat each child as an individual," "be flexible and "'play it by ear,'" and "maintain a sense of humor."

An example of a teacher responding to a personal maxim and abandoning her lesson plan as a consequence is seen in the following extract from one of the narratives in Cortazzi's study:

"Most of the teaching has to be very planned, sometimes things might crop up.

Well, you know we're doing this book about your school, well, it was somebody's birthday in the unit (for partially hearing children).

So I decided, 'Right, how old are you?' So I taught them to lip read the question, 'How old are you?' And they've learnt to write 'I'm 5,' 'I'm 6,' 'I'm 7.'

And then cropped up, something I hadn't planned for but which cropped up because one of the children in the unit, she was 8. She's in the other class.

And I just jumped on it. So whatever else I had planned for the day I just didn't do because something else had come up that was much more exciting. I mean, it may not sound exciting to you, but for me . . . we have to make things exciting, we have to grasp anything we can use.

Well, basically my teaching is planned because I've got to have a scheme of work in my mind, but I do play it by ear to a certain extent you've got to, if you've got something of interest you'll get far more from the children using it there and then." (Cortazzi 1991: 68–9)

In this extract the teacher explains how she abandoned what she had planned for a lesson and improvised a lesson around her pupils' ages, based on the children's response to something that occurred in the book they were reading. The teacher made an interactive decision because "something else had come up that was much more exciting." The teacher rationalizes in saying, "we have to make things exciting, we have to grasp anything we can use." This teacher is responding to the following implicit maxim:

THE MAXIM OF INVOLVEMENT: Follow the learners' interests to maintain student involvement.

When faced with a choice between following her lesson plan and doing something more exciting, the teacher opted for the latter because it would be more engaging for her learners.

An example of another second language teacher using a similar maxim is given in Woods (1996), which includes case studies of two teachers teaching the same ESL course in a Canadian university. One of them reported that the primary belief that influenced his approach to the course centered on the importance of student involvement in course content and the notion of student responsibility. The teacher believed in a learner-centered rather than teacher-centered classroom.

In discussing the teacher's approach to his teaching, Woods describes how this belief influences the teacher's decision making:

For this teacher, moment-to-moment decisions in the lesson were influenced by the students. In the videotaped lesson, there were many points at which his decisions were affected by a consideration of the learners which overrode the curriculum and his lesson plan. One activity in the lesson had two planned components; but the second one was abandoned when it became clear that the lesson had evolved in a different direction led by the interests of the learners. He made particular decisions on the spot on how to group the students for an activity in order to avoid certain personality clashes, and then he joined the groups in a certain order and dealt with the students in specific ways, decisions which were later elaborated on while watching the videotape in terms of his past experiences with these students, in terms of their personalities and working habits, and in terms of the preparation they had done for the activity. All of these factors influenced who he sat down with and what issues he broached.

Even at the most local level of his classroom decision-making, his style of speech with the students reflected an attitude of working things out with the students as the lesson proceeded. For example, when a learner brought up a point that he had not planned, he said "OK, I agree with you there." When he discussed his planning in the interviews as well, the content of his discourse as well as the style revealed a readiness to go wherever the students took him. (Woods 1996: 195)

Woods attributes this teacher's beliefs about effective teaching to his own experience as a language learner and his teaching experience. In contrast, Woods describes a case study of another teacher working in the same ESL program for whom the planned curriculum was the primary reference point in her teaching. Her concern throughout was to cover the material prescribed in the curriculum and consequently to ensure that the material she had planned to teach was taught. A maxim she operated from was:

THE MAXIM OF PLANNING: Plan your teaching and try to follow your plan.

Woods gives an example of how this maxim influences the teacher's decision making during a lesson. The teacher is presenting a lesson on definitions and has a carefully planned outline for the lesson. During the lesson a student volunteers an alternative interpretation of a definition pattern she is presenting. But the teacher downplays the student's comments to enable her to keep to her plan. She later comments:

"After I did it [elicited the students' opinions] I was glad that I did it because I thought it worked out well . . . and the information they provided me with *helped lead me to where I wanted to go*, although I had to kind of fill out what they said because they were on the right track but *they weren't exactly giving me what was necessary.* In the afternoon class I did the same thing . . . and that time it didn't work as well because the students *didn't give me the kind of information I was looking for.*" (Woods 1991: 10–11; italics added)

Woods comments that the preplanned curriculum was central in this teacher's thinking. She involved the students only to the extent of helping her implement her preplanned lesson and was not prepared to depart from it in response to student feedback. Woods comments about this teacher: "At various points in the course when there was a conflict between sticking with her planned curricular activity and following another direction initiated by the students, she made the decision to carry out the planned activity" (p. 10). This teacher's approach could be attributable both to her personal style as well as her views about how a language is best taught. She explains: "I like things to be organized or else I feel out of control and nervous. . . . I'm one of those who spends a lot of time organizing and planning" (Woods 1996: 168). She viewed many aspects of language learning as mastery of a progression of items, "beginning with the most basic in a simplified and decontextualized form, and leading to the more complex and more contextualized. Her comments reflected a view that learning starts with explicit information, which first has to be consciously understood, and then has to be applied and practised in order to be used in other contexts" (Woods 1996: 218).

Differences between the implicit maxims underlying these two teachers' practices does not imply, however, that the "student-centered" teacher was superior to the "curriculum-centered" one. As Woods points out, Teacher A's focus on the curriculum "does not imply a lack of concern for the students, but rather a particular view of the roles of the curriculum and the students in the instantiation of the course" (1996: 27).

The way in which personal maxims can lead to very different approaches to teaching is further illustrated in a case study of two ESL teachers in a Hong Kong secondary school, described in Tsui (1995). For one, a central principle in her teaching was to keep the class disciplined and orderly so that students can learn most effectively from her lessons:

THE MAXIM OF ORDER: Maintain order and discipline throughout the lesson.

The teacher was a Chinese woman with eight years of teaching experience who was teaching a secondary four (10th grade) class. Her class was regarded as one of the best in the school because of the students' academic results and their well-disciplined behavior. She conducted her class in a somewhat formal "teacher-centered" manner and judged her lessons as effective according to whether they accomplished what was planned and achieved their learning outcomes. She saw her role as ensuring that the classroom was a place where students could learn in a well-disciplined manner. Tsui attributes much of the teacher's approach to her cultural and educational background:

May Ling had been brought up in the Chinese culture, which valued subservience to authority and emphasized observation of protocol. She had been educated in a system that viewed teachers as people with knowledge and wisdom, and in a society that held teachers in great respect. In this culture, the teacher's role was to impart knowledge, the students' role was to receive knowledge, and the relationship between students and teachers was formal. . . .

May Ling observed the traditional classroom protocols as an accepted means of showing respect for the teacher. To her, the classroom is a place where students learn in a well-disciplined manner, and the teacher should be in control of herself, her students, and her subject.

Despite her wish to encourage student participation in her classes, her students "seldom volunteered answers, and she sometimes had to call on someone and wait for a long time before a response was forthcoming." (Tsui 1995: 357)

Tsui compares this teacher with another teacher, whose students were of the same level and in the same school, but whose class was very different from May Ling's. For him, a different maxim was central in his approach to teaching:

THE MAXIM OF ENCOURAGEMENT: Seek ways to encourage student learning.

This teacher was a New Zealander with three years of teaching experience, who attempted to break away from typical Hong Kong classroom practices in his class.

Students did not have to stand up to greet him, and they did not have to raise their hands or stand up when they answered questions. The classroom atmosphere was very relaxed. The students were noisier in the sense that they volunteered answers from their seats, and there was a lot more laughter. George was quite happy to accept whatever contributions they made, whether they raised their hands or not. (Tsui 1995: 357)

In comparison to the students in May Ling's class, George's students were much more confident and outspoken. When asking questions, he would give students time to discuss the question among themselves before answering, because he felt it made responding in front of the class less threatening. He encouraged an informal relationship with his students. He felt he was not obliged to follow conventional seating arrangements with single rows, but did whatever he felt was necessary to promote student-student interaction. Tsui attributes this teacher's approach to teaching to his Western cultural background.

George had been brought up in the Western culture and had gone through a Western education system, in which more emphasis was placed on the individual, most classrooms had done away with the traditional protocol, and the relationship between students and teachers was much less formal. These differences in cultural and educational backgrounds seemed to permeate the practical theories underlying the two teachers' classroom practices. (Tsui 1995: 359)

These examples demonstrate that teachers possess rational orientations toward teaching as well as personal beliefs about what constitutes good teaching, and these lead them to try to create specific conditions in their classrooms. These conditions reflect the teachers' view of the role of the teacher and of the learners, their beliefs about the kind of classroom climate they think best supports learning, what they believe constitutes good methodology, and the quality of classroom interaction and language use they seek to achieve. The maxims that teachers develop reflect their personal and individual understanding of the "best" or "right" way to teach, and provide the source for much of the teacher's interactive decisions throughout a lesson.

Other maxims that teachers refer to in describing their teaching philosophies and that appear to account for many of their preactive and interactive decisions include:

THE MAXIM OF ACCURACY: Work for accurate student output.

THE MAXIM OF EFFICIENCY: Make the most efficient use of class time.

THE MAXIM OF CONFORMITY: Make sure your teaching follows the prescribed method.

THE MAXIM OF EMPOWERMENT: Give the learners control.

K. M. Bailey (1996) studied the interactive decisions of teachers during lessons and the reasons they departed from their lesson plans, and identified a number of principles underlying their decision making, including "serve the common good" and "teach to the moment" (see Chapter 6). Teachers presumably have a range of principles such as these that they employ, and in any particular lesson they choose the ones that seem most likely to help them create a successful lesson. Maxims that a teacher seeks to realize in a low-level class may be different from those the teacher feels are appropriate for an advanced class. The constraints of the classroom, however, often restrict the choice of maxims, accounting for the fact that teachers sometimes do not "practice what they preach." For example, Yim (1993) describes a study of second language teachers in Singapore, who in articulating their approach to teaching professed a clear preference for a communicative methodology in which the focus was on authentic, meaning-focused activities. But when observed in their classrooms, many of them made greater use of accuracy-focused activities, since they felt these were necessary in order to prepare students for examinations. This problem was encountered by Julian, an experienced ESL teacher at the British Council in Hong Kong who is committed to a communicative approach to teaching and who sees his role as a facilitator who should create an optimum learning environment. In one of his observed lessons, however, this philosophy was less in evidence. It was more of a grammar-focused series of activities that culminated in a writing task. When asked if this lesson reflected his beliefs in a communicative approach to teaching, he commented:

"I don't necessarily apply teaching principles all the time. My general principle is just to make things student-centered and communicative. The problem with this class is that I can't always do that because people are very shy. So you can't really make it student-centered because the students don't say anything. You have to call everyone by their name which makes it a little bit more teacher-centered. It was communicative in a sense that they were writing together in groups rather than on their own. That's why I got them around the table to emphasize they are not just working on their own."

Ulichny (1996) provides a detailed account of how a teacher renegotiates during teaching by replacing one working principle with another. The teacher is an experienced ESL teacher of a college ESL reading class. Among the principles she sought to bring to her teaching was a belief in the need to help students see reading as the building of meaning from texts (rather than focusing on linguistic forms), to create lessons that were at an appropriate level of difficulty but not discouraging to students, and to provide lessons where students were actively engaged in reading rather than directed by the teacher. In a segment of a lesson Ulichny describes in detail, the teacher has assigned students to read a chapter from a sociology text. She has given the class a simplified lecture that restates some of the main points that they have read and the students are asked to locate some these points in the text. As the lesson proceeds according to the teacher's first principle of "helping the students make meaning from the text," she discovers that they have not understood the main points of her lecture. So she decides to adjust her planned lesson in order "to make the text and talk comprehensible to the students." A different principle now comes into play, the principle of creating a lesson at an appropriate level of difficulty, which she does by creating a scaffold, or propositional structure, of the text through questions and answers with the students. Gradually the teacher takes on more of the tasks she had originally planned for the students to do.

Her first recourse in the face of difficulty is to simplify the level of the task and to provide the class with more guidance to complete it. But when these techniques fail, she pushes them forward onto the next question by completing the task herself. (Ulichny 1996: 191)

Ulichny's study demonstrates the interaction of different beliefs and principles during teaching as the teacher unconsciously weighs one factor against another.

Teachers' maxims thus can be viewed as outcomes of their evolving theories of teaching. They are personal working principles that reflect individual philosophies of teaching and are developed from experience of teaching and learning, from teacher education experiences, and from teachers' own personal beliefs and value systems. Maxims are more specific and practical than the "images" that have been described by researchers such as Clandinin (1985) and Johnston (1992). They can be regarded as images that have been transformed into models for practical action. The development of personal working principles, or maxims, can be viewed as an important goal in teacher development.

At the initial stages of teacher development, what Shulman (1987) terms "instructional skills" are a central component of the teacher's expertise (see Chapter 1). Instructional skills refer to strategies for organizing and presenting content and for the effective management of teaching and learning in the classroom. Developing skill in these aspects of teaching involves the mastery of routines and procedures that teachers can call upon in order to move successfully through the agenda of a lesson (Berliner 1987). Moving to the next level involves the development of a personal theory of teaching, one containing a coherent set of beliefs, values, and principles that provide an orientation to teaching and a framework for practice. Elbaz (1981) refers to this growth from use of procedures to the employment of principles by distinguishing between "rules of practice" and "principles of practice," the latter corresponding to the notion of teaching maxims presented here.

According to Elbaz, rules of practice are brief, clearly formulated statements prescribing how to behave in frequently encountered teaching situations. Implementation of a rule of practice is a simple matter of recognizing a situation and remembering the rule. In contrast a principle of practice is a more general construct than a rule of practice, derived from personal experience, and embodying purpose in a deliberate and reflective way, which can be drawn upon to guide a teacher's actions and explain the reasons for those actions. (Clark and Peterson 1986: 290)

Implications for teacher education

The view presented here offers a perspective on teacher development that has some useful implications for teacher education. The focus on subjective accounts of the principles underlying classroom practice offers an important perspective on what teaching is and how people acquire the capacity to teach, particularly since beliefs and principles serve as a filter through which new information and experience is interpreted. If teachers are guided in their teaching and in learning to teach both by personal maxims as well as by general instructional considerations, the nature, status, and use of such maxims clearly deserve recognition in teacher education programs. Teachers' beliefs about the principles underlying successful teaching form part of the knowledge base student teachers bring to SLTE programs. Hence they are a key element in determining how student teachers respond to training experiences. Almarza (1996: 59) emphasizes the importance of recognizing the nature and role of teachers' beliefs:

Although their ideas might not have been put forward in academic discourse, they may serve as a basis on which to make the connections between theory and practice which are crucial in their professional development. Yet we won't be able to establish what kind of contribution teacher education courses make to student teachers' development and how they contribute to student teachers' education if we do not know what was already there and how this old knowledge relates to practice.

Teachers' implicit theories provide a useful perspective for student teachers to examine in the course of their professional preparation, as they explore both their own thinking-in-action as well as that of others. The making explicit of beliefs, principles, and values can be an ongoing focus of teacher development programs, since as Clandinin and others have demonstrated, teachers' images and perspectives often have a powerful and lasting influence on their thinking and practice, and may also create resistance to alternative modes of thought and action. Identifying the maxims that teachers and student teachers use to guide their teaching can be achieved in a variety of ways, including narratives, journal writing, discussion, and other forms of critical reflection. Prior to a lesson, teachers can articulate the principles they hope to apply during the lesson. Following the lesson they can then review to see in what ways the lesson reflected their principles. K. M. Bailey (1996) suggests that student teachers discuss ways in which their lessons departed from their lesson plans, and in the process identify the principles that accounted for such departures: "Preservice teachers can learn by discussing these issues with one another and with more experienced cooperating teachers after their own lessons, or by examining videotapes or transcripts of lessons taught by other teachers" (p. 37). Once identified, student teachers' maxims can serve as one source of information that can help them interpret and evaluate their own teaching, as well as the teaching of others.

However, as with images of teaching, it is not the case that teachers' maxims should go unchallenged (see Calderhead and Robson 1991; Johnston 1992). A supervisor may conclude that a teacher is teaching with an inappropriate maxim, for example, or that a maxim is being overused to the detriment of student learning. While a supervisor may not agree that the maxims a teacher follows represent an appropriate way of teaching, recognizing them and examining their role in shaping thoughts and actions can be a useful step in facilitating the student teacher's future professional growth.

Part II Perspectives on teacher thinking

4 Teacher beliefs and decision making

Conceptualizations of the nature of teaching determine the way the process of teacher education is approached. As was illustrated in Chapter 2, if teaching is viewed as a science, scientific investigation and empirical research are seen as the source of valid principles of teaching. Good teaching involves the application of research findings, and the teacher's role is to put research-based principles into practice. Alternatively, teaching may be viewed as accumulated craft knowledge, and the study of the practices of expert practitioners of their craft may be seen as the primary data for a theory of teaching. In recent years, an alternative metaphor has emerged within the field of teacher education and is now making its way into SLTE. This is the notion of teaching as a thinking activity, which has been characterized as "a common concern with the ways in which knowledge is actively acquired and used by teachers and the circumstances that affect its acquisition and employment" (Calderhead 1987: 5). Calderhead points out that interest in teachers' thinking was a response to dissatisfaction with behaviorist approaches to the study of teaching in the 1970s:

Ideologically, viewing teachers as active agents in the development of their own practice, as decision-makers using their specialist knowledge to guide their actions in particular situations, underlined the autonomous, responsible aspects of teachers' work, and provided an appealing rationale for considering teaching as a worthy, complex, demanding profession, especially when contrasted with the previously dominant view of teaching as the mastering of a series of effective teaching behaviours. (Calderhead 1987: 5)

The teacher-as-thinker metaphor captures the focus on how teachers conceptualize their work and the kinds of thinking and decision making that underlie their practice. Rather than viewing the development of teaching skill as the mastery of general principles and theories that have been determined by others, the acquisition of teaching expertise is seen to be a process that involves the teacher in actively constructing a personal and workable theory of teaching. Burns comments:

Interest in the relationships between classroom behavior and teacher thinking and decision-making is partly the result of an acknowledgement that the enactment of the curriculum is not the linear "ends-means" process of discrete sequential stages, suggested by earlier curriculum theorists. Rather,

65

it is grounded in personally evolved theories or sets of beliefs about teaching and learning. (1992: 57)

This orientation to teaching is the focus of this chapter, which seeks to clarify the concept of teaching as a thinking process, to describe research on second language teachers that has been carried out from this perspective, and to examine implications for the field of SLTE.

Any attempt to characterize the thinking processes underlying a process as complex and multifaceted as teaching is fraught with difficulties. Fortunately, several scholars have tried to tease apart some of the issues that are involved (e.g., Calderhead 1987; Clark and Peterson 1986; Clark and Yinger 1979) and reveal something of what Clark and Peterson refer to as the "cognitive psychology" of teaching. In their survey of teachers' thought processes, Clark and Peterson (1986) identify three major categories of teachers' thought processes: (a) teachers' theories and beliefs; (b) teachers' planning or preactive decision making; and (c) teachers' interactive thoughts and decisions. This chapter focuses on teachers' theories and beliefs and their interactive thinking. (Preactive decision making is the focus of Chapter 5.) While research on teachers' theories and beliefs tries to identify the psychological contexts underlying teacher thinking and decision making, research on teachers' preactive and interactive thinking seeks to identify the thinking and decision making employed by teachers before and during teaching. In studying the knowledge and cognitive skills used by teachers, a variety of different research approaches has been employed, including questionnaires, interviews, think-aloud procedures (in which teachers verbalize their thoughts while engaged in tasks such as lesson planning), planning tasks, stimulated recall (in which teachers examine a videotape or audiotape of a lesson and try to recall their thought processes or decisions at different points in the lesson), as well as written accounts of teaching, such as case studies, journals, and narratives. While data obtained from such sources provide only indirect evidence of teachers' thought processes during teaching, they can serve to broaden our understanding of the role of beliefs and decision making in teaching.

The nature of teachers' belief systems

A primary source of teachers' classroom practices is belief systems – the information, attitudes, values, expectations, theories, and assumptions about teaching and learning that teachers build up over time and bring with them to the classroom. Shavelson and Stern (1981) suggest that what teachers do is governed by what they think, and that teachers' theories and beliefs serve as a filter through which a host of instructional judgments and decisions are made (see Chapter 1). Teacher beliefs form a structured set of principles that are derived from experience, school practice, personality, education theory, reading, and other sources. Cummings points out:

The kinds of practical knowledge which teachers use in teaching, appear to exist largely in very personalized terms, based on unique experiences, individual conceptions, and their interactions with local contexts. It tends to have a personal significance which differs from prescribed models of educational theory. (1989: 46–7)

For example, in a questionnaire study of the beliefs of English teachers in Hong Kong schools, Richards, Tung, and Ng (1992) found that the 249 teachers sampled held a relatively consistent set of beliefs relating to such issues as the nature of the ESL curriculum in Hong Kong, the role of English in society, differences between English and Chinese, the relevance of theory to practice, the role of textbooks, and their own role in the classroom. In comparing English and Chinese, most of the teachers felt that English has more grammar rules than Chinese; most disagreed that English has a larger vocabulary or more colloquial expressions or more flexibility in communication than Chinese. When asked what they thought was the best way to learn a language, they said that learners should expose themselves to the language as far as possible, interact with native speakers, and read books in English. They did not believe that either studying the rules of the language or repeating and memorizing chunks of language was helpful. Compared with the experienced and trained teachers, inexperienced and untrained teachers were more likely to think that grammatical theories of language are useful to language teaching, and believe more strongly in the value of requiring students to memorize dialogues. The teaching methods they thought most useful were identified as a grammar-based approach, a functional approach, and a situational approach. Differences in their beliefs, however, resulted from the amount of teaching experience they had and whether they subscribed to a primarily functional or grammar-based orientation to teaching.

Burns (1992) investigated the beliefs of six ESL teachers and identified a core of underlying beliefs that appeared to influence their approach to language teaching and their instructional practices. These beliefs related to:

- the nature of language as it relates to beginning language learning
- the relationship between written and spoken language in beginning language learning
- the nature of beginning language learning and the strategies relevant to language learning at this stage
- learners, their ability to learn, and their ability to learn English
- the nature of the language classroom and the teacher's role within it

Of the latter belief, Burns comments:

The establishment of positive and non-threatening classroom "dynamics" was considered to be a crucial element of the language classroom. Teachers saw themselves as having a central role and responsibility in facilitating good relationships among students and between themselves and their students. This represents "the mirror image" of the concern with affective learning factors and is viewed as an essential contribution to such things as building confidence, making learners feel "comfortable" and "at ease," lessening their passivity and helping them to relate positively to each other. (1992: 62)

Teachers' beliefs may differ significantly from those of their learners, leading to misperceptions about various dimensions of teaching. Brindley (1984) points out that beliefs held by many Western language teachers can be stated as:

– Learning consists of acquiring organizing principles through encountering experience.
– The teacher is a resource person who provides language input for the learner to work on.
– Language data is to be found everywhere – in the community and in the media as well as in textbooks.
– It is the role of the teacher to assist learners to become self-directed by providing access to language data through such activities as active listening, role play and interaction with native speakers.
– For learners, learning a language consists of forming hypotheses about the language input to which they will be exposed, these hypotheses being constantly modified in the direction of the target model.

(1984: 97)

Learners' beliefs, however, particularly if they come from an Asian cultural background, are more likely to be these:

– Learning consists of acquiring a body of knowledge.
– The teacher has this knowledge and the learner does not.
– It is the role of the teacher to impart this knowledge to the learner through such activities as explanation, writing and example.
– The learner will be given a program in advance.
– Learning a language consists of learning the structural rules of the language and the vocabulary through such activities as memorisation, reading and writing.

(Brindley 1984: 97)

Here there is a clear basis for a conflict between the teachers' and the learners' views about the nature and value of teaching and learning activities.

A number of studies have sought to investigate the extent to which teachers' theoretical beliefs influence their classroom practices. K. E. Johnson (1991), in a study of this kind, used three measures to identify ESL teachers' beliefs: a descriptive account of what teachers believe constitutes an ideal ESL classroom context, a lesson plan analysis task, and a beliefs inventory. In the sample of teachers studied, she identified three different methodological positions: a skills-based approach, which views language as consisting of four discrete language skills; a rules-based approach, which views language as a process of rule-governed creativity; and a function-based approach, which focuses on the use of authentic language within situational contexts and seeks to provide opportunities for functional and communicative language use in the classroom. The majority of the teachers in the sample held clearly defined beliefs that consistently reflected one of these three methodological approaches. Teachers representing each theoretical orientation were then observed while teaching, and the majority of their lessons were found to be consistent with their theoretical orientation. A teacher who expressed a skill-based theoretical orientation generally presented lessons in which the focus was primarily on skill acquisition. A teacher with the rule-based orientation tended to employ more activities and exercises that served to reinforce knowledge of grammatical structures. She constantly referred to grammar even during reading and writing activities, for example, by asking students to identify a key grammatical structure and to explain the rule that governed its use. The function-based teachers, on the other hand, selected activities that typically involved the learners' personal expression, teaching word meaning and usage through a meaningful context, choosing reading activities that focused on the concepts or ideas within the text, and using context-rich writing activities that encouraged students to express their ideas without attention to grammatical correctness.

In exploring the relationship between teachers' beliefs and classroom practices, Woods (1991) carried out a longitudinal study of two teachers with different theoretical orientations who taught the same ESL course in a Canadian university (see Chapter 3). According to Woods, one teacher had a "curriculum-based" view of teaching and the other a "student-based" view. A curriculum-based view of teaching implies that decisions related to the implementation of classroom activities are based primarily on what is preplanned according to the curriculum. Student-based teaching, on the other hand, implies that decisions are based primarily on factors related to the particular group of students in the classroom at that particular moment. Woods found that for each teacher there was strong evidence that:

1. The decisions made in planning and carrying out the course were internally consistent, and consistent with deeper underlying assumptions and beliefs about language, learning and teaching; yet
2. Each teacher's decisions and beliefs differed dramatically from the other along a number of specifiable dimensions.

(Woods 1991: 4)

For example, the teacher with the "curricular" view of teaching explained her goals and evaluated her teaching in terms of planned curricular content. Although she often mentioned the students in talking about her lessons, they were not typically for her a starting point in making instructional decisions. She tended to evaluate her teaching in terms of how successfully she had accomplished what she had set out to do according to the curriculum. When there was a choice between following up something that developed in the course of a lesson as opposed to keeping to her plan, she invariably followed her plan. The second teacher, on the other hand, was guided much more by student responses. He was much more prepared to modify and reinterpret the curriculum based on what the students wanted.

Smith (1996), in another Canadian study of ESL teachers in postsecondary ESL classes, found that teachers' instructional decisions were highly consistent with expressed beliefs, and that personal belief systems influenced how teachers ranked their institution's explicit course objectives for the courses they were assigned to teach. Among teachers teaching the same course, those with a structured grammar-based view of language selected different goals from teachers holding a functionally based view of language.

In each of the studies described here, the teachers were relatively free to put their beliefs into practice. However, there are also well-documented accounts of situations where there is not a high degree of correspondence between teachers' expressed beliefs and their classroom practices. Duffy and Anderson (1986) studied eight reading teachers and found that only four of them consistently employed practices that directly reflected their beliefs. Factors cited as likely to prevent teachers from teaching according to their beliefs include the need to follow a prescribed curriculum, lack of suitable resources, and students' ability levels. Hoffman and Kugle (1982) found no significant relationship between teachers' beliefs about reading and the kinds of verbal feedback they gave during reading lessons. Yim (1993) likewise found in studying ESL teachers in Singapore that while they were able to articulate beliefs about the role of grammar teaching from a communicative orientation, these beliefs were not evident in their classroom practices, which were driven more by exam-based, structured grammar activities of a non-communicative kind.

Teacher belief systems have also been studied in terms of how they influence the thinking and practice of novice teachers. The belief system of novice teachers as they enter the profession often serves as a lens through which they view both the content of the teacher development program and their language teaching experiences (see Chapter 1). For example, Almarza (1996) studied a group of four student teachers in a foreign language teacher education program in the United Kingdom, and examined how the relationship between their internalized models of teaching, often acquired informally through their experience as foreign language learners, interacted with the models they were introduced to in their teacher education program. The teachers responded quite differently to the method they were being trained to use in their teacher education program – a modified direct method. One teacher welcomed the structure introduced by the method, because it provided her with a tool to manage her teaching and gave her confidence. She measured her own success in terms of how closely she was able to follow the method. For her, the method superseded any instinctive views she had about the nature of teaching:

"Now having applied it [the method] with . . . both classes and private students, I can see why it's been called the 'miracle' method! Even my least confident students have been speaking the language with good pronunciation and without making mistakes and I know they'll never forget what they've learned. . . . With this method they never hear an incorrect version – so, of course, they don't make mistakes.

The method was without question the decisive factor in my carrying out TP successfully. It gave me absolute confidence and it had a positive attitude on the pupils towards French or Spanish and towards me, as it allowed me, for the first time, to really achieve something in the language and feel that they had achieved something." (quoted in Almarza 1996: 60)

By contrast, others rejected the method because it conflicted with their own theories of teaching. One said she could not believe in a methodology that did not consider the learner as the center of the learning process.

"I feel first that it is not respecting the students' intelligence, in a way. Students may not have the word in the foreign language for a book or a chair, but they know very well that it is a book and a chair and to have to spend 10 minutes arguing or not arguing, but deciding that this is a book and this is a chair, seems to insult the students. . . . The students may not be very motivated by that kind of presentation. . . . Why should the student want to learn, I mean, to learn those items in the first place? . . . I am just wondering to what extent, where is the balance on that scale, where can you sort of exert your knowledge as a teacher in order to choose the right kind of input, to guide the students to look into, let's say, certain texts, or certain whatever, but at the same time keeping up motivation in the student." (quoted in Almarza 1996: 60)

Almarza's study shows that while a teacher education program might be built around a well-articulated model of teaching, the model is interpreted in different ways by individual trainee teachers as they deconstruct it in the light of their teaching experiences and reconstruct it drawing on their own beliefs and assumptions about themselves, language, teaching learners, and learning.

The ways in which teachers' personal theories influence their perception and evaluation of their own teaching was further illustrated in a study of a group of novice teachers completing an introductory teacher preparation program in Hong Kong, the UCLES/RSA Certificate in TEFLA (Richards, Ho, and Giblin 1996). One of the issues that was studied was the theories of teaching held by each of the teachers in the program. Data were provided by written reports of their planning, classroom observations, interactive and evaluation decisions, as well recordings of discussions with their supervisors. The individual differences in the way the five of them planned, monitored, and described their own teaching suggested different ways in which they conceptualized teaching. These differences can be summarized in the following way.

A *teacher-centered perspective* sees the key features of a lesson primarily in terms of teacher factors, such as classroom management, teacher's explanations, teacher's questioning skills, teacher's presence, voice quality, manner, and so on. In this view, a lesson is a performance by the teacher. A different view of a lesson, which can be termed the *curriculum-centered perspective,* sees a lesson in terms of a segment of instruction. Relevant focuses include lesson goals, structuring, transitions, materials, task types, and content flow and development. A third perspective on a lesson can be called the *learner-centered perspective.* This views the lesson in terms of its effect on learners and refers to such factors as student participation, interest, and learning outcomes. These different perspectives on a lesson are summarized in Table 4.1.

Any lesson can be conceptualized in terms of any or all of these perspectives. In the study, although each of the teachers (Teachers A, B, C, D, and E) referred to all three aspects of lessons in describing their teaching, Teacher A's focus of awareness was more consistently on teacher factors than other dimensions of her lessons. Teacher B included all three perspectives in her discussions of her lessons and moved throughout from one perspective to another, though the role of the teacher was a recurring focus. For Teacher C, the learner perspective had priority. For Teachers D and E, lessons were discussed more frequently from the teacher's point of view and in terms of the design of the lesson. In discussing each other's teaching in group sessions, these different perspec-

TABLE 4.1.   DIFFERENT PERSPECTIVES ON A LESSON

Teacher-centered focus	The teacher is the primary focus; factors include the teacher's role, classroom management skills, questioning skills, presence, voice quality, manner, and quality of the teacher's explanations and instructions.
Curriculum-centered focus	The lesson as an instructional unit is the primary focus; factors include lesson goals, opening, structuring, task types, flow, and development and pacing.
Learner-centered focus	The learners are the primary focus; factors include the extent to which the lesson engaged them, participation patterns, and extent of language use.

tives often emerged. For example, Teacher B, commenting on one of A's lessons, described it from the "curriculum" perspective:

"You did a good job on building it up, starting with revision. You didn't waste any time on setting up the lesson. It flowed through beautifully."

Teacher A herself, however, commented on her lesson from the teacher's perspective:

"I thought the lesson deteriorated as it got to the end. I wasn't happy with the drilling. I didn't give myself enough time to do it properly."

Teacher C commented on the same lesson from the learners' perspective:

"I liked the way your lesson went at the end. The students were being expressive. They put feeling into it."

The differences in the individual teachers' views of a successful lesson can be seen by listing the three different perspectives according to the priority of each teacher (Table 4.2).

Interactive decision making

While teachers' belief systems shape the way teachers understand teaching and the priorities they accord to different dimensions of teaching, the thinking that teachers employ during the teaching process itself is also crucial to our understanding of the nature of teaching skills. In classic articles on educational research, Clark and Yinger (1979), Shavelson and

TABLE 4.2. PRIORITIES FOR EACH TEACHER ACCORDING TO THEIR PRIMARY
FOCUS OF CONCERN

	1 (highest priority)	*2*	*3 (lowest priority)*
Teacher A	teacher	curriculum	learners
Teacher B	teacher and learners		curriculum
Teacher C	learners	curriculum	teacher
Teacher D	curriculum	teacher	learners
Teacher E	teacher	curriculum	learners

Stern (1981), and Clark and Peterson (1986) identified interactive decision making (decisions teachers make while teaching) as constituting a
key dimension of teachers' thought processes. According to their model
of teacher decision-making processes, teaching is a type of improvisational performance. During the process of teaching, the teacher fills out
and adapts the lesson outline based on how the students respond to the
lesson. While the teacher's planning decisions provide a framework for
approaching a lesson, in the course of teaching the lesson that framework may be substantially revised as the teacher responds to students'
understanding and participation and redirects the lesson in midstream
(see Chapter 6).

How does this reshaping and redirection come about? Shavelson and
Stern (1981) introduced the metaphor of "routines" to describe how
teachers manage many of the moment-to-moment processes of teaching.
Teachers monitor instruction by looking for cues that the students are
following the lesson satisfactorily. They teach using well-established routines. Berliner has commented on "the enormously important role
played by mental scripts and behavioral routines in the performance of
expert teachers" (1987: 72):

These routines are the shared, scripted, virtually automated pieces of action
that constitute so much of our daily lives [as teachers]. In classrooms, routines
often allow students and teachers to devote their attention to other, perhaps
more important matters inherent in the lesson. In [a study] of how an opening
homework review is conducted, an expert teacher was found to be brief,
taking about one-third less time than a novice. She was able to pick up
information about attendance, and about who did or did not do the
homework, and identified who was going to get help in the subsequent lesson.
She was able to get all the homework corrected, and elicited mostly correct
answers throughout the activity. And she did so at a brisk pace and without
ever losing control of the lesson. Routines were used to record attendance, to
handle choral responding during the homework checks, and for hand raising
to get attention. The expert used clear signals to start and finish lesson
segments. Interviews with the expert revealed how the goals for the lesson, the

time constraints, and the curriculum itself were blended to direct the activity. The expert appeared to have a script in mind throughout the lesson, and she followed that script very closely.

Novice teachers, by comparison, lack a repertoire of routines and scripts; creating them and mastering their use occupies a major portion of their time during teaching (Fogerty, Wang, and Creek 1983). In the study of teachers completing the RSA Certificate program discussed earlier, for example, a recurring concern of the teachers was the use of such basic techniques as eliciting, drilling, checking concepts (i.e., checking that students understood new teaching points), monitoring (i.e., attending to student performance and giving feedback on errors), and how to use the overhead projector and the white board. Discussion of how to carry out these procedures effectively occupied a substantial portion of time in group feedback sessions with their tutors.

This is in line with findings of a body of research on differences between the knowledge, thinking, and actions of experts and novices. Experts and novices have been found to differ in the way they understand and represent problems and in the strategies they choose to solve them (Livingston and Borko 1989). Novices have less fully developed schemata. In this context, schemata are described as abstract knowledge structures that summarize information about many particular cases and the relationships among them (Anderson 1984). Studies of expert teachers have shown that they are able to move through the agendas of a lesson in a cohesive and flexible way, compared to the more fragmented efforts of novice teachers:

The cognitive schemata of experts typically are more elaborate, more complex, more interconnected, and more easily accessible than those of novices. Therefore expert teachers have larger, better-integrated stores of facts, principles, and experiences to draw upon as they engage in planning, interactive teaching, and reflection. . . .

In the lessons we observed, the success of the experts' improvisation seemed to depend upon their ability to provide examples quickly and to draw connections between students' comments or questions and the lesson's objectives. In terms of cognitive structure, successful improvisational teaching requires that the teacher have an extensive network of interconnected, easily accessible schemata and be able to select particular strategies, routines, and information from these schemata during actual teaching and learning interactions based on specific classroom occurrences. (Livingston and Borko 1989: 36)

Experienced teachers hence have well-developed mental representations of typical students, of typical tasks, and of expected problems and solutions. As Calderhead (1987) points out, experienced teachers

75

seemed to know the kinds of home backgrounds of students, they knew what to expect in the way of knowledge and skills in their classrooms, they had an image of the likely number of students who would need help, they had an image of the types of behaviors and discipline problems that could be expected. They knew what the students might possess in the way of previous experience, skills, and knowledge. . . . This kind of pedagogical knowledge is learned from thousands of hours of instruction, and tens of thousands of interactions with students. It is knowledge that influences classroom organization and management and is the basis for intercepting the curriculum. (quoted in Berliner 1987: 64)

Decision-making models of teaching propose that when problems arise in teaching, a teacher may call up an alternative routine or react interactively to the situation, redirecting the lesson based on his or her understanding of the nature of the problem and how best to address it. Teachers' overriding concern, according to Shavelson and Stern (1981), is to maintain the flow of the lesson, and the use of routines during interactive teaching enables activity flow to be maintained. This process has begun to be examined in the context of second language teaching.

Nunan (1992) studied the interactive decisions of nine ESL teachers in Australia by examining with teachers a transcription of a lesson they had taught and discussing it with each teacher. He found that the majority of the interactive decisions made by the teachers related to classroom management and organization, but also that the teachers' prior planning decisions provided a structure and framework for the teachers' interactive decisions. K. E. Johnson (1992b) studied six preservice ESL teachers, using videotaped recordings of lessons they taught and stimulated recall reports of the instructional decisions and prior knowledge that influenced their teaching. Johnson found that teachers most frequently recalled making interactive decisions in order to promote student understanding (37% of all interactive decisions made) or to promote student motivation and involvement (17%). Reasons for other interactive decisions reported are shown in Table 4.3. Johnson comments:

These findings confirm previously held characterisations of pre-service teachers' instructional decisions as being strongly influenced by student behaviour. In addition these findings support the notion that pre-service teachers rely on a limited number of instructional routines and are overwhelmingly concerned with inappropriate student responses and maintaining the flow of instructional activity. (K. E. Johnson 1992b: 129)

Ulichny (1996) describes a case study of an ESL teacher presenting a classroom activity to an ESL class, using a detailed microanalysis of the discourse of the event together with the teacher's own reflections and interpretations of the classroom talk. The teacher in Ulichny's study was an ESL teacher in an American university ESL program, and the teach-

TABLE 4.3   TEACHER'S REASONS FOR INTERACTIVE DECISIONS

Reason for decision	Percentage of all decisions made
Student understanding	37
Student motivation and involvement	17
Instructional management	15
Curriculum integration	9
Subject matter content	8
Students' language skill and ability	8
Students' affective needs	6

Source: K. E. Johnson (1992b: 127).

ing moment she examines was an ESL reading class for incoming students. The teacher had a well-developed schema for teaching a reading lesson in this situation. The course was content based and included a close reading of a chapter from a sociology textbook. The teacher planned to lead the students through the chapter, section by section, helping them grasp the meaning of the text. She assigned part of the chapter to be read for homework. Ulichny notes: "She has given them a simplified lecture that restated the five main points about why, according to the book, nuclear families are more functional in industrialized societies, and she is planning to have the students locate those five points in the words of the author in the text" (1996: 11). However, once the teacher began her lesson, she discovered that the students' comprehension of her lecture was unclear, and she could not elicit the ideas she was looking for. Thus she rethought her plan and began trying to build up their comprehension of the points of her lecture. Ulichny traces the teacher's thinking through a series of steps, which started with discovering a problem, assessing the problem, and then unsuccessfully attempting to elicit what she was looking for from the students. Then she took over and did the work for the students, modeling and scaffolding the content of the text – a task she had originally planned for the students themselves to do. From her longitudinal analysis of the teacher's evolution of her teaching methodology through interaction with the students, Ulichny concludes:

Teaching is a constant mediation between enacted planned activities and addressing students' understandings, abilities and motivation to carry out the activity. How a teacher determines which activities to engage the class in, how she assesses the students' participation in the task and what she determines are reasons and remedies for lack of adequate participation are the basic units of the teaching moment. The particular construction or sense-making of the moment is a product of an individual teacher's past learning and teaching experiences, beliefs about teaching and learning – from both professional training as well as folk wisdom gleaned from fellow teachers – and her particular personality. (1996: 178)

Implications for SLTE practice

The metaphor of the teacher as thinker provides a conceptual framework that offers a rich alternative to behaviorally oriented views of teaching and also provides a useful research agenda. As Freeman observes:

It focuses research on the teacher and recognizes the central importance of his or her cognitive world. It also provides a methodologically accessible architecture which can lend itself to both qualitative and quantitative study. (Freeman and Richards 1996: 362)

Freeman also points out the limitations inherent in this framework, which he ascribes to "the fixed nature of decision-making as an a priori construct, the lack of attention to the context of decision, and the potential to overlook language as both the substance and the research vehicle of decision-making" (Freeman and Richards 1996: 362). Notwithstanding these limitations, the analysis of teaching as an activity that is grounded in the teacher's belief systems and cognitive world offers several important implications for the practice of second language teacher education, and I would like to conclude by examining some of these implications as I understand them.

Modeling the cognitive skills of expert teachers

An important goal of preservice experiences for language teachers is to expose novice teachers to the thinking skills of expert teachers in order to help them develop the pedagogical reasoning skills they need when they begin teaching. While many current resource books in SLTE make extensive use of tasks that student teachers carry out at their own level of pedagogical expertise, the value of these activities can be enhanced if they are followed by presentation of expert teachers' solutions of the same tasks, together with the thinking that accompanied them. For example, in my methodology classes with preservice teachers, after assigning students a planning task, such as planning a reading lesson around a short text, feedback on their efforts includes not only peer and instructor responses to their lesson plans but a think-aloud "walk through" of the same planning task, during which I try to model the thinking that an experienced teacher would bring to the task. This strategy is also appropriate for cooperating teachers.

To promote knowledge development in student teachers, we believe that co-operating teachers should be able and willing to explicate the routines and

strategies they use, provide systematic and constructive feedback, and engage with the student teacher in joint problem solving about pedagogical issues. They should also model pedagogical thinking to student teachers by demonstrating and then explaining how they transform subject matter into pedagogically powerful forms. By making their thinking explicit, they reveal the connection between their actions and their knowledge structures.
(Livingston and Borko 1989: 40)

Using case studies

Case materials, including both written and videotaped cases, provide another rich vehicle for helping student teachers develop the capacity to analyze situations, to explore how teachers in different settings arrive at lesson goals and teaching strategies, and to understand how expert teachers draw on pedagogical schemas and routines in the process of teaching. In 1986, the report by the Carnegie Task Force on Teaching as a Profession, *A Nation Prepared: Teachers for the 21st Century,* proposed the use of teacher cases in teacher education, recommending that "teaching cases illustrating a variety of teaching problems should be developed as a focus of instruction" (1986: 76). Case accounts allow access not only to the problems teachers encounter but the principles they bring to bear on their resolution. Information revealed in teachers' case accounts reminds us that teacher education is concerned with far more than preparing teachers in the use of instructional strategies, materials, and methods: It must focus on the beliefs and thinking that teachers employ as the basis for their teaching, how they frame and problematize issues, and the ways in which they draw on experience, beliefs, and pedagogical reasoning skills in teaching. Case-based approaches are widely used in other professions, such as business, law, and medicine, but have only recently begun to be used more generally in teacher education (Shulman 1992). Case reports can reveal ways of thinking about a significant teaching incident, and when accompanied by "deconstruction" through questioning and critical interpretation, can help reveal how the teachers' beliefs, knowledge, personality, and pedagogical reasoning shapes a particular event.

A number of advantages have been suggested for using case studies in this way in teacher education (Kleinfeld 1992):

1. Students are provided with vicarious teaching problems that present real issues in context.
2. Students can learn how to identify issues and frame problems.
3. Cases can be used to model the processes of analysis and inquiry in teaching.
4. Students can acquire an enlarged repertoire and understanding of educational strategies.

5. Cases help stimulate the habit of reflective inquiry.

The building up of a collection of case reports that can be effectively used in this way is invaluable for use in SLTE programs. Examples of two case studies from a collection developed for use in SLTE (Richards, in press) is given in the Appendix. These consist of three parts—the context in which the teacher works, the problem that occurred, and the strategy or solution the teacher put in place to address it.

Providing focused field experiences

The inclusion of goals related to the cognitive and interpretative domain of teaching also suggests a different focus for field experiences such as practice teaching and classroom observation. In practice teaching, for example, providing student teachers with multiple opportunities to teach the same content enables them to develop their schematic knowledge of teaching and to appreciate the effect of context on their understanding of teaching incidents.

The opportunity to repeat and fine-tune instructional strategies and explanations increases the likelihood that novices will incorporate these elements into their cognitive schemata. Similarly, critically analyzing performance and revising it for another session helps novices to elaborate and connect existing knowledge structures. This revision process contributes to the development of pedagogical content knowledge and pedagogical reasoning skills. (Livingston and Borko 1989: 40)

Such experiences can also be linked with the preparation of case reports for use as part of the on-campus program.

A focus on interactive decision making also provides a rationale for a different focus to classroom observation. During observations, student teachers can be engaged in watching how an experienced teacher uses routines and scripts in teaching and how the teacher's improvisational performance helps resolve problems that occur during a lesson. Such activities can help novice teachers understand the interpretative nature of teaching and realize the conceptual basis for such interpretation.

Conclusion

While a focus on cognitive processes is not new in applied linguistics and TESOL, as seen in a growing literature on learning strategies and the cognitive processes employed by second language writers and readers, interest in the cognitive processes employed by second language teachers is more recent. At present, the conceptual framework for such research has been borrowed wholesale from parallel research in general education, and only recently have attempts been made to incorporate a language or discourse orientation into that framework (see Freeman 1996b). The cognitive analysis of second language teaching is, however, central to our understanding both of how teachers teach as well as how novice teachers develop teaching expertise. There is an important message in this research, which can be expressed (with slight overstatement) in the following way: "There is no such thing as good teaching. There are only good teachers."

In other words, teaching is realized only in teachers; it has no independent existence. Teacher education is hence less involved with transmitting models of effective practice and more concerned with providing experiences that facilitate the development of cognitive and interpretative skills, which are used uniquely by every teacher.

Appendix: Examples of teacher case studies*

Dealing with Different Learning Styles by Al Bond

CONTEXT

The EAP program (English for Academic Purposes) in which I teach is located at a large urban university in the heart of a thriving city in the southeastern United States. As in many larger cities in the U.S., there is an ever-growing international population, including a large number of students interested in studying at American universities. My class was an academic writing class, designed as the first in a series of 3 writing courses in a full reading, writing, grammar, and oral skills program preparing EAP students for university work here, or at whichever university they might decide to attend. Students entering this program test into levels 1 through 5 in each area and then work their way up. The writing classes here start at level 3, because at levels 1 and 2 the writing and grammar classes are combined. After level 5, the students can enter normal university classes:

I had lived abroad for 13 years and done a lot of English tutoring and language learning of my own, but this was my first teaching experience in which I had a full class of students. My writing class met each Tuesday and Thursday from 7:45 to 10:00 for a total of 19 class meetings during that quarter. The class had 15 members, of which 7 were women. There were 4 Vietnamese, 3 Russian, 2 Chinese, 2 South American, 2 African, 1 Indian, and

---

*The case studies in this Appendix are from "Using Authentic Materials in China," by Rodney Jones and from "Dealing with Different Learning Styles," by Al Bond. Both studies are in *Teaching in Action: Case Studies from Second Language Classrooms* (forthcoming). Copyright 1997 by Teachers of English to Speakers of Other Languages, Inc. Used with permission

1 French student in the class. Their ages ranged from 18 to 35. The writing assignments and tests in the course were based on reading assignments in an American history textbook in order to give them an academic focus.

PROBLEM

The problem I was having in my class had to do with my attempt to do group (mostly pair) writing in class and with the fact that with such a diverse group of students it did not always run smoothly. We did a good deal of writing and editing in pairs. We called these sessions "writing workshops." Students generally read each other's plans for an essay or one of the drafts of an essay they had worked on in class or at home. They then edited each other's work by writing or making comments about the content (facts), organization (logical progression), or English (complete sentences, etc.) of the work. My main reason for this pair work was that I wanted to help the students to get ideas from and function as models for each other by reading each other's work and by getting feedback about their own work. I also wanted students to get into the habit of reading critically, so that this critical reading might be used to better write and edit their own work.

Some students seemed very positive about group writing and editing in class. One Vietnamese student wrote in her evaluative essay of the class, "reading other people's essay has really helped me to improve grammar and also helped me to see other people's errors. . . . After I finished writing my essay, I usually check . . . But I could not find any error even I read all my composition over several times." Students like this were very enthusiastic any time they found out that we were going to do group writing in class. Other students, such as one Russian student who wrote, "Also, I prefer to work in class by myself. I don't like to work with someone," were much less enthusiastic and showed little cooperative spirit in such groups.

Whether this lack of enthusiasm on the part of some students was due to the great variety of cultural backgrounds in the class, or simply was the result of differences in personal learning styles present is difficult to say. What concerned me was that often these learners with completely different types of learning styles would be paired together if I did the pairing randomly. It did neither learner any good when one who was very enthusiastic about working with others and hoped that it would help a great deal with his or her writing was paired with another student who believed that the best way to improve writing was concentrated personal effort, and thought that group work was mostly distracting and a waste of time. The result of this kind of combination was simply two very frustrated learners.

SOLUTION

The solution I came up with was to give them a choice in how things were to function in order to get them more invested in the class. I let the students decide on their own partners. I did not disagree with the students about what was best for them as far as learning strategies went. They may have known themselves and their own learning styles better than I did. By this time, most students had, at some point or another, worked with most of the other students in the class. So now they were at a point when they could select permanent partners for the rest of the quarter.

Students generally chose partners whom they had enjoyed working with previously, and these were generally partners who had the same style of pair participation. Some of these new pairs enjoyed pair work a great deal and did every step of the way together, using a great deal of discussion (in English) to get their writing done. Others tended to work alone on some parts and simply to do final readings of each other's work at the end of each stage of a first writing or a rewrite and then to make corrections and offer suggestions. I encouraged these learners to work together and learn from each other as much as possible. They agreed that in some parts of each task "two heads are better than one," but their ideas of which parts this was true of was more limited than that of other pairs. In the end, each pair found a workable and time efficient arrangement, and there were a number of different levels of "pair participation."

Working together with partners who had similar styles of learning seemed to generate a great deal less anxiety and frustration both for those who liked to work alone better and for those who preferred to work in groups. In this way, during these sessions, the students in each pair could choose to what extent they wished to communicate, based on what each student thought was to his or her advantage. I think students felt more in control of their learning situations and were more motivated because of this.

Using Authentic Materials in China by Rodney Jones

CONTEXT

Luoyang is a small industrial city in central China. It's situated on the banks of the Yellow River in Henan Province about 70 km east of Xian. Most of the "work units" in the city (including factories, schools, and hospitals) come under the auspices of the Ministry of Machine Building. In 1985 when I taught there the reforms that were taking hold in the coastal cities and the more open attitudes towards Western ideas and education that generally accompanied the reforms still had not reached the inland provinces. The people in Luoyang were, at that time, mostly conservative, provincial, and suspicious of foreigners. Western goods, and even goods manufactured in Shanghai and Guangzhou, were very scarce in Luoyang. There was one Foreign Language Bookstore which actually stocked no foreign language books except for a few musty simplified versions of *Jane Eyre*.

I was employed to teach young teachers of technical subjects at the Luoyang Institute of Technology. The students were ostensibly learning English so they could cope with technical documents in their respective fields, but most of them also saw improving their English proficiency as way to gain a better posting in a larger city, and so they were highly motivated and keen to develop their speaking skills.

83

PROBLEM

The problem I encountered teaching these young teachers was one of both materials and methods. The English Training Program they were enrolled in predictably stressed reading. The texts available, however, were severely limited. The students were using *English for Today* (Alexander). When I arrived, they had already worked through Books 1 and 2 and were about half-way through Book 3. The English Department stocked no other texts, and showed no willingness to order more resources. Unfortunately, most of the essays in *English for Today* were neither relevant nor challenging to these learners; they bore little resemblance to the technical texts the students had to deal with in their work, and the topics they covered were remote and boring to these young men and women, whose interests ran more towards contemporary issues, politics, economics, and science. Attempting to find alternate texts was extremely frustrating. At first I suggested that the students bring in English books from their own fields to work with, but even those were extremely rare and usually could not be taken out of the library or laboratories where they were stored. I had brought a few things with me, and more arrived later in care packages from home, but the institute had no xerox facilities. Anything I wanted duplicated I had to type onto carbon stencils for mimeographing, and the result was often unreadable.

What the students were reading was only half the problem; the other half was how they were reading. In the past the course had been taught as an intensive reading course. Students read and analyzed passages from the textbook, checking their dictionaries and writing Chinese translations in the margins. In class they were meant to answer the lecturer's questions regarding lexis and grammatical structures and possibly to recite portions of the text from memory. This method was clearly doing nothing for their proficiency, as they hardly had any time to attend to meaning or speak spontaneously. The strategies they were using were making them into slow, laborious readers who were capable of diagramming sentences without an inkling of what they meant, and awkward, reluctant speakers, hesitant to utter anything they hadn't first committed to memory.

SOLUTION

The solution to the problem of materials presented itself when I noticed that when my students visited me at my residence they were fascinated by the magazines and newspapers I had received in the post. I had thought of using articles from them as reading texts but dismissed the idea because of the problem of reproduction. It then occurred to me that there was no reason why everyone in the class had to read the same thing, and a single magazine contained enough material for every one in the class to have at least one article. So I gathered together all the copies of *Time* and *Newsweek*, *Scientific American*, and *The China Daily* that I had and brought them into the class along with scissors, glue, and a stack of heavy file folders. I told the students that we were going to construct a classroom library, divided them into groups, and gave each group a stack of magazines. Their first task was to search for texts they thought were interesting and useful and attempt to classify them according to either topic or text type. This forced the students to look at the texts more globally before plunging into the grammatical structures. Getting the students to cut out the texts and paste them into the file folders proved the most difficult part of the exercise; at first they couldn't believe I would invite them to cut my precious magazines to shreds. But eventually they got the idea, and after two weeks of sorting, cutting, and pasting we had a substantial stack of file folders, each containing a single text, arranged in categories like: Economics, Science and Technology, China, Movies, Popular Music, etc. The folders were kept in the classroom, and throughout the semester the students were asked to use them to perform particular tasks, such as pair and group discussions based on their reading, writing review paragraphs or imitations to be kept in the folders along with the texts, and giving oral reports based on texts they had read. After several months, the students had enough exposure to different text types that they were ready to write and edit their own class magazine.

On my visits to other institutes it became apparent that other foreign teachers were experiencing similar problems. After I described the technique I had used to teachers at Yellow River University in Zhengzhou, we decided to start a materials exchange. Folders from my class (along with my students' written responses to the texts) were exchanged with folders from similar classes at Yellow River University. The students not only were exposed to a greater variety of texts, but they also got a chance to read the written work of students from another institute.

Interestingly, after I had dealt with the problem of materials, the problem of method seemed to solve itself. As soon as the students were confronted with authentic materials and communicative tasks, they began to focus less on structure and vocabulary. Since many of the texts contained idioms, slang words, and technical terms not included in their dictionaries, they had no choice but to resort to alternative reading strategies. And, since the students had chosen the texts themselves, they were much more inclined to pay attention to the content.

5 Exploring pedagogical reasoning skills

Jack C. Richards, Benjamin Li, and Angela Tang

In Chapter 1, a central issue in SLTE was identified as understanding the specialized thinking and problem-solving skills that teachers call upon when they teach. Shulman's concepts of *pedagogical reasoning skills* and *pedagogical content knowledge* provide a useful framework for examining these dimensions of teachers' expertise. He characterizes pedagogical reasoning as a process of transformation in which the teacher turns the subject matter of instruction into "forms that are pedagogically powerful and yet adaptive to the variations in ability and background presented by the students" (Shulman 1987: 15). He characterizes pedagogical content knowledge as,

for the most regularly taught topics in one's subject area, the most useful forms of representation of those ideas, the most powerful analogies, illustrations, examples, explanations, and demonstrations – in a word, the ways of representing and formulating the subject that make it comprehensible to others. . . . [Also], an understanding of what makes the learning of specific topics easy or difficult: the conceptions and preconceptions that students of different ages and backgrounds bring with them to the lessons. (1986: 9)

While it is generally assumed by teacher educators that the content of teacher education programs provides knowledge and skills teachers can employ during teaching, whether they do in fact make use of such information when they enter the profession is seldom explored. Teacher education is thus often built upon unexamined assumptions of considerable significance. As teacher educators we need to ask, for example, in what ways courses on the sociolinguistics of language use, pedagogical grammar, second language acquisition, or second language reading are likely to influence teachers' thinking and practices in teaching and the extent to which they contribute to teaching expertise. These questions are the focus of this chapter.

Teachers with differing degrees of teaching experience, professional training, and subject matter knowledge presumably adopt different solutions to instructional problems and tasks. A teacher who has taken a course on second language phonology or on the teaching of pronunciation, for example, would be expected to have a different understanding and response to students' pronunciation errors than a teacher without such knowledge or training. Likewise teachers with training but with little or no classroom experience will have a limited store of schemata to draw on in planning and teaching lessons. One way of investigating these assumptions, and of uncovering the different types of knowledge and thinking used in teaching, is to give teachers with different levels of experience and training teaching tasks to consider and then compare the kinds of thinking they bring to such tasks. This is the approach that was taken in the two following studies.

Example 1: How novice and experienced teachers approach a reading lesson

The first study[1] compared how student teachers and experienced teachers planned a reading lesson. Ten student teachers in their second year of a BA TESL degree constituted the novice group. They had little or no teaching experience apart from simulated experiences provided as part of their degree but had completed a number of basic courses on TESL methodology. Ten graduate secondary school teachers, all with a postgraduate TESL qualification and an average of five years' teaching experience, constituted the experienced group. Each group was given the same lesson planning task, which required them to plan a 40-minute supplementary reading lesson around a short story for a class of average-ability Form 4 Arts-stream students in a Hong Kong secondary school, in a functional scenario constructed for the study. Each was asked to spend about one hour planning the lesson. Following the planning task they were asked about why their plans took the form they did, what problems they had encountered in preparing them, and how these were resolved.

The text the subjects were asked to plan their lessons around was a short story entitled "Puppet on a String," by Patrick Gordon (see Appendix). It was deliberately selected to provide opportunities for teachers to demonstrate their pedagogical reasoning skills. The story centers on a problem encountered by a handicapped child the first time he leaves home alone and travels by bus. During the journey he is tricked into carrying a package by a man on the bus. He becomes confused and decides to go to the police station, where the package is discovered to contain drugs. The police officer believes the boy is faking his mental illness, and the story ends with the officer discussing sending the boy to prison. Planning a lesson around the story is a relatively challenging task since it involves a moral dilemma, and it also presents a number of linguistic difficulties since it contains both dialogue and narrative with many words

1 This research was undertaken by Benjamin Li as part of his MA TESL degree at City University of Hong Kong, 1993–4.

and expressions that might cause difficulties for Form 4 students. How did the novice and experienced teachers approach the planning of a lesson around this text?

Novices

The novice teachers spent an average of 62 minutes planning their lessons. Most reported that they had little previous experience in preparing lesson plans, and so drew on their previous experience as students as well as ideas they had encountered in their teacher education degree. They followed a format that had been presented in a methodology course as the basis for their lesson. This consisted of a three-part lesson:

1. prereading activities
2. while-reading activities
3. postreading activities

On the whole, the novices had few opinions about the story and had difficulty developing pedagogical ideas from the text and building a lesson around it. They found the story difficult to understand and felt the situation in the story would not be accessible to Hong Kong students. They also worried about the dialogue section in the text and the difficult vocabulary and syntax the writer uses:[2]

"There may be some difficult words. The situation is also difficult. Since this is extracted from a publication in England for students not familiar with the context, it may be culture bound." (Teacher 9)

"Personally I don't think it's a good reading text. I think it's better to cut off the conversation part and just present the narrative part to the students." (Teacher 1)

The objectives the novices developed for their lessons focused mainly on building up literal comprehension of the text and helping students understand the vocabulary and structures in the story. Hence they approached the text in terms of language and did not identify broader objectives for using the story in an ESL class.

"I was more concerned about the level of the students. Since the target students are of Form 4 level and of average ability, I think the most important thing is for them to learn the useful sentence structures and vocabulary from the reading. So when I tried to design activities for the reading lesson I put much emphasis on these areas. I perceive this as a remedial lesson for the students, so the ultimate aim should be to increase students' knowledge of English, right?" (Teacher 2)

---

2 Extracts are from the participating teachers' responses to the planning task.

Another feature of the novices' lesson plans and their conversations about them was a rather mechanical view of reading. Their plans usually began with the teacher asking warm-up questions, reading the text, and then answering comprehension questions. Either during or after reading the text, the teacher would explain unfamiliar vocabulary items or unfamiliar grammatical structures in the text. The lesson usually ended with a teacher-led discussion.

Their lesson plans hence typically approached the story from the teacher's perspective, and their plans focused on such dimensions as timing (to ensure that they could get through the whole text during the lesson) and explaining the text clearly and comprehensively to the students. Students would be led through the text by the teacher, and questions about the story would be teacher led.

"I'll give them the text and allow ten minutes for reading. Then they will be divided into groups of five to seven. Then I'll give them a worksheet which consists of some questions for group discussion." (Teacher 7)

The main factor they tried to address in their plan was the interest level of the lesson and whether the teacher could create a pleasant reading environment for the students, factors they considered crucial to the success of a reading lesson.

"I think it is very important to arouse students' interest in reading. Once they are interested in reading, they will pick up a book from time to time and start reading." (Teacher 5)

"I will have the students read the story aloud. I think this will make the reading lesson more interesting. From my experience as a private tutor, I find my students very interested in reading aloud. This may not be relevant to a reading lesson, but if students can read aloud to each other I think this can enhance their interest and they can learn better." (Teacher 3)

When asked about the type of problems they would anticipate in teaching their lessons, most of the novice teachers expressed concerns about whether the students would be able to use English in answering questions, in discussion, and in follow-up activities such as drama and role play. The solutions the novices favored, however, indicate they give priority to the smooth running of the lesson. Instead of preparing alternate approaches to deal with the problem, they would rather do it "the teacher's way":

"The students are expected to talk in English but in reality this is usually not the case. So the teacher will need to exercise her power to force students to speak in English." (Teacher 2)

"If this really happens, I'll provide them some clues to help them to answer the questions. If they still don't answer, maybe I'll answer them myself since it's important to follow the sequence of the lesson. I don't want to interrupt the procedure." (Teacher 3)

In addition, in the novices' lesson plans there were no attempts to go more deeply into the text and deal with character traits or the moral theme of the story. Students were not asked to respond personally to the incident in the story or to think about its social meaning.

Experienced teachers

The experienced teachers produced quite detailed lesson outlines in their lesson plans, and spent an average of 42 minutes on their plans. In general, they reported that the use of detailed lesson plans was unusual in their teaching.

"I won't write a lesson plan in detail for my daily teaching. I would just have a brief mental plan and conduct the lesson in a very flexible way. I often change some parts of my plan when necessary." (Teacher 3)

"To tell you frankly, I seldom write lesson plans. Sometimes the lesson plans jump in my brain the moment I'm walking towards the classroom. If I'm in the good mood, I may come up with wonderful ideas." (Teacher 9)

In comparison to the novice teachers, the experienced teachers generally found the text interesting, and although acknowledging the language demands of the text, saw it as providing a good basis for a reading lesson, one that contained many interesting opportunities for classroom exploitation.

"I think the story is interesting in that it involves moral conflicts. I would try to make use of the situations and get students to talk about their feelings and opinions." (Teacher 4)

"I think it's a very interesting text. I think it has a lot of opportunities for teaching. But I think it's a sensitive text in that it deals with mentally retarded people . . . so this sensitivity of the text plays an important issue on my planning." (Teacher 7)

In comparison with the novice teachers, the experienced teachers developed a wide variety of objectives for their lessons. These included:

- to raise students' awareness of handicapped conditions (T1)
- to promote autonomy in learning (T9)
- to involve the students in reading not only as interpreter but also as creator (T8)
- to instill in students some common sense (T6)
- to practice for prediction and coherence (T3)
- to integrate reading skills with oral practice (T7)

One teacher expressed her goals in the following way:

"I think the text is interesting because it involves moral conflicts – one person is trying to cheat another person, and a handicapped person is put into jail. I'll try to transform my understanding of the text into an activity that would allow my students to experience the emotional and intellectual struggles that are involved in the moral conflicts. Let them have a feel of what the writer is trying to express." (Teacher 4)

The experienced teachers' plans suggest they would spend little time on vocabulary problems but would encourage students to guess or ignore difficult words. They would focus more on global understanding of the story.

"I won't focus too much on the vocabulary, which seems to be the worry of most teachers, and the students seem to believe in the myth that understanding the vocabulary means understanding the whole passage. But I myself believe in global understanding rather than local understanding." (Teacher 3)

In discussing the problems they would try to address in teaching from the text, the experienced teachers typically focused on a learner rather than a teacher perspective. Thus they discussed how to present the text from the point of view of the students, how to involve the students in the lesson, whether the students would find the story interesting, and how the students could arrive at an interpretation of the broader meaning of the story. In their lesson plans, the students were seen as actively engaged with the text rather than as recipients of the teacher's decoding.

"I wondered what attitudes the students already had about the handicapped." (Teacher 1)

"I was concerned about how I would involve the students emotionally and imaginatively in the passage. The students come from the Arts-stream and most of them are girls. I think they are emotionally prepared for the appreciation of good literary materials. I really would like to think of a dramatic, imaginative, feeling-oriented and involving approach to present the text." (Teacher 8)

The experienced teachers thus operated from a complex understanding of the nature of reading. Their lesson plans revealed an attempt to deal with the overall social meaning of the story as a primary goal, rather than approaching reading as decoding language. They emphasized "meaning-making" and developing a shared understanding through suggesting scenarios, making predictions, identifying and empathizing with the characters, and relating the situation in the story to the students' lives.

In preparing students to read the text, the experienced teachers probed the students' background knowledge. Some started by looking at attitudes toward the handicapped in general and then moved to consider the students' attitudes; others started by examining the kind of sympathy

91

students would have for physically challenged people and then moved to the issue of mental retardation.

In helping students make sense of the text, the teachers introduced prediction skills and prepared comprehension questions that involved inference and creation of meaning.

"I would not give them the entire text. I would give them the text in three parts. I would divide the text at places where we might consider them cliffhangers – places in the text that ask a question quite naturally. I'll ask questions that would involve the students using their imagination to fill the gap; And of course all these questions will end with the question, 'What will happen next?'" (Teacher 5)

"I'll give the students a series of questions . . . inferential questions, such as 'Who is Andy?' because students simply don't know him from the text. Through discussion with others they can use their imagination to make sense of the story." (Teacher 10)

The teachers also worked toward a broader view of reading through having students think more deeply about the plot, the character construction, and the story, and through the use of activities such as drama, role play, and constructing monologues for the characters.

"I want them to bring characters and setting to life. So I would divide them into groups and each group would act out a scene which is one of the numbered part divided from the story. They have to create scripts in their own particular scenario." (Teacher 8)

Included in the mental plans of the experienced teachers were alternative approaches that took into consideration the dilemmas and complexities that arise in teaching the lesson. It seems that they had already planned for these contingencies by drawing on their pedagogical expertise.

"If there is time, I would try to focus on their own feelings about the handicapped, because of course in Hong Kong, there is the housing estate, Tun Tau, where some residents are very resistant to the idea of having mentally retarded people within the area. (Teacher 1)

"I'm sort of torn between having them complete the story or having them write a newspaper article for the story." (Teacher 5)

In addition, the teachers' plans involved pair work and group discussion of issues raised in the text. These questions would allow multiple interpretations. Some teachers suggested follow-up writing activities to develop critical thinking skills through adding new perspectives to the story.

"To arouse students' awareness that there could be different ways of ending the story, I will integrate the idea of reading and writing by asking them to find out what is happening in the story and to write an ending for the story." (Teacher 4)

The differences between the inexperienced and experienced teachers' approach to the lesson can be summarized as follows.

Inexperienced teachers	*Experienced teachers*
one hour of planning time needed	40 minutes of planning time needed
limited lesson formats	varied lesson formats
relatively little detail in plans	detailed lesson plans
teacher-focused lesson	learner-focused lesson
language-focused objectives	both linguistic and broader objectives
limited range of objectives	wide range of objectives
saw limited teaching potential in the text	saw the text as offering lots of teaching potential
presented a narrow view of reading	presented a broad view of reading
whole-class teaching	small group teaching

Example 2: Effect of subject matter knowledge and experience on the teaching of literature

The second study compared how twelve teachers approached the teaching of literature in an ESL context.[3] All of the teachers had at least a bachelor's degree and a teaching certificate and a minimum of four years' teaching experience. However, they differed in the following ways.

Group A: teachers with a BA in English literature and with experience teaching literature in an ESL context
Group B: teachers with a BA in literature but without experience in teaching literature
Group C: teachers with a BA but without a literature specialization and with no experience in teaching literature

The teachers in the study could therefore be described as having a similar degree of general instructional knowledge and skills, but with respect to literature, different degrees of pedagogical content knowledge and pedagogical reasoning skills. How would these differences be reflected in their approach to the teaching of literature?

In order to answer this question, the teachers were given three sets of literary texts, each containing a short story or short literary extract and a poem:

3 This research was conducted by Angela Tang as part of her MA TESL degree at City University of Hong Kong, 1993–4.

Set 1: "The German Boy," by Ron Butlin
"The Sound of Silence," by Paul Simon
Set 2: "The Illiterate Despatch Rider, the Army Clerk and
the Love Letters," by Christopher Leach
"Those Winter Sundays," by Robert Haden
Set 3: "Stig of the Dump," by Clive King
"The Mid-Term Break," by Seamus Heaney

The teachers also completed (1) a questionnaire that contained questions about their background, their approach to teaching, their attitudes toward literature, and their approach to teaching it; (2) a response sheet in which they were asked to record their reactions to the texts; and (3) a response sheet in which they were asked to describe how they would use the literary texts in a Form 6 ESL class in Hong Kong. The teachers completed the information in their own time and were later interviewed in order to further explore their experiences, attitudes, beliefs, and teaching strategies. The interviews were audiotaped.

The texts selected for the study were thought to present a good opportunity to explore the teachers' abilities to access literature-related pedagogical content knowledge and reasoning skills. Literature poses special problems in an ESL context, since apart from helping students understand literature texts, in teaching literature teachers also seek to develop students' personal understanding and response to a text, as we saw in the first case study. Students read literature to develop a level of response and understanding that goes beyond the level of words and syntax. Cultural, aesthetic, humanistic, and other values are also involved, as well as recognizing such literary conventions as metaphor, ambiguity, analogy, polysemy, and other stylistic conventions. Much of the meaning of a literary text lies outside of the text itself, so interpretation, evaluation, ideology, and reconstruction come into play. In addition, the texts selected for the study were of different genres and were examples of contemporary writing on universal themes such as love, relationships, and family, which are likely to appeal to young readers.

In presenting the teachers' responses to the tasks in the study, we will first describe their approaches to literature and then compare their lesson plans.

The teachers' views of literature and their responses to the texts

GROUP A (LITERATURE MAJORS WITH EXPERIENCE
TEACHING LITERATURE)

The teachers in this group were enthusiastic about the value of literature and its role in ESL classes. For them, literature can "help students gain self-discovery and articulation of personal views" and "widen their horizons." Teaching literature is challenging and stimulating for the teacher, but literature should be used to develop appreciation and not to achieve others' ends, such as moral education or developing grammar awareness. They believed that authentic literature should be used. One of the teachers reported that she brings literature extracts (poems, short stories) to class regularly to complement topics that come up in other areas of the curriculum (e.g., delinquency). In general, the teachers favored a broad approach to literature. They enjoyed reading literature themselves and reported that they read often. They regretted that literature does not have a greater role in the curriculum in Hong Kong secondary schools.

GROUP B (LITERATURE MAJORS WITH NO EXPERIENCE TEACHING LITERATURE)

Like the teachers in Group A, most of the teachers in this group were enthusiastic about literature. They enjoyed literature themselves but had not had the opportunity to teach it. They believed in the value of literature, though they had varying concerns about teaching it. One teacher believed students might have difficulty coping with literature but that it could be used to develop students' self-awareness. Another felt that literature should be taught as literature and not downgraded to serve linguistic purposes. However, she believed that available literature resources were often too difficult for Hong Kong students, and local literary materials at a suitable level should be prepared. One of the teachers commented: "Learning through literature can not only promote language learning but is also an effective way to consolidate other subjects, such as history and geography."

Nevertheless, the teachers felt that text selection was difficult for teachers, particularly those without training. In addition, students needed to have a good reading level in English before they could start reading literature. One of the teachers reported that he enjoys reading literature but finds the teaching of literature irrelevant to the school exams. According to him, a major problem is dealing with the mismatch between students' experience and available materials. Other materials were available that could be used instead of literature. Exposure to literature was not really necessary, since newspapers and other printed sources could be used to develop reading skills.

GROUP C (NO LITERATURE TRAINING AND NO EXPERIENCE TEACHING LITERATURE)

The teachers in this group had mixed opinions about the value of literature, and saw its role in teaching ESL simply as a way of supporting the development of reading skills. They felt it could be helpful in developing students' moral and personal growth. However, in general, the teachers believed that teaching literature in ESL classes was too difficult, both for teachers and students.

"I worry that unmotivated students would reject literature and it would be hard to locate suitable texts for them."

"It is too demanding for teachers who need to digest a text and read it critically before they can teach students."

The teachers' own reading of literature was more limited than that of teachers in Groups A and B, and was mainly confined to popular fiction. Even so, what they would teach is not really what they enjoy reading, as they believe the students are too naive to understand the issues raised in the literary texts. Some had mixed feelings about teaching and about teaching English, which was not their first subject of choice.

The teachers' plans for using the texts

All three groups of teachers were able to conceptualize ways of using the texts in ESL classes in order to develop both reading skills and students' personal responses and appreciation. However, there were significant differences in their plans. Teachers with a major in literature (Groups A and B) were able to interact with the texts more critically and creatively than the nonmajors (Group C). They were less troubled by abstraction and ambiguity in the texts. Teachers in Group C felt insecure when confronted with difficulties in interpreting something in a text. Teachers in Group A differed from those in Group B in how they prepared the texts for classroom use. They showed considerable variety and flexibility in their use of the texts, suggesting the use of activities such as the following:

- using prereading activities to provide links with the students' background knowledge
- using audio and visual aids to help students understand a text
- collecting pamphlets and other printed materials to arouse students' interest in a text
- developing visual analogies from the text
- exploiting the author's use of literary techniques
- using the author's style, technique, or voice to identify the writer's beliefs, attitudes, or feelings
- finding ways to enable students to transfer what they have read to their own lives
- developing postreading activities to extend themes or ideas in a text

Group A teachers hence tended to see richer pedagogical possibilities for use with the texts than teachers in the other groups, who used the texts primarily to practice reading for information or for appreciation.

Though all three groups were able to analyze and understand the texts, Group C revealed a less developed sensitivity to language, style, and approach. They typically commented on the texts in broad and general terms, rarely using literary terms. For example, compare these responses to a text from teachers in Groups A and C:

"The story is complicated in structure, but it's interesting and it's skillfully written." (Group C teacher)

"It's an interesting description and narrative – an adventure story – the encounter of two creatures from two different worlds. But the story doesn't appeal to me. The techniques used are comparatively very simple. It's very hard to analyze an extract. Is it a simplified version?" (Group A teacher)

When encountering difficulties such as abstraction in a text, the literature majors made use of a greater variety of strategies than the nonmajors, including concept mapping, cognitive schema, and visualizing. Group C teachers, on the other hand, tended to stick closely to the texts. In addition, the literature majors addressed such issues as interpretation, mood, alliteration, characterization, setting, style, and technique, which were not addressed by the nonmajors. Teachers in Groups A and B focused on guiding students to discover personal meaning within the text, a strategy not seen in Group C, and used questions to orient the reader to the situation of the character or to look for contrasts or comparisons, to make inferences, and to explore feelings and reactions.

In terms of classroom pedagogy, all three groups employed a mixed approach seeking to involve students in the text through a variety of different tasks. However, Group A was the most successful in identifying ways of using the texts, and was able to employ a wider variety of procedures than the other groups as well as a more flexible approach. Group C tended to focus on reading for information followed by postreading assignments, whereas Group B used a mixture of both A and C's strategies. The differences between the three groups of teachers' approaches are summarized in Table 5.1.

Discussion

The two examples presented in this chapter reveal marked differences in how inexperienced and experienced teachers planned a reading lesson, and in how teachers with different degrees of literature training and experience in teaching literature approached the use of literature texts in ESL teaching. Similar differences have been found in teachers of other subject areas (e.g., Feiman-Nemser and Parker 1990). In drawing conclusions from these studies, it is illuminating to discuss these differences in relation to four dimensions of learning to teach ESL: (a) learning to

TABLE 5.1   SUMMARY OF APPROACHES TO TEACHING LITERATURE

Group A (literature majors with experience teaching literature)	Group B (literature majors with no experience teaching literature)	Group C (no literature training and no experience teaching literature)
Beliefs about the role of literature		
Enthusiastic about literature	Enthusiastic about literature	Doubtful about value of literature
Read literature regularly		Don't read much literature
Favor a broad approach to literature	Misgivings about teaching literature in ESL context	
Authentic literature useful	Doubtful about use of authentic literature	
Favor integration of literature into the ESL curriculum	Favor integration of literature into the ESL curriculum	
Plans for the use of the literature texts		
Saw ways of dealing with difficulties	Saw ways of dealing with difficulties	Worried about anticipated difficulties
Saw wide variety of teaching possibilities	Saw limited variety of teaching possibilities	Texts used primarily for reading comprehension
Addressed literary aspects of texts	Some attention to literary aspects of texts	Did not address literary aspects of texts
Variety of strategies used to help students explore meaning of texts	Variety of strategies used to help students explore meaning of texts	Mainly used questions to check comprehension of texts

think about subject matter from the learner's perspective, (b) acquiring a deeper understanding of the subject matter, (c) learning how to present subject matter in appropriate ways, and (d) learning how to integrate language learning with broader curricular goals.

Learning to think about subject matter from the learner's perspective

Learning to teach involves recognizing which aspects of a lesson are likely to be of greatest interest and relevance to learners, discovering how to anticipate difficulties students might have, and recognizing how they are likely to respond to and process subject matter. The differences between the novice and experienced teachers' approaches to reading

texts illustrate striking differences in these aspects of the teachers' pedagogical learning skills. The novice teachers' lessons centered primarily on
linguistic comprehension of the story, made no use of students' background knowledge, and did not seek to engage students in the deeper layers of meaning of the story. Experienced teachers, on the other hand,
started with students' understanding and suggested strategies for mapping student thinking onto the text.

A similar result was found in the study of literature teaching. The literature teachers were very concerned to make their lessons learner-centered. Besides doing background research in order to find out how the
materials could be used to meet students' needs, they were also concerned with whether the students would be involved in the learning
process, which they saw as crucial for a successful lesson. In considering
how to present subject matter to their learners, they believed teachers
should modify their personal schemas to take into account students'
needs and abilities. Instead of imparting everything the teacher thinks is
important to the students, every effort should be made to enable students
to establish a relationship with the author of a text so that they can share
the author's feelings and thoughts. These features were rarely found
among the teachers who were not literature majors.

Acquiring a deeper understanding of the subject matter

The study of teachers' approaches to the use of literature demonstrated
that without a thorough knowledge of the content of teaching, teachers
will have difficulty turning content into appropriate plans for teaching.
They have an insufficiently developed pedagogical content knowledge to
be able to make content comprehensible to others. Thus the teachers
without literature training, in comparison to those with training and
with both training and experience, were unable to recognize such literary features of texts as mood, style, or technique, lacked the technical
discourse needed to discuss and analyze literary texts, and felt insecure
about using some of the texts with students. They were thus unable to
utilize the opportunities the texts provided for developing lessons. In the
case of the novice and experienced teachers' approach to the reading lesson, a limited understanding of the nature of second language reading
led the novice teachers likewise to see limited potential for using the
story as the basis for a reading lesson.

Learning how to present subject matter in appropriate ways

The experienced teachers in the first study described a variety of interesting ways of using stories in class. The novice teachers, however, used
a standardized format for a reading class and described a much more

limited set of strategies than the experienced teachers reported. The experience of literature teachers likewise described a variety of ways of using the literature texts and demonstrated greater flexibility in their use of texts than the teachers without literature training. The experienced teachers thus interacted with the texts pedagogically, rather than using them as a basis for reading for information.

Learning how to integrate language learning with broader curricular goals

In the first example, the experienced teachers saw reading not as an end in itself, but as a way of exploring social issues, of clarifying values, and of engaging in personal reflection. In the second study, the literature teachers emphasized the aesthetic mode of teaching reading. To them, reading can help broaden the cultural experience of the learners, enhance their analytical and imaginary powers, and engage their minds and feelings in purposeful dialogue so that they can develop new ways of expressing themselves. They viewed literature as part of a "whole person" approach to education in which an individual's responsivity, imagination, and creativity are encouraged through the study of literature.

The experienced ESL teachers and the experienced literature teachers in the two studies were similar in another way, a way that further distinguishes then from the other teachers in both samples; namely, they show evidence of a different mindset toward the use of literary texts. For whereas the inexperienced teachers and the teachers who were not literature majors approach literary texts primarily as a means to an end, the goal being language skills development, the other teachers regard the experience of reading a particular text or set of texts as valuable for its own sake.[4]

In conclusion, the two studies described here illustrate the importance and usefulness of examining how teachers conceptualize lessons and the contribution of subject matter expertise and experience to teachers' pedagogical reasoning skills. The planning of lessons engages teachers in complex processes of comprehension, selection, adaptation, and representation as they transform teaching artifacts such as texts into effective mediums for learning. The better we are able to understand how novice and experienced teachers employ these fascinating cognitive skills, the better prepared we are to provide appropriate activities and experiences to help develop these skills within TESL/TEFL teacher education programs.

---

4 This interpretation was suggested to us by John Green of Salem State College.

Appendix: Reading text used in Example 1*

"Puppet on a string" by Patrick Wolrige Gordon

Paul was a mentally retarded fourteen-year-old. Today he was taking a great step: this was the first time he had ever travelled on a bus and the first time he had ever left home alone. He climbed excitedly up the stairs and sat down on a vandalised seat next to a young man who was chewing gum and reading the *Sun*.

'What do you want?' he asked Paul, offended that this obnoxious boy should sit on his seat when the whole of the upper deck was empty.

'I'm going to play with Andy,' said Paul, his excitement betraying his mental condition. 'This is the first time I've been in a bus.'

'What's your name?'

'Paul.'

'Paul who?'

'Paul who?' came the incredulous reply.

'Yeah.'

'I . . . I don't know what you mean.'

'Ah, I see . . . then I've got something to tell you, Paul. Something very important . . . '

'Oh?'

'I'm a police agent and I want to see your pass.'

'My pass?'

'Yeah . . . to show you've got official permission to come upstairs on a bus.'

'I haven't got permission. I'm sorry,' Paul stuttered, terrified.

'Please don't send me to prison. I'll be good!'

'Normally, of course, I'd have to send you to prison; but there is an alternative.'

'I'll do anything . . . '

'Good lad. Get off the bus at the next stop. You'll see a man there wearing a green coat and jeans, reading a book. Give him this package. Get going now – he'll tell you what to do next.'

As the bus shuddered and lurched to a stop, Paul got out at a run, carrying the package tightly under one arm. No sooner had the bus driven off than a man ran past and seized the package; but Paul's grip was good, and the man only managed to break the wrapping paper and make off with one of the two boxes that were inside. He was wearing a green coat and carried a book. That was odd, thought Paul. Oh well, he had done as much as could be expected. He sat down in the bus-stop shelter.

He waited for a few minutes until rainwater dripping through the roof of the shelter disturbed his dreams. He was still clutching the box in one hand. He was in a sad-looking suburb over which the sky was crying gently. And he was lost. He did not live here and neither did Andy. Oh dear, he thought; and

* From: Inside comprehension, Christopher Woodland (Ed). Cambridge: Cambridge University Press, 1984.

his mother had told him not to get mixed up with strangers. He sobbed to himself for some time. Then with a start he realised what a fool he was.

'I don't think policemen count as strangers,' he said aloud. So he got up and walked down the road in search of a police station.

Presently Paul was climbing a flight of stone steps towards an impressive pair of blue doors with the word POLICE emblazoned above them. He was soon telling a policeman all that had happened. He apologised for not having completely succeeded in doing what he had been told. The police officer opened the box and was in conversation with the Chief Inspector within seconds.

'. . . That's right, sir. Looks like heroin to me. Must be worth a bomb . . . Yes . . . Claims he was told to make the drop by a plain clothes officer . . . If you ask me, sir, it's a load of rubbish . . . No, I don't know why he should give himself up. Fit of remorse, maybe, and I reckon he's putting on an act of being nuts or something so he can get off lightly . . . Yes, we have a cell free . . . No, I understand – no maltreatment. Yes . . . just so – not a leg to stand on in court. Borstal, I should think . . . a touch of the short, sharp shock, eh? That's right – make decent citizens of them . . . Bye.' The policeman put the phone down.

'Can I go home?' asked Paul.

'Look, you can stop your act now, lad. You're in the proverbial hands of the law. This way.'

6 What's the use of lesson plans?

Two aspects of teaching typically receive a major focus in preservice teacher education courses: *lesson planning* and *lesson delivery*. The success with which a teacher conducts a lesson is often thought to depend on the effectiveness with which the lesson was planned. Hence both lesson plans as well as lessons themselves are often assessed when reviewing teachers' performance. Teachers completing the Diploma in the Teaching of English as a Foreign Language to Adults, for example, (University of Cambridge 1991) are assessed for a component called "Preparation and Lesson Plan," which includes the following elements:

- general shape and balance of activities
- patterns of learner-teacher interaction
- timing
- clarity, limitation, and specification of aims/objectives
- clarity of specialization of procedures
- suitability of aids, materials, and methods for the class and its level
- suitability of materials and methods for teaching what is to be taught
- anticipation of learners' difficulties

Lesson plans are thought to help the teacher think through the lesson in advance and resolve problems and difficulties, to provide a structure for a lesson, to provide a "map" for the teacher to follow, and to provide a record of what has been taught (Harmer 1991; Rivers 1981). In this chapter, the ways in which language teachers use lesson plans are examined through studying the reported uses of lesson plans by experienced and less experienced teachers. An understanding of how teachers use lesson plans and what they do when they depart from their plans can help determine the role and value of lesson planning activities in language teacher education.

The nature of lesson plans

The subject of planning for instruction has been dealt with extensively in the general literature on curriculum and instruction (e.g., Clark and Peterson 1986) as well as in the field of second and foreign language teaching. A widely taught model is the behavioral objectives model,

103

which dates from Tyler's (1949) classic *Basic Principles of Curriculum and Instruction*. This offers a rationalistic ends-means approach to curriculum development that begins with considerations of learners and their needs, conceptions of subject matter and its importance, and conceptions of society and its needs, and then proceeds to the development of instructional objectives, which are shaped by educational philosophy and the psychology of learning. From these procedures, content and lesson plans are ultimately developed (Figure 6.1).

Tyler's model has influenced generations of teacher educators, and it appears in modified form in many contemporary texts on curriculum and lesson planning. For example, Pang's book *Lesson Planning* (1992), intended as a guide for teachers of all subject areas, is based on the following framework for lesson plans:

1. Setting objectives
2. Setting the knowledge structure, concepts and the subject matter
3. Determining the approaches and methods
4. Planning key questions
5. Planning the introduction and summary
6. Methods for arousing interest
7. Considering the timing for the different parts
8. Considering appropriate audio-visual aids and their sources
9. Constructing a blackboard plan
10. Writing worksheets and/or handouts
11. Designing the homework or follow-up activities
12. Objectives check, linkages and ways to explain
13. Methods for evaluating learning outcomes
14. Making a list of things to bring or to prepare

(Pang 1992: 17)

Tay (1986) asks why the Tyler model or derivatives of it are still widely taught despite consistent evidence that they do not represent how teachers plan lessons. She suggests that, because it reflects a technical view of teaching that many teacher educators still hold, it is regarded as a legitimate intellectual exercise; it reinforces teacher educators' sense of control and presents a standard format that can be easily taught and tested.

Guidelines for lesson planning in ESL/EFL teacher training texts tend to be more flexible than those found in general education. Hubbard et al., for example, comment:

The planning of a lesson is a highly personal undertaking: only the teacher knows what he can do and what his students are like. We feel, therefore, that it is dangerous and wrong to prescribe what form a lesson should take. This is something that only the teacher can decide. (1983: 319)

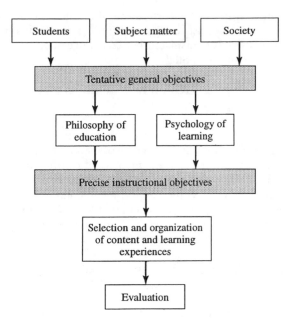

Figure 6.1   Tyler's (1949) model of curriculum development.

Harmer (1991), a widely used text in preservice TESL teacher training courses, provides a sample lesson plan that includes only five major components in comparison to the fourteen listed in Pang:

1. Description of the class
2. Recent work students have done
3. Objectives, which may refer to activities, skills, or type of language to be taught
4. Content, which includes situations, class organization, aids, new language items, possible problems
5. Additional possibilities

Research on teachers' use of lesson plans suggests that the approach recommended by Harmer is more realistic than frameworks based on the Tyler model, since teachers seldom use such detailed planning procedures. Shavelson and Stern (1981: 477) comment:

Most teachers are trained to plan instruction by (a) specifying (behavioural) objectives, (b) specifying students' entry behaviour, (c) selecting and sequencing learning activities so as to move learners from entry behaviours to objectives and (d) evaluating the outcomes of instruction in order to improve planning. While this prescriptive model of planning may be one of the most

105

consistently taught features of the curriculum of teacher education programmes, the model is consistently not used in teachers' planning in schools. Obviously, there is a mismatch between the demands of the classroom and the prescriptive planning model.

Similarly, summarizing research on how teachers plan lessons, Freeman points out:

[Teachers] did not naturally think about planning in the organized formats which they had been taught to use in their professional training. Further, when they did plan lessons according to these formats, they often did not teach them according to plan. Teachers were much more likely to visualize lessons as clusters or sequences of activity; they would blend content with activity, and they would generally focus on their particular students. In other words, teachers tended to plan lessons as ways of doing things for given groups of students rather than to meet particular objectives. (1996c: 97)

This is illustrated in an account of how a second language teacher does lesson planning in a study by Fujiwara (1996: 151):

Though now I do try to articulate objectives, my method of planning still begins with activities and visions of the class. It's only when I look at the visions that I can begin to analyze why I'm doing what I'm doing. I also need to be in dialogue with students, so it's hard for me to design a year's course in the abstract. Just as my language-learning process is no longer in awareness, so my planning process is based on layers and layers of assumptions, experiences, and knowledge. I have to dig down deep to find out why I make the decisions I do.

Nunan (1992) reports on the planning processes employed by nine teachers with different levels of experience, and concludes that the teachers' plans had a significant impact on their lessons, although their lessons were substantially modified during instruction.

While it is naive to assume that what gets planned will equate with what gets taught, and that what gets taught will equate with what gets learned, this does not mean that planning, including the formulation of objectives, should be removed from the equation. While the plans that teachers lay will be transformed, if not metamorphosed, in the act of teaching, such plans provide a framework and structure for the interactive decisions which the teacher must later make. They also provide a set of criteria against which such interactive decisions may be evaluated. (Nunan 1992: 161)

Studies such as Nunan's, as well as more recent studies (e.g., Woods 1996), have been conducted within the framework of teacher decision making (see Chapter 4) and have sought to identify the "on-line" decisions teachers confront while teaching, which often require them to depart from their lesson plans. K. M. Bailey (1996) followed this approach in a study of how six experienced ESL teachers departed from their plans during lessons. She interprets the basis for their interactive decisions in terms of the implicit principles they hold (see Chapter 3). Teachers gave the following justifications for departing from their plans:

1. *Serve the common good* (e.g., an issue raised by an individual student was thought to be worth pursuing because it would benefit the whole class)
2. *Teach to the moment* (e.g., the teacher drops the lesson plan and pursues a current issue likely to be of particular interest to students at that moment)
3. *Accommodate students' learning styles* (e.g., the teacher decides to incorporate some explicit grammar instruction since the learners have a preference for this mode of grammar learning)
4. *Promote students' involvement* (e.g., the teacher drops a planned activity to give students more time to work on an activity that they have shown a high degree of interest in)
5. *Distribute the wealth* (e.g., the teacher keeps one student from dominating class time to enable the whole class to benefit from a learning opportunity) (Bailey 1996: 24–35)

Nunan makes similar comments on the role of a teacher's personal philosophy of teaching on her interactive decisions:

Most of the interactive decisions made by the teacher reflected her personal philosophy of language learning and teaching. She is committed to a "communicative" orientation with an interactive focus, and this is reflected in the major modifications which she made to the original lesson suggestions made by the authors, as well as a number of the interactive decisions made in the course of the lesson. (Nunan 1992: 154)

In view of the importance attributed to lesson planning in TESL teacher preparation texts and programs, as well as an interest in the interaction between lesson plans and the interactive decisions teachers make while teaching, a study was undertaken that explored how language teachers with different levels of experience use lesson plans. The study sought to clarify the extent to which teachers depart from their lesson plans while teaching and the factors that appear to account for these departures.

A study of teachers' uses of lesson plans

In order to find out how ESL teachers use lesson plans, a study was made of sixteen teachers with different levels of training and experience, teaching English classes at the British Council, Hong Kong.[1] The study sought to find out the teachers' reported purposes for using lesson plans, the content of their plans, the uses made of plans during teaching, and whether experienced and less experienced teachers differ in their use of lesson plans.

The teachers

The sample of sixteen teachers was selected to constitute two groups – an experienced and a less experienced group. The experienced teachers all held both the RSA Certificate and the RSA diploma, in addition to other qualifications such as a first degree or master's degree, and had an average of 9.6 years of ESL teaching experience. Of the less experienced group, all but one held the RSA Certificate (the other had a professional teaching certificate), and they had an average of 1.6 years of ESL teaching experience. All of the teachers were teaching either general English courses (elementary or intermediate level) or business writing courses. Materials used in their classes were either commercial textbooks or materials provided by the British Council.

Data sources

Information was obtained from the following sources:

1. *Questionnaires* Each teacher completed a questionnaire consisting of the following questions:
   (a) *Teaching philosophy:* Please describe briefly how you view yourself as a teacher and the kind of lessons you try to create. When do you feel you have achieved a successful lesson? How do you see your role in the classroom?
   (b) Please describe your approach to lesson planning. What do you see as the purpose of a lesson plan?
   (c) What kind of lesson plan is useful – e.g., a "mental plan" or a "written plan"?
   (d) What do you normally include in a lesson plan?
   (e) How often do you make use of a lesson plan?

1 This project was supported by a small-scale grant from the City University of Hong Kong (Project Number 9030351). I am grateful to the British Council, Hong Kong, for permission to conduct the study of teachers' use of lesson plans, at the British Council, and to the support of the Director of Studies at the British Council, Mr. Rod Pryde. I am particularly grateful for the willing collaboration of the following teachers who took part in the study: Diana Cox, Nick Florent, Ian Fortescue, Anne Hill, Loraine Kennedy, Kevin MacKenzie, Julian Peachey, Martin Peacock, Francoise Phillips, Carol Schroeder, Stewart Smith, Sally Trainor, and Rebecca Vane. Acknowledgment is also gratefully made to my skillful research assistant, Ms. Min Kyong-Ju.

2. *Classroom observations*   Two classes taught by each teacher were observed. During the observation, a written description of the lesson was prepared that focused on what the teacher did and the activities that were employed. Lesson plans for each lesson were provided by the teacher.

3. Recorded follow-up interviews   Following each lesson the teacher was interviewed about the lesson, asked to identify points in the lesson that departed from the planned lesson, and the reasons for the departure from plan.

Results

THE TEACHERS' BELIEFS ABOUT A SUCCESSFUL LESSON

In their questionnaires and in the follow-up interviews, the teachers were asked to describe how they viewed a successful English lesson and the criteria they used to evaluate if a lesson was successful or not. A summary of their responses is given in Table 6.1. As can be seen from their answers, the two groups of teachers shared similar beliefs about the nature of a successful lesson. Their concerns represented a student-centered view of teaching and addressed the interest level of the lesson as well as student learning and language use.

Both groups of teachers were able to articulate well-developed personal theories of teaching that addressed their own role in the classroom, the learners' role, and their teaching strategy. For example, one of the less experienced teachers described her teaching philosophy in the following way:

"I feel that I create a relaxed classroom environment in which the students will participate and learn. I feel that if a teacher has a positive and enthusiastic attitude toward the class, the students will feel the same. I try to prepare lessons that take their previous knowledge and expand on it. In their regular classroom, they have had exposure, but have had little or no actual speaking practice. By using simple instructions, encouraging group participation and spontaneity, the students can develop more self-confidence. In Asian cultures, spontaneity is difficult to achieve because of 'losing face,' therefore praise is essential to encourage the student to try. At the same time, the teacher must tactfully correct, and also have students correct each other in group activities.

By using a variety of activities, students remain interested and when the class is over, they can take what they've learned and use it in 'real life.' I feel the class is successful when the students are actively participating and using the target language in free activities, games, etc.

I see my role in the classroom as an instructor, or resource person. I'm able to present a language point and, being culturally sensitive, show how they can use it effectively when necessary. I would and do encourage them to ask questions to better understand. In each class, I strive to help the student to use

TABLE 6.1   THE TEACHERS' CRITERIA FOR A SUCCESSFUL LESSON

Criteria	Less experienced teachers	Experienced teachers
Achieves aims	2	1
Active student participation and language use	4	3
Students use and practice target language	2	1
Lively and enjoyable, interesting lesson	3	3
Students feel they are learning	–	1
Covers all four skills	1	–
Variety of tasks	1	–
Students feel positive	1	2
Students learn new and useful things	–	1

what they know and expand that knowledge, overcoming the obstacle of 'peer pressure' or acceptance – losing face among their classmates. By encouragement and praise, help them to verbalize what they already know or are learning."

One of the experienced teachers likewise describes a student-centered view of teaching:

"As the years go by, I feel less and less a 'teacher' and more and more a 'guide' or 'conductor' trying to extract what is inside my students; trying to give them the courage and develop a trust between themselves so that their learning experience will be faster and easier and fun in the process! With that philosophy of a more humanistic approach behind me, I always try and create a lesson which enhances communication and co-operation between the learners where I take a back-seat and they depend on each other more – a more student-centred lesson. So naturally a successful lesson would have incorporated all of this – me as a guide, an example, initially, someone they can rely on for help and where slowly I can dissolve into the background while they are discussing in English the task they are doing – and where I re-appear only to help, encourage and apologize for the lesson being over."

The similarities of the teaching philosophies described by the teachers may reflect the fact that they were all working in the same institution, which has an identifiable philosophy and teaching approach. These comments also confirm the role of "lesson images" noted by Tay (1986); that is, teachers try to create a positive environment for learning in their classrooms, and their mental picture or image of a successful classroom often serves as a powerful influence on their planning (Senior 1995).

TEACHERS' REPORTED USES OF LESSON PLANS

As research on the use of lesson plans has found elsewhere, the experienced teachers reported less frequent use of lesson plans than the inexperienced teachers, made greater use of mental plans than written plans, and because their plans were much briefer, included less information in them (see Table 6.2). In discussing their approach to lesson planning, the inexperienced teachers typically presented a managerial and organizational function for lesson planning and lesson plans. That is, lesson plans were seen as a necessary aid in ensuring that the teacher addressed the

TABLE 6.2 THE TEACHERS' REPORTED USE OF LESSON PLANS

	Less experienced teachers	Experienced teachers
Frequency of use		
Every lesson	7	3
Mental plan only	1	3
Only for new or unfamiliar material	–	2
Purposes of lesson plan		
Provide framework for lesson	3	–
Ensure balance of four skills	2	1
Help realize aims	3	–
Help see lesson as whole	1	5
Help think through teaching process	2	4
Help remember what to cover	4	3
Provide record for future use	3	–
Help identify problems and solutions	1	1
Determine content and sequence	3	2
Reminder of props needed	5	1
Ensure sufficient amount of material	–	1
Achieve good pace and timing	–	1
Contents of lesson plan		
Aims and objectives	8	1
Activities and sequence	8	7
Materials to be used	4	1
Timing	6	3
Language points	4	3
Anticipated problems	4	2
Procedures to use	7	–
Grouping arrangements	1	1
Important reminders	1	1
Homework assignment	–	1
Assessment	6	3

different elements of a lesson, maintained structure and timing, and remembered different details such as aids, OHTs, and flashcards:

"It helps me clearly organize how I'm going to present the language to the students."

"It provides a framework for me to follow during the lesson."

"It helps me clarify my aims and gives the lesson structure."

"The lesson plan is essential for me in creating a cohesive lesson. It reminds me of the different elements I need to pay attention to in bringing the whole lesson together."

"I find unless I have a lesson plan I tend to forget things, and never get half the things done that I planned to do."

While these dimensions of planning were also referred to by some of the experienced teachers, many of them focused more on the process of planning rather than the plan itself. They distinguished between the written plan and the mental plan, the mental plan being the result of thinking through the lesson and identifying problems, strategies, and procedures.

"The written plan helps me to formulate the mental plan. Writing something down helps me develop a plan. The clearer the mental plan, the simpler the written plan."

"There is not always time to write formal lesson plans as required by training courses. Thus what often materializes is a short plan in note form or, in some cases, a mental plan. I find a written plan helps me to remember what I'm going to do (even if I don't look at it!) and to clarify my ideas."

"At first I found lesson planning very difficult, being able to take all things necessary into consideration and writing it down. Now the 'writing it down' is not always necessary as long as the 'process' of lesson planning has been gone through."

"It helps me think through the lesson *before* teaching – it helps get the lesson into my head!"

"I find a mental plan much more useful than a written plan as I invariably find that I divert from a written plan during the course of a lesson. Having a mental plan allows you to focus on the students more. I often find that ideas come to me in the classroom that didn't occur to me before."

"I don't find it helpful to write things down. I look at the materials and I see what I am going to do. And I have a mental picture of what I am going to teach in the class. But I don't find it particularly helpful to write it down. Usually, what I have is a mental plan of the first hour or so of the lesson and then the second part of the lesson comes up while I'm teaching. I used to always write lesson plans down for all the class. And then I did the RSA Diploma and I got used to writing plans and doing lessons. In the end I often

112

found my lessons would be the same as I've been doing for a long time. So I didn't mean to write it down. I knew the format and I knew what it was going to be like. And then I just got out of the habit of this. I can't go back into the habit of writing plans."

Examples of the type of lesson plans made use of by the teachers in the study are given in Appendixes 1 and 2. Appendix 1 is a detailed lesson plan from one of the less experienced teachers that describes aims, activities, procedures, and language items. Appendix 2 is a plan in outline form used by one of the experienced teachers and lists only the activities to be presented during the lesson.

USE OF PLANS DURING LESSONS

Each teacher was observed in two of their regular classes. They provided their lesson plan and their teaching materials prior to each class, and these were used to help the observer follow each lesson. Immediately after the lesson, the teacher was asked to describe any departures made from the plan and the nature of the major interactive decisions made during the lesson. The extent to which teachers made use of their lesson plan is summarized in Table 6.3.

As can be seen from the table, all of the teachers used their lesson plans to some extent. This was to be expected, since they were all teaching to a prescribed syllabus, using materials that had been assigned by a coordinator or prepared by the teacher based on the course specifications. However, the two groups differed in their use of lesson plans while teaching. Most of the less experienced teachers, working with more fully elaborated plans, tended to follow these fairly closely, adding to their plans or dropping activities mainly as a result of time factors. For four of the lessons of the inexperienced teachers, however, only outline plans were used, and these were elaborated on during the course of the lesson. The experienced teachers made much greater use of this mode of teaching, elaborating on brief outlines while teaching or using the materials as the plan and improvising as they taught.

TABLE 6.3 EXTENT TO WHICH THE TEACHERS USED A PLAN

	Less experienced teachers	Experienced teachers
Followed the plan closely	9	2
Followed the plan but added or dropped activities	3	2
Followed a brief outline and filled it out while teaching	4	9
Used the materials as the plan	–	3

This latter mode of teaching can be described as "improvisational performance" (Yinger 1987). It involves the teacher working with a brief outline of the lesson and filling in the details while teaching, drawing on his or her repertoire of teaching routines as a response to the performance of the students. Improvisational performance accounts for the fact that teachers rarely teach the same lesson twice in the same way. Interactive decision making is a crucial dimension of this teaching mode. No matter how brief or detailed a lesson plan a teacher has, during a lesson the teacher monitors students' performance and makes many individual decisions based on assessment of how the lesson is proceeding. These decisions may involve providing an explanation of a concept or procedures to complete an instructional task, questioning students about knowledge of a concept topic or procedure, or encouraging students' initiations and using them during instruction (see K. E. Johnson 1992b). It is through interactive decision making that a teacher shapes and redirects a lesson during the course of instruction.

In the study, the kinds of interactive decisions made by the teachers were identified by interviewing them immediately after each lesson about the lesson as a whole. Since the lessons were not videotaped, it was not possible to probe each lesson with the teacher in an attempt to elicit recollections of specific decisions at various points throughout the lesson. The interview focused instead on the major unplanned departures from the lesson plan that each teacher remembered. The teachers had little difficulty recalling this level of interactive decision making. The results are seen in Table 6.4.

The major interactive decisions were classified into four categories: timing, affective factors, pedagogical factors, and language focus. As can be seen from Table 6.4, timing was an issue that both groups of teachers responded to, though the inexperienced teachers had greater difficulty in carrying out their plans within the time available. One of the less experienced teachers described her concern with timing in the following way:

"The students finished quicker than I thought they would, so I kind of filled in a little at the end. That's why I went back and had them do some sentences at the end. Because I originally planned that when they had done the game on the board and then copied it on paper, that would be the end of it. So it all went in sequence and I just had to add some extra at the end. I think sometimes you can prepare a lesson plan but you don't know often how fast or slow it will go in the classroom. Perhaps with time or maybe when you are into a course or a term you will be able to predict more accurately either how much or how fast they will catch on. So what I'm saying is if you are not sure where their academic level is, you can come into a lesson and you can determine that it's gonna take x number of minutes, but if the students are very confident at that level, instead of something that would probably take 15 or 20 minutes it will take 10. So you can plan a lesson plan for x number of minutes, but if their

TABLE 6.4   INTERACTIVE DECISIONS DURING LESSONS

	Less experienced teachers	Experienced teachers
Timing factors		
Dropped activity because of time	6	3
Added activity to fill out time	2	1
Affective factors		
Added activity to liven up class	2	3
Modified activity to increase interest level	2	5
Pedagogical factors		
Changed sequence of activities	1	1
Elaborated an activity	1	7
Changed grouping arrangements	4	3
Changed or dropped activity because of difficulty	4	2
Dropped activities that didn't seem necessary	–	1
Added activities to strengthen lesson	–	3
Language focus		
Modified activity to change language focus	1	3
Added activity to provide more language work	2	6

academic background is such that they are already comfortable and confident in it, you may not know that necessarily and so you have to come in and all of a sudden your 20 minutes time slot slips down into 10, so then you have to compensate a lot."

For this teacher, timing is a problem that cannot be resolved in advance.

Both groups reported on-the-spot modification of planned activities in order to maintain students' engagement and interest level. This was more frequently reported by the experienced teachers, for whom the students' interest in the lesson was often as much of a concern as the content of the lesson itself. The two groups also reported many modifications they made to activities that were prompted by pedagogical factors, such as the need to make a task easier to accomplish or a change in procedure to make an activity more "communicative." Since many of the experienced teachers were teaching from brief lesson outlines or cues, they reported instances of interactive decision making as they considered alternative procedures while carrying out an activity; they then selected the one they thought most appropriate.

"After I gave them the dictation, I'd not decided then how I was going to feed it back when I wrote this written plan. I thought about using an OHT, but I didn't because there are too many people here. I just put it up on the white board. Even until the last minute I couldn't decide whether to let them do it. I decided it would be more efficient if I did it. If they'd not done it so well, and looking around, they had, I would probably have got them to write it up. That's all impromptu."

They also described how they elaborated activities, confirming the improvisational dimension of teaching noted earlier.

"I hadn't worked out how to do the game before I started the lesson. So I wasn't sure whether it would work better in pairs or groups. Then when I counted the number of people in the class, I decided to do it in pairs, and I quickly modified the way it works to make sure it would fit with pairs."

The experienced teachers also reported adding unplanned activities as necessary, when they diagnosed a point in the lesson that needed what one of the teachers referred to as "instructional repair."

"I realized they were having difficulty with the vocabulary, so I decided to add extra vocabulary work and spent more time eliciting vocabulary than I'd planned. By building in an extra vocab activity, they were able to do the writing task much more successfully."

Many of the less experienced teachers also reported changes to activities or grouping arrangements within a lesson, in order to strengthen the effectiveness of the lesson.

"One of the main changes I made to my plan was in the first part, where I was supposed to introduce a sentence. I was going to write it down on the blackboard. But because the students weren't too involved in what I was doing, I decided to play a game instead of just giving the sentence. I thought if I play a game that'll make them more involved in what they were doing. So I did a backward dictation. That worked quite well. I diverted it here as well. Students were supposed to give each other their opinions and respond to the opinions. I found that they weren't too involved in what was going on. So instead of that I made them write down their actual response and then write down the reasons why. At least that gives them a focus to work on. For the feedback I was going to ask them about their opinions and they were going to answer me. But students were very shy about what they were saying because someone was watching them. They weren't saying anything. So instead of doing that I made them cross-group and asked one student to ask another student. Instead of teacher to student, I made it student to student."

Both experienced and less experienced teachers also reported interactive decisions that were prompted by the need for more language-focused teaching at points within lessons. This was more frequent among the experienced teachers. Nunan reports a similar finding: "Only 12% of the comments and decisions made by the inexperienced teachers were driven by language issues. In contrast 21% of the decisions of experienced teachers were language related" (1992: 157). The greater focus on language factors among experienced teachers may reflect the fact that they have routinized many other instructional decisions that arise during lessons, giving them more opportunities to focus on the explicit linguistic content of lessons.

The working principles, or maxims, that appeared to account for how the teachers used their lesson plans and the interactive decisions they made during the lesson may be summarized as follows:

Maxims used more frequently by the less experienced teachers
Cover your lesson plan.
Fit your plan to match the time available.

Maxims used by both groups of teachers
Provide students with sufficient guidance for tasks.
Maintain a communicative focus to the lesson.
Find the most effective grouping arrangement for tasks.

Maxims used more frequently by the experienced teachers
Build on students' difficulties.
Maintain active student involvement.
Develop a language learning focus for the lesson.

Conclusions and implications

The view of lesson planning seen in the educational and second language literature sometimes presents a "deficit" view of lesson planning – that is, lesson planning models or frameworks are seen as checklists that teachers should use in order to achieve an idealized conception of an effective lesson. Teachers' "capacity to teach" is viewed as an empty box that is gradually filled as decisions are made by selecting from a predetermined hierarchy of categories. Planning is often depicted as an activity that is mainly concerned with the effective management of instruction or as a set of procedures teachers should employ in order to prevent them departing from established methods of teaching. Studies of how teachers plan and use lesson plans, however, suggest that lesson planning should be regarded more positively and creatively, since the process of making the teachable learnable is a central dimension of teacher cognition.

In the study described in this chapter, both experienced and less experienced teachers reported the usefulness of planning in teaching, though experienced teachers tended to make more use of the improvisational mode of teaching than less experienced ones. This suggests that as teachers develop their teaching skills, they are able to draw less on preactive decision making (the type of planning that occurs prior to teaching) and make greater use of interactive decision making as a source of their improvisational performance. On-the-spot decision making and problem solving are central dimensions of teaching for both experienced and inexperienced teachers, but the experienced teachers in this study did more interactive decision making to create lessons as they taught, using brief outlines or lesson notes as prompts rather than as maps or plans. This raises a number of implications for the role of lesson-planning activities in teacher preparation programs.

An emphasis on planning as a process rather than a product

Many of the teachers in the study emphasized the value of the process of planning, rather than the actual plan itself. Shulman (1987) has described the process of planning as constituting the essence of teaching. He refers to this process as pedagogical reasoning, which can be thought of as a process of deconstruction and re-creation. On examining the potential content of a lesson, be it a textbook lesson or a set of materials assembled by a teacher or coordinator, the teacher's problem is how to make the content learnable. Drawing on his or her knowledge of the students, their interests and prior knowledge, as well as his or her own beliefs and principles, the teacher formulates ideas about how the material can be used in ways that will make sense to the learners and allow the teacher to realize his or her personal teaching style. Discussion of how this can come about is an invaluable activity for student teachers, who can work collaboratively on lesson planning. The goal of such activities is not to produce detailed lesson plans, but to acquire the skills of determining what might constitute the implicit difficulties or challenges of a lesson, what activities and procedures might be effective and why, and what adaptations might be needed. By analyzing and problematizing a lesson in this way, student teachers can develop pedagogical reasoning skills that can be employed in many future planning tasks. Interviewing experienced teachers or reading case reports on their approaches to lesson planning can also provide useful insights for student teachers into such thinking processes.

An emphasis on improvisation and decision making in teaching

The teachers in this study also demonstrated the central role of flexibility and adaptability in teaching and the importance of being able to monitor, evaluate, elaborate, and revise plans while teaching. These skills can become a useful focus in teaching practice and microteaching, if student teachers are encouraged to see interactive decision making and problem solving as constituting the essence of the teaching moment. Teaching can

118

be viewed not so much as the process of realizing plans, but as a creative interaction between plans, student responses, and teacher improvisation. Journal accounts and case studies of how teachers transform lessons while teaching can provide useful documents for reflective review in seminars and postlesson review sessions (see Burns and Hood 1995). This can also be accomplished through the use of video recordings of lessons, particularly if these are accompanied by the teacher's account of some of the principal decisions he or she had to consider during the lesson. At the same time, the validity of teachers' individual and personal solutions to problems should be highlighted. Two teachers may create two very different lessons from identical lesson content, through the unique elaborations each teacher creates while teaching a lesson. Lesson-planning activities can hence play a useful role in teacher preparation programs, but plans should be seen as records of teachers' adaptations of lessons and stimuli for creative improvisations in the classroom, rather than straightjackets that impede creative teaching.

Appendix 1: Lesson plan of a less experienced teacher

Aim: teach duration of time with "for/since" in present perfect tense.

I. Revision / "Just" with pres. perfect tense
   1. Show pic./Write 2 verbs "buy/sold"
      Elicit: She has just bought ————— .
               just sold ————— .

Mime: sit down ⎫
       open book ⎬ Elicit ⎧ just sat down
       drink soda ⎭   ⎨ just opened the book
                       ⎩ just drunk

   2. Draw T. Line to show "just"

II. Draw 2 T. lines on board
  (a) *Ask:* When did we start class? (5:30)
           Show on T.L.
           What can we say?
           We have been in class ————— .
     Write on board under T.L.
     Ask: What time is it now?
           How long have we been in class?
     Elicit: We have been in class ————— .
     Write up on board.
  (b) When did you start F2? (Sept.)
     Ss: We have been in F2 (since Sept.)

    Ask: How long have you been in F2? (for 3 months)

(c) Show pix of boy.

    He was sick on Sun./Not today but —————— .

    Ask: How long has he been sick?

    Ss: He has been sick (since yesterday.)

    Ask: How long?

        He has been sick (for 2 days.)

(d) I've lived in H.K. a long time.

    I came in 1975.

    When did I start living here? (1975)

    Ask: How long have I been living here?

    Ss: You have been living in H.K. (since 1975.)

    Ask: How long?

    Ss: You have been living here (for 19 years.)

(e) Show pic. of girl/McDonald's/ hungry

    She went at 4:00

    Show on T. line

    Ask: When did she go to McD's?

        How long?

        She's been at McD's (since 4:00)

        Write 4:30 on T.L./Now it is 4:30.

    Ask: How long has she been there?

        She has been at McD (for half an hour.)

For/Since   used to tell how long something has been happening

    Since: tells when it began or started.

    For: tells us the time or how long.

H.O.1

III. H.O.2 to Ss

Fill in blanks with "for since"

Check with partner

F.B. OHT

IV. Grid Game/X O

Draw grid on board

Make 2 teams

Explain one team X, one team O

Use "for/since"

Demo 5 min.

Team 1 checks Team 2

Team 2 checks Team 1

T writes ans. in boxes

If time Ss write answers on H.O.3 from grid on board.

Appendix 2: Lesson plan of an experienced teacher

GEB 1 – Lesson   Transport

1. Warmer
2. Vocab check – adjectives
3. Pronunciation check of vocab
4. Match adjective with form of transport – Ex in workbook p22
5. Elicit questions for journey to Council with diagram on w/b
6. Write Qs in full – drill
7. Q&A with partner
8. Change partners – report information
9. Write paragraph about partner
10. If time/homework – workbook p23C

Part III *Examining teacher education practices*

7 Textbooks: Help or hindrance in teaching?

The most commonly found elements in second and foreign language classrooms around the world are teachers, learners, and textbooks. While the roles of teachers, teaching, and learners have been the focus of a vast body of discussion and research over the years, much less attention has been given to textbooks. Yet in many schools and language programs the textbooks used in classrooms *are* the curriculum. If one wants to determine the objectives of a language program, the kind of syllabus being used, the skills being taught, the content the students will study, and the assumptions about teaching and learning that the course embodies, it is often necessary to look no further than the textbooks used in the program itself. Textbooks and other commercial materials in many situations represent the hidden curriculum of many language courses and thus play a significant part in the process of teaching and learning. In this chapter, the roles of textbooks and their impact on teachers and teaching are examined.

The extent of textbook use in language teaching

Every year millions of language textbooks are sold worldwide. A diversity of commercial textbooks is available to support practically every kind of language program, from general international courses to country-specific texts aimed at, for example, elementary school children in Singapore, immigrant factory workers in Australia, or university botany students in Poland. Increasingly, the audience for today's textbooks is specific groups, each with particular requirements. This is a somewhat different picture from the 1970s, when basic series such as *English 900* (English Language Services 1964) were designed to be used worldwide. Today there are fewer global course books and an increasing demand for country-specific textbooks. The design and production values of textbooks have also changed significantly. Contemporary language textbooks are visually appealing, with full-color art and sophisticated magazine-like design, printed on high-quality paper and supported by an assortment of supplementary resources, such as workbooks, cassettes, CDs, CD-ROMs, and videos. Today's textbooks are also much more culturally sensitive than their predecessors. Publishers are increasingly responsive to the need to ensure that their textbooks reflect progressive and politically acceptable values. Efforts are made to avoid social bias and ethnocentrism and to reflect universal human concerns, needs, and feelings in the content of the books. Some publishers provide guidelines for authors on these issues. For example, Macmillan/McGraw-Hill has developed a set of multicultural guidelines for the use of writers of educational materials. To avoid physical stereotypes in book illustrations, the guidelines state:

– Maintain a 50–50 balance between the sexes – numerically and in terms of the significance and prominence of the activity illustrated, within schools and across the series.
– Aim for a gender-neutral style of illustration.
– Use illustrations that include all physical types, with occasional evidence of physical disability. Avoid stereotypical association of images.

(*Reflecting Diversity* 1993: 38)

Haines (1996: 27) characterizes differences between current and past trends in ESL/EFL textbooks in the following way:

Then	*Now*
1. author and academic centered	1. market led
2. uncertain global market	2. specific, fragmented markets
3. European focus	3. Pacific Rim and Latin America focus
4. sell what is published	4. publish what can be sold
5. culture of origin, methodology of origin	5. international or local culture
6. English for its own sake	6. indigenous learning situations
7. UK/US publisher dominance	7. English for specific purposes
8. native speaker expertise	8. rise in local publishing
9. culturally insensitive	9. non-native speaker competence
10. low risk/competition	10. culturally sensitive
11. little design	11. high risk/competition
12. artificial text and task	12. design rich
13. single volume titles	13. authenticity
14. multi-component/multimedia	

Not all schools and institutions encourage the use of commercial textbooks, however. Reasons for discouraging their use include (see also Crawford 1995):

– Teacher-made materials are more relevant and appropriate than commercial materials.

- Textbooks cannot provide the basis for a comprehensive language course.
- Textbooks are often culturally inappropriate (e.g., they might have British cultural content that would not work in a non-British context).
- Textbooks are not compatible with a learner-centered philosophy of teaching.
- Textbooks should not be needed by good teachers, who can create their own materials.

However, situations where textbooks are not used are in a minority, to judge from the diversity of textbooks published each year. It is not surprising that most teachers capitalize on their availability. For many teachers, the commercial textbook is hence the primary source of teaching ideas and materials in their teaching. Indeed, the extent of English-language teaching activities worldwide could hardly be sustained without the help of the present generation of textbooks. In many parts of the world, much of the teaching of English goes on outside the state school sector in private language schools. Teachers in these schools may or may not be native speakers of English, but they often have little or no formal teacher training. The textbook and the teacher's manual are their primary teaching resources.

Even in state school systems, where teachers with a better level of training may be employed, commercial textbooks are often the major teaching resources used. For example, in a survey of ESL teachers in Hong Kong secondary schools ($N = 149$), the teachers reported that their primary teaching resources were textbooks, supplementary materials, and audiotapes. The primary functions of the textbook were to provide practice activities (64%), a structured language program for teachers to follow (56%), language models (55%), and information about the language (50%). Most teachers reported that they do not rely on a single textbook (83%), but use a separate textbook for listening (86%), reading practice (66%), and writing (56%). Only 28% of the teachers reported that they made a significant use of exercises and materials that they prepared themselves (Richards, Tung, and Ng 1992).

The dominant role of textbooks within school systems is reflected in the bureaucratic apparatus that has evolved in many situations to place and maintain textbooks in schools, often with minimal input from classroom teachers themselves. Thus in many countries a chain of events takes place in which the Ministry of Education produces test formats or guidelines, publishers produce textbooks to match the guidelines, school districts set in place procedures by which textbooks are reviewed and adopted, lists of approved textbooks are published, and teachers (or their supervisors) then select the books they will use.

The reasons for the widespread use of commercial textbooks are obvious. There are time and cost benefits to teachers and schools in the use of commercial materials. If teachers were not allowed to use textbooks, they would need additional training in the preparation of materials. Schools (or teacher training institutions) would have to plan for such training. In addition, if materials preparation were to be an ongoing and central aspect of a teacher's work, teachers would need reduced teaching loads in order to take on these additional responsibilities. Even if such allowances are made, the quality of school-produced materials can rarely compete with that of commercial materials, which often are supported by large budgets for development and production. In addition, commercial materials offer teachers a considerable variety of resources to choose from, and since they represent no personal investment on the part of the teacher, they can easily be replaced if a more interesting textbook comes along.

In addition to the obvious practical advantages of using textbooks, it has been argued that the dominance of commercial textbooks in education generally since the 1950s has been supported by a convergence of assumptions and interests involving educators, teachers, and publishers (Apple 1986). One point of view in the educational establishment has been that improvement in the quality of teaching will come about through the use of instructional materials that are based on findings of current theory and research. Publishers sometimes see their role as bringing new theories and approaches to teachers by setting up teams to write materials based on currently approved pedagogical models (e.g., communicative language teaching or the whole language approach). Good teaching will then result from the use of scientifically based textbooks developed by experts. This idea was stated long ago with respect to reading materials: "One of the most potent factors in the spreading of the results of research is through a well prepared set of readers and their manuals" (Donovan 1928: 106, cited in Shannon 1987). Current language teaching approaches such as communicative language teaching attribute a primary role to instructional materials. Materials are seen as an essential component of instructional design and are often viewed as a way of influencing the quality of classroom interaction and language use (Richards and Rodgers 1986).

Textbooks as a positive or negative influence on teachers

For many educationists, textbooks are seen as having a positive impact on teachers and teaching. The practical benefits teachers gain from using textbooks in terms of time benefits and access to a varied choice of professionally produced resources was noted earlier. Harmer (1991: 257) observes:

> Where a textbook is involved there are obvious advantages for both teacher and students. Good textbooks often contain lively and interesting material; they provide a sensible progression of language items, clearly showing what has to be learnt and in some cases summarizing what has been studied so that students can revise grammatical and functional points that they have been concentrating on. Textbooks can be systematic about the amount of vocabulary presented to the student and allow students to study on their own outside the class. Good textbooks also relieve the teacher from the pressure of having to think of original material for every class.

R. L. Allwright describes one point of view about the role of textbooks as the *difference view:*

> [This] holds that we need teaching materials as 'carriers' of decisions best made by someone other than the classroom teacher, not because the classroom teacher is deficient, as a classroom teacher, but because the expertise required of materials writers is different from that required of classroom teachers – people who have the interpersonal skills to make classrooms good places to learn in. . . . [This] frees the teacher to develop the expertise needed for dealing with practical and fundamental issues in the fostering of language learning in the classroom setting. (1981: 6)

Hutchinson and Torres (1994) argue that a well-prepared textbook is more than just a set of potential lesson plans, and that textbooks survive and prosper because they are a convenient way of providing structure to a learning program. They suggest that both teachers and learners see textbooks as providing a guide that can help them teach and learn more effectively. From a survey of teachers' views they report:

> Teachers see managing their lessons as their greatest need. Most of their responses centre around the facilitating role of the textbook: it 'saves time, gives direction to lessons, guides discussion, facilitates giving of homework', making teaching 'easier, better organized, more convenient', and learning 'easier, faster, better'. Most of all the textbook provides confidence and security. (Hutchinson and Torres 1994: 318)

The idea that commercial materials are technically superior to teacher-made materials because they are based on a more systematic and carefully developed syllabus has had a long history in education.

> [Commercially] prepared materials are, as a rule, more skill-fully organized and are technically superior to those developed daily in classrooms. Because they follow a sequential plan, the chance for so called 'gaps in learning' is greatly reduced. (Gray 1936: 90–1; cited in Shannon 1987)

For both teachers and learners, the textbook provides a map that lays out the general content of lessons and a sense of structure that gives coherence to both individual lessons as well as an entire course. Students, too, often appreciate studying from an attractively produced class text, since they feel it is an authoritative and accessible tool that can both facilitate learning and make it more enjoyable. This view is reflected in the following comments from teachers on their reactions to a commercial textbook they are using:

"My students really enjoy coming to class. The book has made learning much more fun for them."

"This book has totally turned around the listening program in our school. We really didn't know what to do with listening before, and the book we were using didn't help. Now we have a great program which both teachers and students like."

"The students love the topics and the art. They don't feel as if they are learning English but just having fun."

For learners, as Hutchinson and Torres point out, textbooks can provide an orientation to their learning program, enabling them to see what they will be studying, in what sequence, and how much material will be covered. This can give learners a sense of autonomy, which dependence on daily or weekly lesson handouts does not provide. Crawford notes:

It may well be this sense of control which explains the popularity of textbooks with students. Consequently a teacher's decision *not* to use a textbook may actually be a "touch of imperialism" . . . because it retains control in the hands of the teacher rather than the learner. (Crawford 1995: 28)

Another view of the value of textbooks is that textbooks and teacher's manuals can help inexperienced teachers develop skills in teaching. Many teacher's manuals for ESL course books are hence not only guides on how to use the book but also serve as teacher training manuals for inexperienced teachers, with detailed advice on such things as how to use small group teaching, approaches to grammar teaching in a communicative class, strategies for error correction, or the philosophy of process writing and how to implement it – information that goes well beyond the context of a particular text.

However, others see textbooks as an impediment to teacher development. Swan (1992: 33), for example, warns:

The danger with ready-made textbooks is that they can seem to absolve teachers of responsibility. Instead of participating in the day-to-day decisions that have to be made about what to teach and how to teach it, it is easy to just sit back and operate the system, secure in the belief that the wise and virtuous people who produced the textbook knew what was good for us. Unfortunately this is rarely the case.

Allwright describes a *deficiency view* of textbooks based on the notion of "teacher-proofing." Teacher-proofing is based on the assumption that teachers cannot always be trusted to teach well and that textbooks should be designed to compensate for the inadequacies of teachers. Textbooks that are based on sound theories and organized along scientific principles provide a system, a predetermined content, and a set of instructional tasks, and can therefore compensate for the variations that are found in individual teaching skill in the real world.

According to this view, we need teaching materials to save learners from our deficiencies as teachers, to make sure, as far as possible, that the syllabus is properly covered, and that exercises are well thought out, for example. This way of thinking might lead, at one extreme, to the idea that the 'best' teachers would neither want nor need published materials. At the other extreme we would have 'teacher proof' materials that no teacher, however deficient, would be able to teach badly with. (Allwright 1981: 6)

Another potentially negative consequence of the use of textbooks is that they can lead to reification. Reification refers to the unjustifiable attribution of qualities of excellence, authority, and validity to published textbooks, a tendency often supported by the promotional efforts of publishers. In promoting their products, publishers often support the idea that their books represent the theories of experts or the most recent scientific research. With or without publishers' efforts, however, there is the general expectation among teachers that textbooks have been carefully developed through consultation with teachers and specialists and through field testing, and that the exercises and activities they contain will achieve what they set out to do. In some situations, this belief may be reinforced by culturally based views on the attributes of the printed word. Teachers in some parts of the world, for example, tend to assume that any item included in a textbook must be an important learning item for students, and that explanations (e.g., of grammar rules or idioms) and cultural information provided by the author are true and should not be questioned; they assume that they do not have the authority or knowledge to adapt the textbook. They likewise believe that activities found in a textbook are superior to ones that they could devise themselves. Ariew (1982: 11) observes:

A textbook is often regarded as an immutable and almost mythical object. Our attitude about a text may border on reverence. Many of us will defend our chosen text passionately, at least for the first two years after its adoption. We rarely ask how the text came into being, or what forces were at work during its preparation.

Reification of textbooks, if it occurs, results in teachers failing to look at textbooks critically and assuming that teaching decisions made in the

131

textbook and teaching manual are superior and more valid than those they could make themselves.

A further consequence of the use of textbooks by teachers is that it may lead to a reduction of the level of cognitive skills involved in teaching if teaching decisions are largely based on the textbook and the teacher's manual. This has been described as "deskilling" (Apple and Jungck 1990; Shannon 1987), or the loss of skills through their lack of use. Apple and Jungck (1990) see deskilling as a consequence of viewing teaching as a labor process in which there is a rationalization and standardization of people's jobs. They identify two significant consequences.

The first is what we shall call *separation of conception from execution*. When complicated jobs are broken down into atomistic elements, the person doing the job loses sight of the whole process and loses control over her or his own labor because someone outside the immediate situation now has greater control over both the planning and what is actually to go on. The second consequence is related, but adds a further debilitating characteristic. This is known as *deskilling*. As employees lose control over their own labor, the skills that they have developed over the years atrophy. The are slowly lost, thereby making it even easier for management to control even more of one's job because the skills of planning and controlling it yourself are no longer available. A general principle emerges here: in one's labor, lack of use leads to loss. (1990: 230)

If some of the essential skills of teaching are lost, such as inability to use the pedagogical reasoning skills that are involved in the preparation of instructional materials, the teacher's role is trivialized and marginalized to that of little more than a technician. The teacher's job is to study the teacher's manual and follow the procedures laid out there. Rather than viewing teaching as a cognitive process that is highly interactional in nature, teaching is seen as something that can be preplanned by others, leaving the teacher to do little more than act out predetermined procedures. Teachers now have little control over the goals or the methods of instruction, and more and more class time is occupied with students completing workbook tasks or working from the textbook under the teacher's direction. If teachers allow textbooks to make most of their decisions for them and see their role as primarily managing the students through the materials, it is argued that the level at which teachers are engaged in teaching is reduced to a very superficial one.

Studolsky (1989), on the other hand, questions the assumption that classroom instruction, particularly in elementary school, is dominated by textbooks. She suggests that it is necessary to distinguish three areas of influence on teaching and teacher planning: topics that occur in textbooks, the actual material and exercises that occur on the pages of a book, and teaching suggestions given in the teacher's manual. A teacher might teach a topic presented in a book but use his or her own materials to supplement or replace the presentation in the book; a teacher might use teaching suggestions given in the manual without using the student text itself; or the teacher may use materials from other textbooks or workbooks to supplement the treatment given in the book. Studolsky argues that too little attention has been given to how teachers actually make use of textbooks and points out that "exactly what the presence of textbooks [in the classroom] signals about their use has not been adequately studied or analyzed" (p. 159).

In a review of research on textbook use, A. Woodward (1993) concludes that use of textbooks depends on the teacher's experience (inexperienced teachers use textbooks more extensively than experienced teachers) and on the subject matter being taught (subject matter teachers use textbooks as a source for lesson content but not necessarily for teaching procedures, whereas reading teachers tend to follow textbooks more rigidly).

Freeman and Porter (cited in Studolsky 1989), in an investigation of how teachers use textbooks, found that even when the choice and sequence of topics to be taught was determined by the textbook, teachers still had to make significant decisions concerning time allocation, expected standards of performance, and modifying instruction to suit different student abilities within the same class. Teachers were also selective in the topics they chose from their textbooks.

Studolsky (1989) examined teachers of math and social studies to determine the extent to which topics taught were from the book, which sections of the book or other materials were used, and the extent to which teachers followed suggestions in the teacher's manual. She found that the six teachers she observed varied considerably in their use of textbooks, the greatest area of influence being choice of instructional topics, though this did not extend to sequencing of topics. The teachers differed most in their use of classroom practices and teaching techniques and their use of activities from the teacher's edition. Teachers were extremely selective in what they used from the textbooks and in following through on recommendations in the teacher's manuals. Studolsky's study suggests therefore that teachers' abilities to teach and to employ pedagogical reasoning skills were not negatively affected by the use of a textbook. Rather, the book served simply as a resource, which they drew from in different ways. Hence she concludes:

We have found little evidence in the literature or our case studies to support the idea that teachers teach strictly by the book. Instead, we have seen variation in practice that seems to result from teachers' own convictions and preferences, the nature of the materials they use, the school context in which they teach, the particular students in their class, and the subject matter and grade level they are teaching. (Studolsky 1989: 180)

Textbooks as products of compromise

Two factors are involved in the development of commercial textbooks: those representing the interests of the author, and those representing the interests of the publisher (Byrd 1995a; Werner et al. 1995). The author is generally concerned to produce a text that teachers will find innovative, creative, relevant to their learners' needs, and that they will enjoy teaching from. The author is also hopeful that the book will be successful and make a financial profit, since a large investment of the author's personal time and effort is involved. The publisher is primarily motivated by financial success. However, in order to achieve a profit, publishers generally recognize that a book must have qualities of excellence that will distinguish it from its competitors. Ariew describes the compromises authors and publishers often have to make in order to achieve their sometimes conflicting goals.

A truly innovative approach may be unfamiliar to teachers and so meet with their resistance; it may be threatening to the public responsible for text adoptions, and it may create public controversy. A publisher's success is based on the ability to satisfy the majority of the public; thus, the preference to aim for the mainstream, to sterilize situations and vocabulary and arouse as little controversy as possible. These products of compromise may be as boring as the innovative materials are threatening. Falling too close to either end of the spectrum can have a catastrophic impact on a text's marketability. Finding a perfect balance between innovation and saleability is maddeningly difficult. (Ariew 1982: 12)

In an attempt to make an author's manuscript usable in as large a market as possible, the publisher often has to change it substantially. Some of these changes are necessitated by the fact that teachers with very different levels of experience, training, and teaching skill might use the book. Exercises should have explicit goals, procedures for using activities should be obvious and uncomplicated, and teachers should not have to spend much time working out how to use the material. In addition, content that would not be welcome in particular markets may have to be removed. As a consequence, much of the "flavor" and creativity of the writer's original manuscript may disappear.

At the same time, the publisher will try to satisfy teachers' expectations as to what a textbook at a certain level should contain. For example, if an introductory ESL textbook does not include the present continuous, teachers may feel that it is defective and not wish to use it. Ariew describes the process of making the textbook usable in the widest possible market as "homogenization":

Many publishers systematically delete all (or all but traditional considerations of) topics believed to be controversial or taboo. This tendency has several significant consequences. Besides making texts look alike, these biases affect the treatment of target cultures and may result in inaccurate descriptions or characterizations. The text becomes an ethnocentric clone of the most conservative expression of our own culture. (Ariew 1982: 12–13)

However, no matter what the circumstances are that lead to the publication of a textbook, the end result is still a very special kind of teaching resource. The process of writing a textbook calls on the writer's pedagogical reasoning skills (see Chapters 2 and 3) – that is, the ability to transform content into effective plans for lessons. The processes a textbook writer employs in writing a textbook are hence the same processes that a teacher employs in planning the content of a lesson. For example, in the case of commercial textbook writing, the writer (in conjunction with editors and consultants, many of them classroom teachers) first develops a syllabus for the book, specifying the topics, structures, skills, and other features that the book will cover. Once the writing process begins, the writer has to confront the problem that is at the essence of teaching – how to create a sequence of activities that leads teachers and learners through the content in a way that is at an appropriate level of difficulty, that is engaging, and that provides both motivating and useful practice. The preparation of a one-page activity in a textbook may hence represent many hours of time on the part of the writer, as well as feedback from editors, reviewers, and field testers. The textbook writer has to draw on a considerable depth of knowledge regarding teachers, teaching, language, and learners in producing what might appear to be the simplest of lessons on the page. As Byrd observes:

For the writer of textbooks, possibly the most demanding of the differences between writing for a particular class and writing for publication is the search for coherence. At its best, a textbook is a unified, seamless whole rather than a random collection of materials. The creative energy demanded for writing textbooks involves more than the ability to present language learning materials that are in some way different from those that have been published previously. Textbooks need to be different in conception and organization from the files of materials that all of us develop over the years as we teach our various ESL courses. (1995b: 7)

Yet despite an author's best efforts, textbooks seldom provide a perfect fit for the situations in which they are used; nor can they, because of the factors of compromise and homogenization described earlier. Teachers should therefore approach textbooks with the expectation that deletion, adaptation, and extension will normally be needed for the materials to work effectively with their class. These processes can be thought of as "deconstruction" and "reconstruction," as teachers tailor the materials more closely to their students' needs and to their own teaching style – processes that constitute the art and the craft of teaching.

Textbooks and teacher training

Since it seems evident that despite the availability of other instructional resources, teachers and schools will continue to use commercial textbooks extensively in the future, what can be done to ensure that textbooks support rather than dominate teaching and that they enhance teachers' level of involvement in teaching rather than hinder it? In order for textbooks to be able to serve as sources for creating teaching, teacher education programs need to provide participants with skills in evaluating and adapting textbooks and other commercial materials and prepare teachers for appropriate ways of using textbooks. Yet in many such programs, student teachers get conflicting messages about the role of textbooks. In one course, the lecturer might discourage teachers from using textbooks, suggesting that current approaches to language teaching are not compatible with the use of commercial textbooks. In another course, the lecturer may suggest that textbooks are a useful resource. In many programs, however, the role of textbooks in teaching is not sufficiently acknowledged, and teachers get inadequate preparation in how to use textbooks in appropriate ways (Ball and Feiman-Nemser 1988). In the remainder of this chapter, activities for use in in-service courses and workshops for teachers are described. These activities seek to develop an understanding of the nature of textbooks and their role in teaching through the processes of analyzing what textbooks set out to do and how they do it, developing criteria for evaluating textbooks, providing experience in preparing instructional materials, giving experience in adapting textbooks, and monitoring the use of materials in teaching.

Examining the content of textbooks

A study of the content of language textbooks is a useful activity in courses on curriculum design, methodology, and materials development. A wide variety of content issues can be examined, including cultural content, linguistic content, and pedagogical content of textbooks. For example, in the area of *cultural content,* teachers may work in groups and examine a set of materials in terms of how they portray women, ethnic minorities, or the elderly, through identifying both the ways in which they are presented as well as the frequency with which specific types of people appear. A focus on the *linguistic content* of a textbook might involve examining a particular linguistic item or set of items in a textbook (e.g., how "if-clauses" are presented) and comparing the treatment given in the textbook with information in a reference grammar or language corpus. A focus on the *pedagogical content* of a textbook involves examining the teaching items and teaching strategies that occur in a book. This will be illustrated in more detail.

136

The first stage in reviewing the pedagogical content of a textbook is to determine exactly what it is that a book or unit from a book sets out to teach. For example, is the focus of a unit linguistic competence (e.g., grammar, pronunciation), language skills (e.g., listening, reading), learning strategies (e.g., dealing with unfamiliar vocabulary), test-taking skills (e.g., answering multiple-choice questions), or real-world tasks (e.g., filling out a job application)? The next stage involves examining the tasks employed in the textbook and identifying the different kinds of formats that are used to teach or practice different teaching items. For example, in examining tasks for the teaching of reading skills, one useful activity centers on a discussion of Barrett's taxonomy of levels of reading comprehension. Barrett's (1968) taxonomy describes reading comprehension in terms of five levels of response to a text:

1. Literal comprehension (recognizing or recalling information stated explicitly in the text)
2. Reorganization (analyzing, synthesizing, and organizing information that has been stated explicitly in the text)
3. Inferential comprehension (using information that has been explicitly stated along with one's own personal experience as a basis for conjecture and hypothesis)
4. Evaluation (making judgments and decisions concerning the value of ideas in a text)
5. Appreciating (responding to the psychological, literary, or aesthetic impact of the text on the reader)

Teachers can first examine exercise types that can be used with a reading passage to focus on each of the five levels of comprehension, and then develop their own exercises for each level to accompany different kinds of texts. Commercial ESL reading materials are also examined to determine the levels of reading comprehension they set out to teach and how they do so.

Developing criteria for evaluating textbooks

Evaluation can take the form of a group activity in which teachers identify criteria they would use in assessing a textbook, a unit of material, or an exercise. The focus is initially at a macro level (i.e., developing criteria that could be used with any kind of textbook), and then at a micro level (e.g., developing criteria for a specific kind of textbook, such as a conversation text). For the macro-level evaluation, criteria are identified under teacher factors, learner factors, and task factors. Under *teacher factors*, a group of teachers identified the following:

– The book has a good teacher's manual.
– It is relatively easy to use.

137

Teacher education practices

– It can be easily adapted to fit my class needs.
– It is culturally appropriate for my learners.
– The teaching points are easy to identify.
– It is not dependent on the use of equipment.
– It can be used with classes of mixed ability.

Under *learner factors* they identified:

– The content interests the students.
– The level is appropriate.
– The cost is acceptable.
– It is motivating and challenging.
– The format is attractive and colorful.

Under *task factors*, they specified:

– The tasks achieve their objectives.
– The tasks are self-explanatory.
– The tasks provide an element of challenge.
– The tasks are engaging and interesting.
– The tasks progress in difficulty throughout the course.

For the micro-level evaluation, the teachers came up with the following criteria for evaluating a conversation text:

– It motivates learners to speak and provides a purpose for speaking.
– It works on the three essential skills of accuracy, fluency, and intelligibility.
– It promotes interaction (two- or three-way) and generates plenty of speaking practice.
– It develops awareness of cultural norms.
– It develops practical, usable skills; it has transfer value.
– It is practical in classroom terms.
– It involves information/opinion sharing.
– It reflects students' needs and experience.
– It practices relevant conversational functions.
– It provides all the support needed for completing tasks.
– It moves from controlled practice to fluency.
– It reflects conversational registers.
– It practices conversational strategies.
– It reflects authentic language use.

Checklists from published sources are also examined (e.g., Daoud and Celce-Murcia 1979), and those, together with the teacher-generated criteria, are used in examining textbooks and determining priorities for adaptation.

Trying out materials design

Experience in writing instructional materials is also invaluable for teachers, enabling them to appreciate the types of planning and decision making that materials design involves. Assigning a group of teachers an identical task (such as developing a set of listening tasks around a listening text) and comparing the different solutions they arrive at is a useful way of comparing not only personal creativity, but also the different types of problems each teacher addressed and how they resolved them. Teachers can also compare their own efforts with those of a textbook writer. For example, they can be given a task to design that is similar to one in a textbook and be given the same goals and resources (e.g., a reading passage). After they have developed their exercises, they can be given the textbook writer's exercises for comparison. Activities of this kind help teachers appreciate the kind of thought and effort that go into textbook preparation and also give teachers skills they can use in adapting textbook exercises or developing their own materials.

Monitoring the use of materials in teaching

The focus of monitoring activities is on collecting data on teachers' use of materials and using the information obtained to reflect critically on teaching. This can involve:

1. self-report forms, in which teachers monitor how they use a textbook, how they adapt it, and how students respond to it. The information obtained may be used later for discussion and comparison with colleagues.
2. journal-writing activities, in which teachers write about their use of materials, focusing on similar issues to those in (1).
3. student reports on materials, either through questionnaires or journal writing.

Parallel teaching

Another useful activity is for a group of teachers to teach the same textbook or materials, to monitor their use of the materials, and then to meet regularly to compare in what ways they use the text, how they adapt and extend it, and how they incorporate it into their own teaching approach. The focus here is not on how to teach the book, but rather on how each teacher uses the book within the framework of his or her individual teaching approach.

139

Conclusion

Textbooks appear to be an undervalued resource in language teaching. Despite their extensive use by teachers, acknowledgment of their role has in the past been somewhat unfashionable. In some situations, it has even been suggested that use of a textbook is an admission of incompetence, and textbook writing has been regarded as a crass commercial enterprise devoid of educational merit. But, as Dubin notes, this situation is changing.

Our own professional universe of language teaching is changing in regard to how large numbers of practitioners view the activity of producing materials for classroom instruction. An earlier era suffered from an abundance of textbooks so void of vitality that the entire genre could be stereotyped under the rubric: *Le livre de ma tante est sur la table*. Throwing brickbats at the textbook – and by extension at the author who produced those kinds of nonmeaningful sentences – used to be commonplace.

More recent paradigms for language learning have widened the scope of materials for instruction, and, in so doing, have helped to legitimize the entire activity of materials production. (1995: 13)

Despite this, we still have relatively little empirical data on how teachers use textbooks and the extent to which they influence their teaching. Clearly, textbooks do have the potential for assuming some of the responsibilities that teachers might wish to assume themselves, such as planning a syllabus, selecting topics and content for teaching, and devising engaging learning experiences. On the other hand, many teachers are happy to leave this task to the textbook writer, and to see their responsibility as personalizing the text for their learners, adapting and supplementing it, building links from the textbook to past and future learning, and developing ways of going beyond the textbook based on the learners' interest and response. Activities such as these are still a fundamental part of every teacher's pedagogical expertise and responsibility, and in no way need lessen the level at which a teacher is involved in the process of teaching.

However, it is also possible for teachers to be relatively uninvolved in teaching, and to see their role simply as presenters of material contained in the textbook. Under circumstances such as these, there is indeed a potential deskilling effect for textbooks. To avoid this possibility, it is essential to give teachers the knowledge and skills needed to evaluate and adapt textbooks – to prepare them to use textbooks as sources for creative adaptation. In this way, the potential negative impact of using textbooks can be minimized and they can find their rightful place in the educational system – namely, as resources to support and facilitate teaching rather than dominate it.

8 Through other eyes: Revisiting classroom observation

Observation of experienced teachers has always played an important role in teacher education. Traditional views of observation argue that through observing how teachers conduct their lessons, solve problems of classroom management, and interact with students, novice teachers can develop a repertoire of strategies and techniques that they can apply in their own teaching (Good and Brophy 1987). Day (1990: 43) describes the following goals for classroom observation:

- developing a terminology for understanding and discussing the teaching process
- developing an awareness of the principles and decision making that underlie effective teaching
- distinguishing between effective and ineffective classroom practices
- identifying techniques and practices that student teachers can apply to their own teaching

Observation is often based on the assumption that acquiring skill in teaching involves learning how to do things – that is, the mastery of specific types of behaviors – and that these are observable in the lessons of good teachers. As Acheson and Gall (1987:28) point out, "The first perspective for identifying characteristics of effective teaching is to examine what teachers do in the classroom." Typical "how to" dimensions of teaching that can form the focus of observation include:

- how the teacher starts and ends a lesson
- how the teacher allots times within a lesson
- how the teacher assigns tasks to students
- how the teacher organizes learning groups
- how the teacher supervises students while they are learning
- how the teacher asks questions
- how the teacher reinforces student answers

Since observation appears to be a relatively simple activity to organize and one that offers immediate tangible benefits, it is not surprising that it plays a core role in many ESL/EFL teacher education programs. However, what we can expect to gain from observation is dependent upon how we understand the nature of teaching. While teaching would *appear* to be an observable phenomenon, only aspects of it in fact are observable. For example, underlying such an apparently straightforward issue as the type of questions a teacher uses when exploring a topic within a lesson (e.g., whether "high-order" or "low-order" questions are asked) lie more complex issues, such as why the teacher opted for one type of question as opposed to another.

> The ability to ask higher-order questions is a competency; clarity is not. There are times when higher-order questions are inappropriate, when the teacher who can ask them should not do so; there is no time when clarity is inappropriate. Research on teacher competencies must take account not only of how teachers behave, but when and why they behave as they do. (Medley 1979: 16)

In other words, the significance of what is observed depends on the theory of teaching (or the particular approach or methodology) the teacher holds (see Chapter 2). One teacher may subscribe to a learner-centered philosophy of teaching and believe that learners "acquire" a second language through engagement with meaningful interactive tasks at an appropriate level of difficulty. Hence that teacher provides a minimum of teacher intervention during a lesson. Another teacher may believe in the need to provide learners with a structured learning program to follow, incorporating explicit grammar-focused tasks. Consequently, the two teachers' classroom behaviors may differ significantly with respect to key elements of a lesson and cannot be understood without knowing the philosophy of teaching (or the maxims) each is operating from. It is for this reason that when different people discuss the same lesson (e.g., a teacher, a supervisor, and a student teacher), they often give contradictory accounts of the same event (Fanselow 1977).

In using classroom observation in language teacher education programs, it is therefore necessary to go beyond a focus on the identification of the techniques and strategies experienced teachers employ and to use observation as a way of collecting information that can be used to develop a deeper understanding of how and why teachers teach the way they do and the different ways teachers approach their lessons. In this chapter, observation is examined in terms of how it can assist both cooperating teachers (those who are observed) and novice teachers to develop a reflective approach to teaching.

Observation of other teachers

In the most frequent type of observation, teachers in training sit in on the classes of experienced teachers. In reality the latter often resent being observed. Many teachers feel distracted by the presence of an observer and feel that despite the intention that observers should observe and not evaluate, it is impossible to watch another teacher teach without forming some sort of impression of how successful the lesson was. It is therefore natural for teachers to prefer not to be put in a situation where inexperienced student teachers are given the opportunity to evaluate their lessons, particularly if they have no choice over who observes them, when, and why. The use of guidelines such as the following go some way toward minimizing the negative consequences of having an observer in the classroom:

1. *Observation should have a focus.* The value of observation increases if the observer knows what to look for. An observation that concludes with a comment such as, "Oh, that was a really nice lesson," is not particularly helpful to either party. On the other hand, giving the observer a task, such as collecting information on student participation patterns during a lesson, provides a focus for the observer and collects useful information for the teacher.
2. *Observers should use specific procedures.* Lessons are complex events with many different activities occurring simultaneously. An observer who wants to observe teacher-student interaction, for example, could use a variety of procedures to make the task more effective, such as using a class seating plan or a class list to check off the frequency of different types of interaction (see Table 8.1).
3. *The observer should remain an observer.* An observer cannot observe effectively if participating in the lesson.

TABLE 8.1   A CODING FORM FOR STUDENT RESPONSES TO QUESTION TYPES

Question number	Question types		Responses		Answers	
	Factual	Inferential	Invited	Voluntary	Key word	Elaboration
1	✓		✓			✓
2		✓	✓			✓
3		✓		✓	✓	
4	✓		✓			✓
5	✓		✓			✓
6		✓	✓			✓
7	✓		✓			✓
8		✓	✓			✓
9	✓			✓		✓
10		✓		✓	✓	
11	✓		✓			✓
12		✓		✓		✓

Note: This observation form consists of categories of classroom behaviors. The observer checks the appropriate category whenever the behavior is displayed during the lesson.

An additional way of improving the value of classroom observation is to establish a nonevaluative role for observers through giving them tasks to complete that involve collecting information rather than evaluating performance, and having the cooperating teacher determine what these tasks are. This means that cooperating teachers need to have a clearer understanding of the role of observation and its potential for helping develop a reflective orientation to their own teaching.

A critically reflective approach to teaching is one in which inquiry and reflection are seen as central to the process of teacher development. The skills of self-inquiry and critical thinking are designed to help teachers move from a level where they may be guided largely by impulse, intuition, or routine, to one where their actions are guided by reflection and critical thinking (Boud, Keogh, and Walker 1985). How can the experience of being observed by a student teacher assist teachers in this process?

Reflection, or "critical reflection," refers to an activity or process in which an experience is recalled, considered, and evaluated, usually in relation to a broader purpose. It is a response to a past experience and involves conscious recall and examination of it as a basis for evaluation and decision making and as a source for planning and action (Bartlett 1990). Bartlett argues:

Becoming critical means that as teachers we have to transcend the technicalities of teaching and think beyond the need to improve our instructional techniques. This effectively means we have to move away from the 'how to' questions, which have a limited utilitarian value, to the 'what' and 'why' questions, which regard instructional and managerial techniques not as ends in themselves but as a part of broader educational purposes. (1990: 205)

Participation in classroom observation is one way of developing a reflective stance toward one's teaching. An observer can assist an experienced teacher in this process by collecting information about aspects of teaching that a teacher wants to learn more about, information that he or she would normally be unable to collect alone. This might involve the observer preparing a written description of the lesson or parts of it, or using checklists or coding systems to capture details of the lesson. The information so collected can be used by the cooperating teacher as the basis for critical reflection and by the observer who is normally doing observation tasks as part of a teacher preparation course.

The following are examples of topics identified by teachers for observers to collect information on during reflective classroom observation of this kind. These topics reflect the teachers' concerns and interests related to their own teaching.

Organization of the lesson: the opening, structuring, and closure of the lesson

144

Teacher's time management: allotment of time to different activities during the lesson

Students' performance on tasks: the strategies, procedures, and interaction patterns employed by students in completing a task

Time-on-task: the extent to which students were actively engaged during a task

Teacher questions and student responses: the types of questions teachers asked during a lesson and the way students responded

Teacher's explanations: how the teacher explained vocabulary items during a lesson

Teacher's action zone: the extent to which the teacher interacted with some students more frequently than others during a lesson

Student performance during pair work: the way students completed a pair work task, the responses they made during the task, and the type of language they used

Classroom interaction: teacher-student and student-student interaction patterns during a lesson

Use of the textbook: the extent to which the teacher used the textbook during a lesson and the types of departures made from it

New teaching activity: class performance during a new teaching activity

Group work: students' use of L1 versus L2 during group work, students' time-on-task during group work, and the dynamics of group activities

The observers were able to collect useful information on these issues, revealing things that the teachers themselves were often unaware of. None of these topics requires the observer to evaluate the teacher's lesson. The observer's role is that of an assistant to the teacher, collecting information that the teacher would like to examine and reflect on.

Procedures used by the observers in collecting the foregoing information included the following:

Time samples: The observer notes down specific behavior displayed at specified time intervals during a lesson.

Coding forms: The observer checks the appropriate category on a set of coded categories of classroom behaviors whenever a behavior is displayed during the lesson.

Descriptive narrative (broad): The observer writes a narrative summarizing the main events that occur during the lesson.

Descriptive narrative (narrow): The observer writes a narrative focusing on a particular aspect of a lesson. For example, the observer describes what a single student did and said throughout a lesson.

Once the observations have been made, the observer provides a copy of any information obtained for the teacher. Information collected in this way forms the first part of the cycle of reflective teaching, which Bartlett

(1990) refers to as *mapping*. This involves collecting information about the observable dimensions of teaching, which can feed into the subsequent cycles of critical reflectivity (Bartlett 1990: 209–13):

Level	Questions
1. Mapping	What do I do as a teacher?
2. Informing	What is the meaning of my teaching?
	What did I intend?
3. Contesting	How did I come to be this way?
	How did my present view of teaching emerge?
4. Appraisal	How might I teach differently?
5. Acting	What and how shall I now teach?

But what can the observer learn from this process? Observers are typically student teachers completing a course in classroom observation as part of a degree or professional diploma and may have no choice about their participation in observation activities. They may have no choice about the focus of their observations, since the aspects of classroom behavior and action they are assigned to observe may be related to issues discussed in other classes and are not chosen by the student teacher. In such cases, it is important for the student teacher and the cooperating teacher to negotiate a focus for the observation that will provide useful information for both parties.

For example, the observation topic for the week for the student teacher may be "teacher's questions." In order for cooperating teachers to benefit from the experience of being observed, they will first have to give some thought to how they approach questioning in the classroom. This will involve considering questions such as these:

What is my philosophy of questioning?
What do I believe to be effective and ineffective questioning behavior?
What are the main purposes for asking questions?
What types of questions are simplest and most difficult for my learners?
What sorts of answers do I encourage from learners?
How do I encourage learners to ask questions?

Posing questions like these is the first step in developing a focus for the student teacher's observation of a lesson. Prompted by an interest in the complexity of the questions she used in her classes, a teacher developed an observation task for a student teacher that required the observer to note down the frequency of different question types during a lesson (see Wajnryb 1992: 47), focusing on:

Yes/No questions
Short-answer questions
Open-ended questions

Display questions
Referential questions

Collecting this information for the cooperating teacher provided the mapping information. Shortly after the lesson, the cooperating teacher and the observer met to discuss the information that had been collected. Conversations such as these are an invaluable teacher training experience, because they enable the experienced teacher to reflect on an aspect of his or her teaching (i.e., they engage the teacher in the informing and contesting phases of the reflective teaching cycle), and they enable the novice teacher to share and understand some of the thinking that underlies how an experienced teacher teaches. This gives a focus to field experiences that is often lacking.

Peer observation

The foregoing approach to observation can also be used as the basis for peer observation. Despite the advantages often claimed for peer observation, it is not a common practice in many schools or institutions, because of its evaluation element and because of logistical difficulties in arranging such activities within the context of teachers' timetables. In addition, the purpose for peer observation is often not clear to teachers. Although it can have practical benefits for individual teachers as well as longer-term benefits for a language program as a whole, clear lines of communication about the nature and purpose of peer observation are essential from the very start. If viewed as simply another initiative from the administration, it may be resisted. Peer observation should be approached as an opportunity for teachers to develop a critically reflective stance to their own teaching. Rather than viewing peer observation as an evaluative procedure, teachers should see themselves as coresearchers collaborating for each others' benefit.

This was the approach taken in a large language department, where it was selected as one of a number of activities teachers could choose to participate in as part of their long-term professional development (Richards and Lockhart 1991). The following guidelines were developed by the participating teachers for implementing peer observation.

1. Peer observation would be voluntary.
2. Participants would select their own partners to work with.
3. Each participant would both observe and be observed. Teachers would work in pairs and take turns observing each other's classes.
4. Preobservation orientation session: Before each observation, the two teachers would meet to discuss the nature of the class to be observed, the kind of material being taught, the teacher's approach to teaching,

the kinds of students in the class, typical patterns of interaction and class participation, and any problems expected. These discussions usually took no more than half an hour, as the participating teachers were often teaching similar classes and covering similar kinds of material. The aim of these discussions was for the teacher being observed to assign the observer a goal for the observation and a task to accomplish. The two teachers would agree on observation procedures or instruments to be used during this session and arrange a schedule for the observations.

5. The observation: The observer would then visit his or her partner's class and complete the observation using the procedures that both partners had agreed on.

6. Postobservation: The two teachers would meet as soon as possible after the lesson. The observer would report on the information collected and discuss it with the teacher.

The teachers who participated in the project reported that they gained a number of insights about their own teaching from their colleague's observations. For example:

"It provided more detailed information on student performance during specific aspects of the lesson than I could have gathered on my own."

"It revealed unexpected information about interaction between students during a lesson."

Some identified specific aspects of their teaching that they would like to change as a result of the information their partner collected:

"It made me more aware of the limited range of teaching strategies that I have been using."

"I need to give students more time to complete some of the activities I use."

"I realized that I need to develop better time management strategies."

Longer-term benefits to the department were also cited:

"It helped me develop a better working relationship with a colleague."

"Some useful broader issues about teaching and the programme came up during the postobservation discussions."

Although none of the teachers felt that the observations were disruptive, a few of the participants pointed out changes in the dynamics of the class:

"I think my students were more enthusiastic than usual."

"There was a greater tendency for English to be used and probably a greater degree of attention to the task."

"The students became a bit more tense."

The teachers also gave a number of suggestions for implementing peer observation:

1. For maximum effectiveness, peer observation should be carried out regularly. Most participants felt that twice during a ten-week teaching cycle would be optimal.
2. A timetable for peer observation activities should be set so that teachers are comfortable with it in light of their teaching and other commitments.
3. Depending on the focus of the observation, a tape recording of the lesson could be useful when reviewing the observer's notes.
4. Teachers are most likely to benefit from peer observation if they want to look at a specific need or issue in more detail. For example, a teacher may be concerned that some students are getting very little language practice during lessons and could invite a colleague to collect information on student output during a lesson.
5. Descriptive narratives are useful as a starting point, since they can help identify areas a teacher may wish to explore in more detail. However, follow-up observations should be more focused, using specific observation forms or procedures.
6. Although participants had been asked not to evaluate the lessons they observed, they felt that once a supportive and collaborative relationship had developed between the two teachers, feedback could sometimes include an evaluative component. It was suggested that the observer could focus on the following questions in the postobservation discussion:

   "What worked best in the lesson?"
   "What was the least effective part of the lesson?"
   "What would you have done differently if you had taught the lesson?"

Three-way observation

While observation usually involves a novice teacher observing an experienced teacher's class, or colleagues observing each other's classes in the case of peer observation, an alternative option is to use students' perceptions of the lesson as a third source of information. A strategy of *three-way observation* was developed in response to a request from a group of new and inexperienced teachers in a language department for assistance in professional development from experienced teachers in the program. In this case, the novice teachers wanted evaluative feedback on their teaching but wanted to combine this with feedback from their students. It was decided to implement the following strategy: (a) Pairs of inexperienced and experienced teachers decided to work together. Usually the novice teacher invited a colleague to collaborate. (b) Each pair of teachers arranged to carry out several observations of each other's classes – that is, to take part in peer observation. (c) Rather than use the procedures for peer observation described in the previous section, data were collected at the end of each lesson on the students', the teacher's, and the observer's perceptions of the lesson. This information was collected in the following way.

At the end of a lesson, the teacher alotted 5–7 minutes to the following activities:

The students' task:
Think back on the lesson that you just had and write answers to these questions.

1. What were the main goals of the lesson?
2. What is the most important thing you learned from this lesson?
3. What did you think was the most useful part of the lesson?
4. Was there anything about the lesson that was not very useful to you?

The observer's task:
As you observe the lesson, try to answer these questions.

1. What were the main goals of the lesson?
2. What is the most important thing the students learned from the lesson?
3. What did you think was the most successful part of the lesson?
4. Was there anything about the lesson that was not very successful?
5. How did you feel about the lesson as a whole?

The teacher's task:
At the end of the lesson you taught, answer these questions:

1. What were the main goals of the lesson?
2. What is the most important thing the students learned from the lesson?
3. What did you think was the most successful part of the lesson?
4. Was there anything about the lesson that was not very successful?
5. How did you feel about the lesson as a whole?

The class teacher then collected the students' comments and arranged for a time to review them together with the observer's comments. Several interesting insights emerged from their subsequent conversations. First, there was often a much closer correspondence between the three sources of information on the goals of lessons taught by experienced teachers than by the inexperienced teachers. In other words, the experienced teachers were often more successful than the others in communicating their goals and intentions during a lesson. And when an inexperienced teacher observed an experienced teacher's lesson, there was a higher degree of agreement as to what the goals of the lesson were. In the case of the inexperienced teachers, however, there was sometimes an apparent mismatch between what they set out to do in a lesson and what either the observer or the students thought the goals of a lesson were. For example, a lesson that a novice teacher had intended to be seen as an oral fluency lesson was thought to be many different things to the students. Some had no clear sense of what they had been learning, some thought vocabulary was the primary focus, and another thought it was a review lesson. This confirms D. Allwright's (1984) observation that learners' interpretations of lessons often differ greatly from those of teachers, and Block's comment on "the existence of a gap between the way teachers and learners 'see' the classroom and all that occurs within it" (1996: 168). In the present case, this gap was greatest with the inexperienced teachers.

Second, the comments on the most successful part of lessons also revealed differences between the views of the experienced and inexperienced teachers. The latter tended to comment on what worked best from their point of view as a teacher – that is, they gave a teacher-based account of the highlights of the lesson. The former tended to focus more on the learners and what was likely to be of most benefit to them. For example, one of the inexperienced teachers thought a spontaneous vocabulary activity was the most successful part of one of his lessons. Based on a student's question, he had spent some time developing pairs of contrasting adjectives, which led into a short oral drill. He thought he had handled this procedure very well. The teacher-observer, however, thought the best part of the lesson was a small group activity, in which he observed the learners engaged in genuine interaction around the task.

The most useful outcome of the three-way observation activities, however, was that they enabled experienced teachers to serve as valued mentors to their less experienced colleagues. In one case, the two participating teachers worked out a program to address specific problems they had identified with the inexperienced teacher's teaching. The fact that the experienced teacher was willing to go through the same process of critical self-reflection gave her greater credibility in the eyes of the novice teacher, but it also enabled her to learn more about her own teaching from the experience. Novice teachers reported the following about participation in three-way observation:

"I have learned how much I can learn from my students."

"It's amazing what you can learn from your own mistakes!"

"It has taught me how much I can learn from my colleagues."

"I have learned the value of evaluating myself. Also now I know more about my strengths as a teacher as well."

"This has given me more confidence as a teacher."

"I have realized the importance of thinking about how the students understand what I am trying to do."

At the same time, it was also found to be a useful activity for the experienced teachers who participated, whose comments included:

"It was useful to work with a less experienced colleague and to find out the kinds of issues that were difficult for him."

"The opportunity to think through how I approach my teaching was very useful."

"It helped me get to know my colleagues better and to realize their strengths."

"It has made me more thoughtful about my teaching."

Conclusion

Our understanding of the role of classroom observation in teacher education has changed in recent years as a result of a movement away from a technical view of teaching, which focuses on identification of the behaviors and skills employed by effective teachers, to a focus on the complex meanings underlying the observable acts of teaching. Reflective observation – that is, observation that is linked to critical reflection – is one strategy that can be used to help teachers develop a deeper understanding of themselves as teachers and so be better prepared to make decisions about their own teaching. As Dewey observed in 1904, preparing teachers to be critically reflective about their practice may be more important in the long term than focusing on mastery of the techniques and skills that form the mainstay of much teacher education practice.

9 Reflective thinking through journal writing

Jack C. Richards and Belinda Ho

The goal of many in-service teacher education programs is to engage teachers in a process of critical reflection upon their current teaching beliefs and practices (see Chapter 8). The notion of reflective teaching, which is a dominant paradigm in teacher education programs around the world, including ESL teacher education programs, seeks to develop teachers who

are willing and able to reflect on the origins and consequences of their actions, as well as the material and ideological constraints and encouragements embedded in the classroom, school and societal contexts in which they live. These goals are directed towards enabling teachers to develop pedagogical habits and skills necessary for self-directed growth and towards preparing them, individually and collectively, to participate as full partners in their making of educational policies. (Zeichner and Liston 1987: 4)

Critical reflection has been much discussed since Dewey (1933: 9) originally conceived of "reflection," which he defined as "active, persistent and careful consideration of any belief or supposed form of knowledge in the light of the grounds that support it and the further conclusions to which it tends." Schon (1983, 1987) further developed Dewey's notion of reflection with the concept of "reflection-in-action":

Reflection-in-action is a reflective conversation with the materials of a situation. Each person carries out his own evolving role . . . 'listens' to the surprises ('back talk') that result from earlier moves, and responds through on-line production of new moves that give new meanings and directions to the development of the artifact. (Schon 1987: 31)

Calderhead (1989) summarizes Schon's view of reflection-in-action as "the exercise of interactive, interpretative skills, in the analysis and solution of complex and ambiguous problems," and points out that teacher educators hold quite disparate assumptions about the nature of reflection and how it informs the applications made of it in teacher education.

A variety of approaches is currently used to help teachers develop a critically reflective approach to their teaching, including action research, case studies, ethnography, and journal writing (Calderhead 1989; Zeichner 1987). Journal writing, or the use of "learning diaries" (K. M. Bailey 1990; Jarvis 1992), learning logs (Porter et al. 1990), and dialogue journals (Barkhuizen 1995) may be used as a form of feedback for the instructor (Murphy-O'Dwyer 1985) or used as a means of promoting reflective inquiry. Procedures used in journal writing include listing topics that aroused the students' interest in lectures or coursework with personal responses to them, personal accounts of professional growth and development, and written conversations between student teachers and the instructor.

Most reports of journal writing stress the positive benefits for both student teachers and instructors. Barkhuizen quotes a student teacher's comments on journal writing:

"Writing up my journal has made me realize that writing about certain issues and forcing myself to reflect and bring them out into the open, has helped me to clarify them. It gets you to think about and express consciously, things that are unconsciously going on in your mind whilst you are learning how to become a teacher." (1995: 2–3)

Teacher educators are also generally positive about the use of journals. Reporting on the use of journals as a feedback mechanism in a teacher training course, Murphy-O'Dwyer writes:

[It] enables receptive teachers to discover the importance of relating their own experience of learning to that of the pupils they teach. The insight is achieved through awareness of, for example, the importance of group dynamics; the role of the teacher as director, facilitator or guide; learners' desire for positive feedback; reactions to different teaching styles; the variety of affective factors which influence learners' attitudes to learning and the processes and strategies used in the classroom and how these affect learners' attitudes to learning.

Secondly, retrospection on, and analysis of, classroom processes and experiences can be a valuable consciousness-raising tool. Teachers see the value of developing their awareness of classroom processes, enabling them to make conscious and informed decisions in relation to their own teaching. (1985: 123–4)

From an account of learning logs in teaching practice, Thornbury (1991) emphasizes the value of journal writing in documenting trainees' developing theories of teaching and in stimulating the development of craft knowledge. Brock, Yu, and Wong (1992: 295) summarize the benefits of journal-writing activities in teacher education:

- They provide an effective means of identifying variables that are important to individual teachers and learners.
- They serve as a means of generating questions and hypotheses about teaching and learning processes.
- They enhance awareness about the way a teacher teaches and a student learns.
- They are an excellent tool for reflection.
- They are simple to conduct.

154

- They provide a firsthand account of teaching and learning experiences.
- They are the most natural form of classroom research in that no formal correlations are tested and no outside observer enters the classroom dynamic.
- They provide an ongoing record of classroom events and teacher and learner reflections.
- They enable the researcher to relate classroom events and to examine trends emerging from the diaries.
- They promote the development of reflective teaching.

However, limitations in the use of journal writing have also been described. Burns (1995) reports the following comments by teachers on journal writing.

- Keeping a journal is time consuming.
- The activity is artificial, unless you are a regular journal writer and enjoy this form of communicating with yourself.
- Comments are unfocused.
- It's an initially interesting, but ultimately tedious, activity.
- Journals are difficult to analyze and interpret.

These comments illustrate the kinds of problems that Jarvis (1992) and Barkhuizen (1995), among others, have commented on. For example, Jarvis (1992) comments on the difficulties some participants have in moving beyond description to a more reflective mode of writing. She notes that teachers' journal entries sometimes fail to make links between what they write about and their own classroom practices, and that sometimes little sense of "reflection on practice" is evident. Barkhuizen points out that while some teachers enjoy journal writing and write meaningfully and reflectively, this is not true of all teachers:

Some writers do not enjoy writing journals. For some reason they lack motivation, they are not interested and are not prepared to give journal writing a chance. These students plod along, writing short uninspired entries until the end of the course. (1995: 25)

The demands journal writing places on instructors should also not be underestimated. Reading and commenting on thirty journal entries a week can prove very time consuming, and entering into a reflective conversation with the student teacher may not come easily for the instructor.

The study described in this chapter was prompted by the concern expressed by Barkhuizen, namely, that journal writing may not necessarily engage teachers in a process of critical reflection, and describes a study of teachers' journals in an in-service teacher education program for second language teachers.

Journal writing in an MA TESL program

Background

Journal writing in the present study was one of several procedures used to develop critical reflection among in-service teachers completing an MA TESL degree (other procedures included action research, case studies, and teaching portfolios).[1] The MA course was aimed at secondary school English teachers in Hong Kong and was offered part-time over two years, during which the participants completed a variety of modules on theory and practice in TESOL. During the first semester of the program, students completed a module called "Reflective Teaching," which sought to orient them toward the reflective philosophy of the program as a whole. The teachers examined a number of central issues in teaching, such as teacher belief systems, teacher decision making, the role of the teacher, learning strategies, and classroom interaction (Richards and Lockhart 1994). The topic that was the focus each week served as the basis for self-observation of the teacher's class and small-scale investigative activities, as well as journal writing. It is the journal writing component that is examined here.

Since the introduction of the MA program in 1989, a number of attempts have been made to use journal writing as a reflective tool, and the procedures used have been modified as a result of feedback. As of this writing, the following procedures had been adopted:

- Teachers are introduced to journal writing at the beginning of the program and given guidelines to follow (see Appendix).
- They are requested to make journal entries on a regular basis, such as once or twice a week, either as a response to the general reflection guidelines, or in response to the topic that is the focus of the weekly lecture session.
- At the end of each journal entry, the teachers pose two or three reflective questions about their entry. They bring their journals to class each week during the tutorial session that complements the lecture/discussion input of the module.
- The teachers read each other's journal entries during the tutorial and discuss the questions they raised.

In line with the philosophy of the MA program, the program itself is subject to ongoing review through critical reflection. In the "Reflective Teaching" module, this has involved critically examining the value of the journal-writing experience in order to convince ourselves that it serves a function other than "busy work." If journal writing helps develop a crit-

---

1 We are grateful to the teachers who participated in this study for allowing us access to their journals.

ically reflective orientation to teaching, what evidence can we look for to confirm that this actually happens? In order to help answer this question, it is first necessary to operationalize the notion of critical reflection.

A number of researchers have attempted to analyze what teachers write about in journals in order to characterize the nature of critically reflective thinking. Roderick (1986) analyzed weekly dialogue journals kept by student teachers over a semester and studied the entries for recurrent themes and patterns. Her focus was on how the students perceived themselves as teachers. She examined the students' journals for the following categories:

general statements about self
statements about teaching in general
positive statements about self as teacher
positive confirming statements
negative statements about self as teacher
statements about changes in self from beginning to end of semester
statements reflecting future goals
statements giving rationale for view of self
statements describing experiences that helped a person develop as a teacher

In the present study, it was decided to focus on four issues in the teachers' journal writing: (1) the questions the teachers asked about their teaching; (2) what they wrote about in their journal narratives; (3) whether their questions and narratives could be described as critically reflective; and (4) whether the journal-writing experience developed the teachers' sense of critical reflectivity over time.

Design of the study

The thirty-two subjects of the study were teachers enrolled in the MA TESL program in 1991–2. They were all teaching regular classes in Hong Kong secondary schools or tertiary institutions and had an average of seven years' teaching experience. We first focused on the questions the teachers posed at the end of their journal entries. The journals of ten of the teachers were then selected for closer analysis in order to identify the topics they wrote about. These journals were from teachers who reported that they spent a minimum of 30 minutes on each journal entry. Each teacher made an average of 8.5 journal entries during the 10-week semester, which were typically two to three pages in length. In order to be able to analyze the journals, the topics each teacher wrote about were identified and coded. This information, together with the full set of teacher questions, provided the data for the study.

157

Results

THE KINDS OF QUESTIONS THE TEACHERS ASKED

The thirty-two teachers asked a total of 348 questions at the end of their journal entries. These questions were of four main types: (1) questions that asked about the purpose, rationale, significance, or meaning of an incident or issue; (2) those that asked for information or explanations about theories, strategies, approaches, and hypotheses; (3) questions that asked for judgments, or reactions to and evaluations of things teachers had done; (4) questions that asked for suggestions about teaching ideas, techniques, and procedures. We classified the questions according to level of reflectivity, based on the distinction used by Bartlett (1990). Table 9.1 shows examples of these categories of questions and their frequencies in the data set. The majority of the questions the teachers posed were not very reflective, since they tended to deal with questions concerning teaching techniques and procedures rather than deeper dimensions of teaching. Only 19% of the questions the teachers asked seemed to "transcend the technicalities of teaching" (Bartlett 1990: 205). We also analyzed the teachers' journal entries in order to find out whether the teachers were writing in a critically reflective mode.

WHAT THE TEACHERS WROTE ABOUT

The teachers' journal entries were first coded by the investigators according to four general categories (Table 9.2). These refer to the expository

TABLE 9.1   FREQUENCY OF QUESTION TYPES ACCORDING TO LEVEL OF CRITICAL REFLECTIVITY

Level of reflectivity	Question category	Example	Frequency	
Highest	1	Will this kind of activity ever be useful to them in real life I wonder?	40 (11.5%)	19%
	2	Is spontaneity something that can be taught?	26 (7.5%)	
	3	Should I have explained the questions in more detail?	164 (47.1%)	81%
Lowest	4	What's a better way of dealing with error correction?	118 (33.9%)	
		Total	348 (100%)	

TABLE 9.2   TOPICS THE TEACHERS WROTE ABOUT

1. Theories of teaching

Theories and beliefs about teaching and learning
- a belief or conviction (e.g., what constitutes good language teaching)
- an expert's views (e.g., referring to Krashen's views about language)
- a justification for something (e.g., describing a theory to justify something the teacher did)
- a personal opinion (e.g., expressing an opinion about the value of classroom observation)

Applying theories to classroom practice
- how a theory was applied (e.g., trying out a questioning strategy described in a lecture)
- contradictions between theory and practice (e.g., describing why a classroom incident does not support a theory)
- how theories changed (e.g., how classroom experience changes the teacher's theories)

2. Approaches and methods

Approaches and methods in teaching
- an approach or a procedure (e.g., the teacher's approach to the teaching of reading skills or the procedures used during a listening lesson)

The content of a lesson (e.g., a description of the content of a grammar lesson)

The teacher's knowledge
- pedagogical knowledge (e.g., knowledge about the demands of class tasks)
- knowledge and experience (e.g., pointing out how one's teaching has become more student-focused)

The learner's background information (e.g., pointing out that students have little opportunity to practice English outside the classroom)

The school context
- The relation between teaching and the school context (e.g., how administrative constraints or school policies affect teaching)

3. Evaluating teaching

Evaluating lessons
- positive evaluations of lessons (e.g., commenting that the lesson went well because all students were active in it)
- negative evaluations of lessons (e.g., pointing out that the lesson failed to achieve its goals)

Diagnosing problems
- student's problems (e.g., difficulties student had with particular grammar items)
- classroom interaction (e.g., a planned grouping arrangement did not work because of problems students had interacting)
- teacher's problems (e.g., the teacher did not have time and energy to mark the students' homework)

Solutions to problems
- alternative ways of presenting a lesson (e.g., beginning a lesson in a different way)
- deciding on a plan of action (e.g., deciding to use role play activities more often)
- seeking solutions from the tutor (e.g., asking for ways of overcoming particular difficulties)

4. Self-awareness

Perceptions of themselves as teachers
- their teaching style (e.g., describing the style of teaching they feel more comfortable with, such as a teacher-centered style)
- comments on their language proficiency (e.g., saying that they do not speak English fluently)

Recognition of personal growth
- how confidence has developed (e.g., describing how the teacher is less affected by problems that arise from teaching than before)

Setting personal goals
- self-development (e.g., identifying aspects of one's teaching to work on in the future)

sections of the journals and include the following topics: (1) theories of teaching, (2) approaches and methods used in their lessons, (3) evaluating their teaching, and (4) teachers' self-awareness of strengths and weaknesses.

SUMMARY OF THE TEACHERS' ENTRIES

The topics that the teachers wrote about and their frequencies are presented in Table 9.3. Looking globally at the teachers' journal entries, the most frequent topics written about were related to the evaluation of their teaching (185 references), followed by descriptions of the approaches and procedures they used (108 references), theories of teaching (93 references), and self-awareness of teaching (20 references). In relation to each category, the following general conclusions can be drawn:

Theories of teaching: The teachers more frequently engaged in citing theories or evaluating them than in trying to apply them to their classroom practices.

Approaches and methods: The teachers wrote more frequently about the methods and procedures they employed than about the belief systems or contextual factors underlying these techniques and procedures. Their focus was primarily on classroom experience, and there were few references that went beyond the classroom to the broader contexts of teaching and learning.

Evaluating teaching: Entries in this category focused primarily on problems that arose and on how problems were resolved.

Self-awareness: There were few entries related to this aspect of teaching.

When we look at the individual teachers, however, we see considerable differences in the choice of topics they wrote about. For example, Teacher 1 had many entries that were related to problems that arose in teaching and solutions to problems. She often referred to the theories of experts and was also interested in the rationale for phenomena or actions. She also went beyond the classroom context, writing about such things as the effect of the learners' backgrounds on their learning as well as about her experiences in teaching.

Teacher 4, however, wrote mainly about the objectives of lessons and teaching procedures. He evaluated his teaching but did not attempt to find solutions to problems by using his own resources or by seeking answers from the tutors.

Teacher 9 was also interested in the problems that arose in teaching. However, in contrast to Teacher 1, she wrote quite a bit about how she solved problems. When she wrote about the theories of teaching, unlike

TABLE 9.3 FREQUENCY OF TOPICS THAT THE TEACHERS WROTE ABOUT IN THEIR JOURNALS

Category	Frequency (total)	Frequency (mean)	Frequency of topics that the teachers (T1–T10) wrote about in their journal entries									
			T1	T2	T3	T4	T5	T6	T7	T8	T9	T10
1. *Theories of teaching*												
Theory	63	6.3	18*	8*	11*	1	3	10*	2	3	4	3
Application	30	3.0	1	2	2	1	0	8*	0	2	10*	4*
Total	93											
2. *Approaches and methods*												
Approaches and methods	56	5.6	4	2	0	7*	8*	8*	5	9*	9*	4
Content	32	3.2	5*	0	0	8*	1	4*	3	9*	0	2
Teacher's knowledge	11	1.1	3*	1	2*	0	0	4*	0	0	1	0
The learners	6	0.6	4*	0	2*	0	0	0	0	0	0	0
School context	3	0.3	0	1*	0	0	0	1*	0	0	1*	0
Total	108											
3. *Evaluating teaching*												
Evaluation	23	2.3	1	3*	1	3*	0	5*	4*	3*	1	2
Problems	110	11.0	28*	8	6	2	7	10	5	9	26*	9
Solutions	52	5.2	10*	7*	8*	0	2	2	2	3	9*	9*
Total	185											
4. *Self-awareness*												
Perception of themselves as teachers	8	0.8	2*	0	1*	0	0	3*	0	0	2*	0
Recognition of personal growth	8	0.8	0	0	0	0	0	6*	0	1*	1*	0
Setting personal goals	4	0.4	0	1*	1*	0	0	1*	0	0	1*	0
Total	20											

*Frequency mean.

Teacher 1 she focused on the application of theories to practice, rather than discussing theories for their own sake. Compared with the other teachers, she wrote the most about self-awareness as a language teacher.

Teacher 10, like Teacher 9, focused on solutions to problems and application of theories. However, he did not write about anything beyond the classroom context, nor did he write anything about his self-awareness as a language teacher.

Analysis

Were the teachers engaged in critical reflection?

A crucial question that this study sought to clarify was the extent to which the journal-writing experience involved the teachers in critical reflection on their own teaching practices. The mere fact of writing about teaching does not necessarily involve critical reflection, since teachers can write largely at a procedural level, focusing on trivial details rather than on deeper issues. The goal of activities like journal writing is to engage teachers in a deeper level of awareness and response to teaching than they would achieve by merely discussing teaching in terms of teaching procedures and lesson plans. Thus, as with the teachers' questions, it was necessary in analyzing our data to distinguish between levels of reflectivity in the teachers' journal entries.

Bartlett (1990) describes five phases in the process of reflective teaching and sees each phase as focusing on the following questions: (1) Mapping: What do I do as a teacher? (2) Informing: What is the meaning of my teaching? What did I intend? (3) Contesting: How did I come to be this way? How was it possible for my present view of teaching to have emerged? (4) Appraisal: How might I teach differently? (5) Acting: What and how shall I now teach? (See Chapter 8.)

We can now look at the topics that the teachers wrote about again and categorize them by those that are primarily descriptive and those that involve critical reflection. From the list of categories identified in the teachers' journal entries, the following were classified as primarily descriptive (cf. Table 9.2):

1. **Theories of teaching**

Theories and beliefs about teaching and learning
– a belief or conviction
– an expert's views

Applying theories to classroom practice
– how a theory was applied

2. Approach and methods

Approaches and methods in teaching

The content of a lesson

3. Evaluating teaching

Solutions to problems
– seeking solutions from the tutor

The following were classified as primarily reflective:

1. Theories of teaching

Theories and beliefs about teaching and learning
– a justification for something
– a personal opinion

Applying theories to classroom practice
– contradictions between theory and practice
– how theories changed

2. Approaches and methods

The teacher's knowledge
– pedagogical knowledge
– knowledge and experience

The learner's background information
The school context

3. Evaluating teaching

Evaluating lessons
– positive evaluations of lessons
– negative evaluations of lessons

Diagnosing problems
– student's problems
– classroom interaction
– teacher's problems

Solutions to problems
– alternative ways of presenting a lesson
– deciding on a plan of action

4. Self-awareness

Perceptions of themselves as teachers
– their teaching style
– comments on their language proficiency

Recognition of personal growth

Setting personal goals

The extent to which the teachers' journal entries can be considered reflective can be seen in Table 9.4.

Summary of the extent of critical reflection

From the information in Tables 9.3 and 9.4, we can see that the teachers differed considerably in the extent to which their journals evidenced traits of reflectivity. For example, Teachers 1 and 9 showed a far greater number of reflective traits than Teachers 4 and 7, whose journal entries more often related to descriptions of techniques and procedures.

Even for the teachers who are classified as reflective, however, there were individual differences in how this reflectivity was manifested. Teacher 1, for example, brought knowledge and experience into the classroom and wrote about issues against a broader context and framework than simply classroom techniques. This teacher often reflected on the rationale behind lessons, the events that gave rise to specific problems, and the range of solutions possible. She was very problem-focused and tried to find solutions to problems. Teacher 6 was reflective in a different kind of way. This teacher wrote more about levels of self-awareness than the other teachers in the sample, and tried to link theories and practice to past and other experiences. Teacher 9 was also very problem-focused and set out to solve problems through reflection and analysis. This teacher tried to link theory to practice and also tried to generate theories from his classroom experience.

Teachers 2, 3, 8, and 10, though still evidencing critical reflection in their writing, did so to a lesser extent than the others. Teacher 2's entries tended to explore theories of teaching. Teacher 3 was often concerned with background factors beyond the classroom. Teacher 10 focused on writing about teaching experiences in order to solve problems that arise in teaching. The teachers who were the least reflective (Teachers 4, 5, and 7) showed no traits of critical reflectivity that have frequencies above the mean in their journal entries.

The link between journals and reflectivity

Another question this study sought to clarify was whether regular journal writing over time increased the teachers' capacity for critical reflection. Many teacher educators regard journal writing as a process by which teachers will develop a more reflective approach toward teaching. Was there any evidence for this in the teachers' journal entries? In order to answer this question, we identified seven traits of development in critical reflectivity through examining the general patterns of each teacher's journal entries: (1) a greater variety of types of critical reflectivity; (2) being better able to come up with a new understanding of theories; (3)

TABLE 9.4   FREQUENCY OF TRAITS OF CRITICAL REFLECTIVITY IN TEACHERS' JOURNALS, BY CATEGORY

Category	Frequency (total)	Frequency (mean)	Frequency of traits of critical reflectivity in the journal entries of each teacher (T1–T10)									
			T1	T2	T3	T4	T5	T6	T7	T8	T9	T10
1. Theories of teaching	45	4.5	13*	6*	4	1	3	4	2	3	5*	4
2. Approaches and methods	20	2.0	7*	2	4*	0	0	5*	0	0	2	0
3. Evaluating teaching	185	18.5	39*	18	15	5	9	17	11	15	36*	20*
4. Self-awareness	20	2.0	2	1	2	0	0	10*	0	1	4*	0

*Frequency mean.

being better able to reflect across time span and experiences; (4) being better able to go beyond the classroom to broader contexts; (5) being better able to evaluate both positively and negatively; (6) being better able to solve problems; and (7) greater focus on "why" questions. We then compared the earlier and later entries of each teacher's journal to discover evidence for development of these features. The results are seen in Table 9.5.

Summary of the extent of change in degree of reflectivity

The overall impression that emerged from this analysis was that there seemed to be no great change in the degree of critical reflectivity that the teachers engaged in over time. Teachers who were classified as showing evidence for critical reflectivity in their journal writing did so as soon as they began and tended to demonstrate the same approach to reflective thinking throughout the semester. Some teachers' later journal entries did show a slight increase in the kinds of traits of critical reflectivity they used. However, there were no clear patterns of development or change.

TABLE 9.5   TEACHERS' JOURNAL ENTRIES: DEVELOPMENT IN DEGREE OF CRITICAL REFLECTIVITY

Traits of development in critical reflectivity	Teachers' (T1–T10) journal entries: development in degree of critical reflectivity									
	T1	T2	T3	T4	T5	T6	T7	T8	T9	T10
A greater variety of types of traits	−	−	−	−	−	−	−	−	−	−
Better able to come up with new understanding of theories	−	−	+	−	−	−	−	−	+	−
Better able to reflect across time span and experiences	+	−	+	−	−	−	−	−	−	−
Better able to go beyond the classroom to broader contexts	−	−	−	−	−	−	−	−	−	−
Better able to evaluate both positively and negatively	−	−	−	−	−	−	+	−	−	−
Better able to solve problems	−	−	+	−	−	−	−	−	−	−
Greater focus on "why" questions	−	−	−	−	−	−	−	−	−	−

Two of the teachers who were relatively nonreflective in their journal entries (Teachers 3 and 7) began to show some traits of reflectivity toward the end of the study, but not to an extent that indicated a significant change in awareness.

Conclusion

We noted that the literature on journal writing makes several claims about the role of journals in promoting reflective thinking. In this study, we sought to determine to what extent we could find evidence for this in the journals that teachers wrote during the first semester of an in-service teacher education program. Our findings are inconclusive. Of the thirty-two journals we examined, about 20% of the questions teachers posed could be described as reflective. Of the six journals we examined in more detail for narrative content, only three teachers wrote reflectively to some degree, and the remaining three wrote in a largely nonreflective manner. There was little significant change in the extent to which the teachers developed a greater degree of reflectivity over time. Would we therefore recommend journal writing as a component of in-service teacher education programs?

We asked the teachers themselves this question in evaluating the journal-writing experience at the end of the semester. Most of the teachers (71%) found it useful, 25% reported that they found it fairly useful, and only 4% thought that it was not useful. Those who thought it useful reported that they did so because it provided an opportunity for them to review and reflect on teaching. Many thought that it helped them to become more aware of what they were doing and to better understand themselves as teachers. Some pointed out, however, that the duration of the journal-writing activity (two months) was too short to allow for any significant impact on their teaching, and that while they began in a spirit of genuine critical reflection, it soon became merely another routine course-related activity.

In conclusion, our experience with journals in in-service TESOL teacher education suggests that journal writing can provide an opportunity for teachers to write reflectively about their teaching, though in itself it does not necessarily promote critical reflection. Teachers differ in the extent to which they can write reflectively, and some initial training in reflective writing may well be necessary as a preparation for journal writing. This could be achieved in a number of ways, such as having teachers analyze different types of journal writing for evidence of critical reflection, giving teachers specific writing tasks that would help clarify the nature of reflective writing, and using checklists to help teachers focus on broader issues and questions, rather than on teaching techniques. Activities such as these may help teachers write in a way that more readily promotes critical reflection. However, whatever type of journal writing teachers engage in, it provides other useful benefits in teacher education. For instructors who have limited opportunities for observing the teachers in their own classrooms, it provides a convenient way of bringing informal classroom data that the teachers themselves have collected to the campus program; it provides a form of dialogue between the instructor, the teacher, and other participants in the program; and it provides an opportunity for them to link the content of the campus program with their classroom experience. However, whatever goals are set for journal writing, it is clear that for these to be realized, a careful structuring and monitoring of journal writing is required in order to determine the extent to which it supports these goals.

Appendix: Journal guidelines[2]

An important goal of the MA TESL program is to engage you in the process of reflecting upon your own teaching and the assumptions underlying your classroom practices. We hope that the information presented in each module will serve to assist you in this process.

A useful way of developing a deeper understanding of issues raised both in the lectures and in your own teaching is by writing about them. Writing can serve as a valuable learning device, and often helps to answer questions or to identify solutions.

This term, we would like all participants in the course to keep a journal, in which you regularly record your reflections and reactions to issues which occur in your teaching.

There are several advantages to reflecting on one's teaching and on one's learning experiences in this way. The journal allows you to explore information and thoughts which may not be accessible in other ways. By later reviewing what was written, things which may not have been obvious when they were recorded may become apparent.

Procedures for the journal

1. You will need a ring binder and writing paper. This way sections of your journal can be removed when needed. Alternatively, you may wish to write on a word processor.
2. Write on one side of the page only. Use A4 paper. Write neatly.
3. The audience for your writing is:
   (a) yourself

---

2 These guidelines were developed by Jack Richards and Charles Lockhart for use in the MA TESL program at City University, Hong Kong.

(b) a fellow course member

(c) your instructors

You should locate a fellow course member in your tutorial group and both of you will read each other's journals regularly, and provide commentary. This commentary will consist of responses to the questions you posed at the end of your entries (see 6 below), or anything else your reader wishes to say.

4. Review your entries once every two or three weeks, using the review questions which will be provided.

5. *How to reflect.* Reflect about a lesson at least twice a week. Put aside five to ten minutes after a lesson you have taught and write your impressions of the lesson. Use the questions in the attachment to guide you but do not try to answer all of them. You may also write about other aspects of the lesson if you wish.

6. After each journal entry, pose two or three questions about what you have written. When your journal reading partner reads your journal entry, he or she will respond to these questions.

Reflection questions
QUESTIONS ABOUT WHAT HAPPENED DURING A LESSON

Questions about your teaching:

1. What did you set out to teach?
2. Were you able to accomplish your goals?
3. What teaching materials did you use?
4. How effective were they?
5. What techniques did you use?
6. What grouping arrangements did you use?
7. Was your lesson teacher-dominated?
8. What kind of teacher-student interaction occurred?
9. Did anything amusing or unusual occur?
10. Did you have any problems with the lesson?
11. Did you do anything differently from usual?
12. What kinds of decision making did you employ?
13. Did you depart from your lesson plan? If so, why?
14. Did the change make things better or worse?
15. What was the main accomplishment of the lesson?
16. Which parts of the lesson were most successful?
17. Which were least successful?
18. Would you teach the lesson differently if you taught it again?
19. Was your philosophy of teaching reflected in the lesson?
20. Did you discover anything new about your teaching?
21. What changes do you think you should make in your teaching?

Questions about the students:

1. Did you teach all your students today?
2. Did students contribute actively to the lesson?
3. How did they respond to different students' needs?

169

4. Were they challenged by the lesson?
5. What do you think students really learned from the lesson?
6. What did they like most about it?
7. What didn't they respond well to?

Reflect about yourself as a language teacher from time to time, e.g., once a fortnight. Try to reflect on your professional development. You may use these questions to guide you as well as other questions of your own.

Questions about yourself as a language teacher:

1. What is the source of my ideas about language teaching?
2. Where am I in my professional development?
3. How am I developing as a language teacher?
4. What are my strengths as a language teacher?
5. What are my limitations at present?
6. Are there any contradictions in my teaching?
7. How can I improve my language teaching?
8. How am I helping my students?
9. What satisfaction does language teaching give me?

Part IV   *Entering the field of language teaching*

10 The first year of teaching*

Jack C. Richards and Martha Pennington

The relationship between the content of a teacher education program and the practices of its graduates is of vital interest to teacher educators. How do teachers teach once they graduate from teacher preparation programs, and how relevant is the preparation they receive to the tasks they confront in schools? Such issues are crucial to reflective practitioners in teacher education and raise central questions about the nature of professional knowledge, the relationship between theory and practice, and the processes of teacher change and development. In this chapter, we seek to explore these questions by describing how five graduates of a BA TESL degree coped with their first year of teaching in Hong Kong secondary school classrooms. Through conversations with the teachers over a one-year period as well as observations of their teaching, we show how nonnative teachers of English as a second language cope with the complexities of teaching and how they develop a variety of principles, or maxims, that guide their behavior. By following the teachers throughout their first year of teaching, we were able to observe how certain principles ended up taking priority over others, and how these affected the functioning of lessons and classroom behavior. In most cases, the teachers' strong adherence to a restricted set of working principles helped them to focus their teaching and to reduce the complexity of classroom management. These working strategies, however, represented an oversimplification of the teaching context and also meant abandoning some of the principles and practices they had been taught in their teacher education program.

Coping with initial experiences of teaching

The experiences of teachers in their initial entry into teaching have been relatively well reported in the general literature on teaching (e.g., Britzman 1991; Bullough 1989; Fuller 1969), but much less documented in the literature on second and foreign language teachers. Fuller's (1969)

*The research on which this paper is based was supported by a Competitive Earmarked Research Grant from the Hong Kong Research Grants Committee for the project, "Learning to Teach English in Hong Kong: The First Year in the Classroom."

173

study of the initiation of preservice teachers into the teaching profession identified four stages of teacher development:

preteaching concerns, in which preservice teachers start to get a grasp of their role as incipient educators; *survival stage,* a phase often characterized by great stress in which teachers confront their teaching practice for the first time and strive to attain control of their classrooms, instructional mastery, and the respect of their supervisors; *teaching situation concerns,* in which student teachers transfer their learning to their teaching situations; *concerns about pupils,* the new teachers need to respond to the demands of their students after they have coped with their own survival needs. (cited in Arias 1994: 8)

Bullough (1989) presented a case study of how a teacher in the United States struggled to develop teaching skills in her first year and a half of teaching and how she dealt with the problems common to beginning teachers. He found that the primary orientation of the teacher he studied shifted in her first year from discipline to motivating students and responding to their needs. In addition, the teacher Bullough studied learned to develop detailed and realistic lesson plans while becoming more consistent in her teaching style. She also became better able to handle the complexities of teaching by responding appropriately to unexpected occurrences in the classroom. Mackinnon (1987) found that novice teachers' initial concerns were with relationships with pupils, which soon gave way to concerns with classroom management, teaching materials, instructional methods, and teacher explanations. Only later were novice teachers able to focus on trying to meet the needs of individual children in their classes.

Far less is known, however, about second language teachers' entry into teaching, either concerning how they manage the complexities of real classrooms or how they make use of the types of experiences offered to them as part of their training. K. E. Johnson (1996) provides a case study of a student teacher completing a teaching practicum in an MA TESL program in the United States, describing the mismatch between the teacher's vision of teaching and actual classroom teaching. The teacher lacked the practical knowledge to deal with the realities of the classroom and responded similarly to student teachers in mainstream classes, who "tend to teach in ways that fail to promote learning, but instead simply maintain the flow of instruction and classroom order" (K. E. Johnson 1996: 45). Almarza (1996) sought to explore the interaction between student teachers' pretraining knowledge and knowledge gained in teacher education, and how this influenced the practice of novice foreign language teachers who were completing a teacher education program in the United Kingdom. Of particular interest in Almarza's study were the different ways in which the teachers responded to the teaching methods that were at the core of their teacher preparation programs, and the difficulties some of them had relating these conceptualizations of teaching and learning to either their own conceptions of good teaching practices or the learning processes they observed in their own classrooms.

Moran (1996) reports a case study of a student teacher of Spanish in the United States completing a one-year internship and identifies four themes as central to her experience:

She drew upon a nexus of *core values* that she used to guide her teaching. Prominent among these was *"legitimacy"* – a fusion of feelings, values, and practices to define what it means to be (or become) a Spanish teacher.

She relied on her views of *students and learning,* to the extent that their reactions to her teaching practices provoked her to reflect upon and to make changes in her practice, as did her own learning experiences as a graduate student in a teacher education program.

She developed *a feeling for subject matter,* Spanish language, and Hispanic culture, specifically of its importance to her mission as an educator, which also motivated her efforts to change her teaching.

She consciously employed models of teaching, Spanish teachers who had taught her, fashioning to varying degrees her own teaching practices after these teachers.

(Moran 1996: 127)

Like the other studies reviewed here, Moran's research underscores the complex nature of teaching and the diverse areas of knowledge and skills that must be brought to bear on the classroom context in order to survive the first year of teaching, and ultimately to succeed in a teaching career.

Certain common themes emerge in studies of novice teachers in both mainstream and second language classrooms. For example, the role of teachers' conceptions of themselves and their sense of professional identity has been noted in Bullough and Baughman (1993) and in Richards, Ho, and Giblin (1996). The development by teachers of personal teaching principles that reflect their beliefs and values is discussed in Bullough and Baughman (1993) and in Chapter 3 of this book, and the development of expertise in handling instructional tasks is discussed as a core dimension of teaching in Berliner (1990) and in Freeman and Richards (1996). Previous chapters of this book discuss how second language teachers develop maxims to guide their teaching. Some of these are general principles, such as "follow the learners' interests to maintain student involvement," while others are specific to individual teachers. In this chapter, we discuss how five novice ESL teachers coped with their first year of teaching, the types of adjustments they had to make in order to deal with the complexities of classroom life, and the extent to which they were able to apply the principles and practices that they had been exposed to in their teacher preparation course.

Study: the first year of teaching

The project teachers

The teachers were volunteer subjects in a project that followed five out of the first graduating class of a BA TESL course at City University of Hong Kong during their first year of teaching in Hong Kong secondary schools. The project teachers included three females and two males teaching at different schools in Hong Kong (see Table 10.1).

All of the teachers were Hong Kong Chinese and were typical of Hong Kong young people of their age and educational background. They had each been through English-medium education schools (where some Cantonese may have been used) and completed an undergraduate degree (the BA TESL) that had been taught entirely in English. Four of the teachers had an advanced level of language proficiency, and their fluency was near native. The fifth was slightly less proficient than the others in his verbal skills. All had chosen to be teachers because they were attracted to teaching as a profession, enjoyed studying and using English, and felt that they could make a positive contribution to secondary education in Hong Kong. Each of the teachers had been assigned as a full-time English teacher in a Hong Kong secondary school.

Teaching English in Hong Kong schools is a very demanding occupation, particularly for new teachers. Secondary school students' language ability and aptitude for learning varies considerably, depending on economic and social background. English is introduced in elementary school, and at secondary level parents can choose to send their children either to an English-medium or Chinese-medium school. The majority opt for English-medium schools, since a knowledge of English is perceived as offering many advantages. In practice, English-medium schools vary greatly in the amount of instruction that occurs in English, since when students' level of English is low, teachers of all subjects make extensive use of Cantonese in presenting material.

TABLE 10.1   CHARACTERISTICS OF TEACHERS, STUDENTS, AND CLASSES

Teacher	Sex	Age	Student's sex	Form/ grade	School level	Class level
K. K.	M	27	M	3/9	High	Mid
Mei Ling	F	24	M/F	1/7	High	High
King Fai	M	23	M/F	2/8	High	Remedial
Ming	M	25	M/F	4/10	Low-mid	Low
Wing Yee	F	23	M/F	4/10	Low-mid	Mid

Note: The names used for the teachers are pseudonyms.

176

English teachers usually teach two to three forms (grades) of English (three classes) and one social science subject (one form, two classes). English teachers are coordinated by a panel chair. Communication with teachers is through the panel chair and form coordinators. New teachers are given fairly precise directions to follow, such as how many compositions and dictations are required for each form each term, and how the composition and dictation will be marked. Coordinators assign tasks to subject teachers. These include designing teaching materials, designing teaching schedules for assigned textbooks, preparing tests and examinations, and preparing supplementary material for each unit in the main textbook.

The teaching of English and indeed of all subjects at Hong Kong secondary schools is often described as examination-based and textbook-driven. Students take their main school examinations at the fifth and sixth forms, and both students and teachers tend to give priority to activities that prepare students for the examinations.

The teachers' TESL preparation

The five teachers had completed a three-year full-time undergraduate BA honors degree in TESL offered by the Department of English at City University of Hong Kong. This degree admits forty students a year, the majority of whom are school leavers with Cantonese as their first language, with a few mature students and students transferring from teacher training colleges. About 30% of the content of the degree addresses English language proficiency and communication skills; the major focus of the rest of the degree is on (a) linguistic and sociocultural studies and (b) theories and practices of language teaching. While the BA TESL aims to provide preparation for teaching English as a second language that is specifically geared to the Hong Kong context, it also offers many opportunities for students to develop broad areas of knowledge in English and the teaching and learning of languages that go beyond this context and that encourage innovation and experimentation. Like any other degree course for future English teachers, it aims to develop not only practical skills, but also theoretical knowledge, content knowledge, and abstract values about the English language and about language learning and language teaching.

Practical classroom skills are developed through microteaching activities throughout the program, and field experiences are provided through a three-week internship experience in the second year, in which the student assists an experienced teacher in the class, and a three-week practice teaching assignment in the third year. Since the degree is offered by an English department rather than a department of education, further access to schools for more extended periods of teaching practice is not available. The courses the students take over the three years of the degree are given in Table 10.2.

On graduation, teachers are expected to be able to teach according to the current methodology that is recommended by the Department of Education for teaching in Hong Kong: communicative language teaching (*Syllabus for Secondary Schools English* 1983). The syllabus guidelines prepared by the Department of Education reiterate the assumptions and principles of communicative language teaching and provide guidelines for implementing this approach in Hong Kong schools. Among the statements included in the syllabus guidelines are:

The principal objective of the English language curriculum in the schools of Hong Kong is to provide every student with the opportunity to develop the maximum degree of functional competence in English of which he or she is capable, given the constraints inherent in the situation, in particular competence in those domains of use which are specially appropriate to the Hong Kong situation. . . . [Teachers must] give consideration to the interests of the learner as well as to his short-term and long-term needs. The instructional materials and the teaching techniques used in the classroom should be designed to stimulate the maximum degree of interest in the learner, to provide him with ample opportunities to do things with English, to experience the feeling of successful achievement that comes from putting the language to use for some purpose. Indeed, it could be claimed that successful use of the language being learned is crucial, since without it he is unlikely to persevere in his efforts. (1983: 12)

In the BA TESL course, students are exposed to both foreign-educated "Western" instructors as well as locally born instructors who received their graduate education overseas (primarily in the U.K., Canada, and the U.S.). Thus, those teaching in the BA TESL course combine some aspects of a Hong Kong educational tradition of translation-mediated, grammar-focused, and teacher-centered instruction with "Western" ideas such as communicative language teaching and learner-centered teaching. Graduates of the BA TESL program are therefore expected to be comfortable teaching according to the principles of communicative language teaching, while at the same time being able to adapt their teaching to student expectations and to the type of class they are teaching. They are also expected to be able to interpret what they have learned in a flexible manner based on their own judgment and are led in several modules to develop such a sense of responsiveness and judgment through reflective and problem-solving activities.

From the principles of communicative language teaching as well as the general principles of language teaching discussed throughout their teacher education course, the teachers in this study could be expected to seek to implement the following principles in their teaching:

TABLE 10.2   BA TESL CURRICULUM

Semester A	Semester B
Year 1	
Introduction to Computing	Contemporary English Grammar
Introduction to Language Learning	English Phonetics and Phonology
Theories	Foreign Language Learning Experience
Human Behaviour	Approaches and Methods in Language
Speaking Skills	Teaching
Listening Skills	Reading Skills
Contemporary English Grammar	Writing Skills
Writing Skills	English as a World Language
	Classroom Observation
Year 2	
Integrated Skills	English and Chinese in Contrast
Hong Kong Society	Internship in TESL
English Discourse	Creative Writing
Interlanguage Studies	Cross-Cultural Discourse
Writing for Academic Purposes	Learner Strategies
Teaching Vocabulary	Electives:
Electives:	Modern English Fiction
Drama in English Language	Modern English Poetry
Teaching	Special Topic in Literature
Computer-Assisted Language	Special Topic in TESL Methodology:
Learning	Communicative Language
Modern English Fiction	Teaching
Language Improvement Workshop	
Year 3	
English in Hong Kong	Project
Teaching Writing and Reading	Drama Workshop
Skills	Public Speaking
Teaching Speaking and Listening	Language Assessment
Skills	Curriculum Development and
	Materials Design
	Electives:
	Teaching English Language through
	Content Areas
	The Teaching of English Literature
	Bilingualism and Bilingual Education

Emphasize meaningful language use.
Give equal attention to form and function.
Focus on learners' needs and interests.
Be in charge of your class.
Plan lessons carefully.
Be responsive to classroom context.
Use English as the medium of instruction.

In following five graduates of the program we additionally predicted that, like graduates of other courses preparing practitioners and like the first-year teacher studied by Bullough (1989), these Hong Kong teachers would go through a period of learning to apply what they had studied in a consistent and comfortable manner. It was further predicted that as they went through this adjustment period, they would fine-tune their teaching performance and contextualize their knowledge in relation to their specific circumstances. By the end of the first year of teaching, it was expected that their ideas and practices would have changed considerably since they graduated from the teacher preparation course and would have come into line with the requirements of the context of Hong Kong education in general and of their particular schools and classrooms.

Data collection

Data were collected from several sources: questionnaires, including a belief-system questionnaire, a first-year teacher questionnaire, and re-flection sheets, completed by each teacher; classroom observations; and monthly meetings.

QUESTIONNAIRES

Belief-system questionnaire. This was adopted from Richards, Tung, and Ng (1992) and requires teachers to describe their beliefs about a wide range of issues related to teaching English in Hong Kong, including aims of English teaching, role of English in Hong Kong, theories of teaching and learning, and characteristics of effective teaching and lessons. The questionnaire was administered at the beginning and end of the study to determine the content of the teachers' beliefs and the extent to which these changed during the year.

First-year teacher questionnaire. This questionnaire, administered at the beginning and end of the project, queried teachers on their use of language, teaching approach, lesson-planning and decision-making behav-ior, professional relationships and responsibilities, and perceptions and values to determine the teachers' changing profile in these five areas over the school year.

Reflection sheets. Twice a month, the teachers filled in biweekly reflection sheets asking about their changing beliefs and practices in the same five areas as the previous questionnaire. This allowed a more microscopic view of the teachers' process of development and their reactions and coping behaviors in specific circumstances.

CLASSROOM OBSERVATIONS

Each teacher was visited eleven times during a 9-month period. During the observations, information was noted on classroom language and general teaching behaviors. The observation was immediately followed by an individual interview to elicit the teacher's reflections on the lesson just taught. Observation reports describing the lesson observed and the content of the follow-up meeting were shared with the teachers to help them reflect on their own performance.

MONTHLY MEETINGS

The teachers met monthly with the researchers to describe their teaching and other school-related experiences, report on difficulties they were encountering, and respond to issues that had been identified during the classroom observations.

Findings

To summarize the results of the study, we will examine how the teachers attempted to implement the maxims that were reflected in their BA TESL program, and the personal maxims each teacher developed during their first year of teaching. The discussion is illustrated by examples from tape recordings of lessons made in March 1995 (Pennington and Lee 1995).

At the beginning of the school year, the five teachers expressed their belief in a communicative teaching methodology; soon, however, they confronted the practical classroom realities of large classes, sometimes unmotivated students, and examination pressure. Mei Ling persisted in her belief in communicative principles and throughout the year experimented with a variety of communicative activities to arouse the students' interests and engage them in communicative language use. At the same time, she also felt grammar teaching was important and made use of regular grammar-focused instruction. Moreover, as the school year progressed, she admitted that her main strategy for stimulating students' interest and motivation was to bring in supplementary materials from other textbooks rather than to focus on communicative methodology.

King Fai and K. K. soon adapted to an approach that emphasized language functions and grammar practice, acknowledging the need for the latter in preparing students for exams. For both of these teachers, review of grammar exercises completed as homework or during class was a principal activity. For K. K., such exercises were often complemented by attempts to develop students' knowledge of language functions for communication. For King Fai, much of lesson time was often spent in reviewing grammar rules, with much of the explanation occurring in Cantonese.

Ming's teaching style was more textbook based, resulting from an expressed lack of confidence to move much beyond the textbook. Perhaps because of his own relatively weak English skills, he was very focused on the students' potential problems comprehending the material. This led him to stick very close to the textbook and to center on the understanding of lexis as the key to English language proficiency. As a consequence, he spent much of class time translating words and explaining the meaning of texts for his students.

Wing Yee started out the school year with a strong belief in the principles of communicative language teaching and throughout the year attempted to implement creative activities to apply CLT principles. However, as a result of discipline problems in her English class, which became increasingly serious as the school year progressed, she often abandoned her planned activities in mid-course. When this happened, the focus of the lesson generally shifted to discipline and routine checking of exercises.

Each of the teachers experimented with ways of adapting textbook exercises and other classroom activities to "make them more communicative." At the same time, they felt the constraints of their teaching context pressuring them away from a communicative approach. For example, in discussing a story in the textbook, King Fai used group discussion to engage the students in information sharing. However, he also avoided certain problem-solving and discussion questions in the reading that he thought would be too difficult for the students. Wing Yee felt that although she would like to use more group work, the noise that resulted would elicit complaints from other teachers. Indeed, when K.K. tried to implement a lesson that centrally involved role plays, the students became so noisy and disorderly that he was discouraged from attempting such a student-centered activity again.

Within their attempts to teach communicatively, the teachers consciously tried to follow the maxim of giving equal attention to both form and function, though for the teachers other than Ming and Wing Yee – that is, the three teaching in high-band schools (schools with a higher academic rating) – form took priority over function, as can be seen in the following example. It comes from King Fai's Form 2 remedial class and refers to an example sentence of indirect speech written on the board:

T: Here, he asked, "Can I come now?" You have to rewrite this as, for non *wh* question words OK such as *do, did, does, have, do* – er – *can, should, may,* we have to use *if* or *whether*, is that right? Now, here is a verb – *can, come* is a verb. Here is subject, we have to change the position, OK? Change the position of the subject and the verb. Subject will come first so: He asked, "Can I come?" – he asked, "Can I come now? The person who asked this question is a boy, so he asked *if I* will be changed to *he*, is that right? This is a question. The boy asked he asked, "Can I come now?" So he asked if or whether he could come – *then*. OK, is that all right? *He could come then.* How about this one?

Another important principle that had been emphasized in the teachers' BA course was the need to focus on learners' needs and interests and to personalize their teaching. All of the teachers made recurring attempts to address this principle through personalizing examples from the textbook. For example, they might make references to the students, to popular Hong Kong entertainers, and to other aspects of teenage culture, as in the following example from Mei Ling's class:

T: Oh – the fifth one is comes from – comes from – for example um – um – Wong Faye [local pop singer] – comes from Shanghai – in China – OK – is it Faye Wong – He's not a Hong oh – Beijing. OK sorry, Beijing. OK comes from Beijing.

Similarly, King Fai, to gain students' interest and attention, mentioned a famous basketball player in relation to a grammar point about commands and then gave examples of commands using students' names:

T: So the teacher told Michael Jordan [Ss laugh] – not to – because of the word *don't* – not to dream – during the lesson – OK? Not to dream during the lesson – this applies to all of you here. OK here is the statement – sorry the commands – sometimes you will have to use er *ask* OK – ask you to do something – *teacher asked you to come in* – er *The teacher asked Alex to shut up* – *The teacher asked Vivian to put her finger down on the table* – *The teacher asked Tim not to eat in the class* – *The teacher told Stella to keep quiet while lining up outside the classroom* – OK – here are some of the examples – and on the first page of this set of notes – please take a look at this – you will also find some examples here . . .

King Fai and Wing Yee, who taught older students in lower-band schools, felt they had to devote considerable time to such personalization of lesson content in order to maintain students' interest. However, none of the teachers departed from their lessons for more than a brief moment to pursue a topic or an example raised by a student, and none allowed spontaneous communicative tangents to develop to any extent as part of their lessons. In fact, more often than not, they followed their textbooks or lesson materials closely and did little teaching that was genuinely communicative. Much of the philosophy of the course was thus stifled by

the overriding concern to maintain an orderly class and to cover the prescribed material of the school syllabus.

The need to maintain order and to teach a prescribed amount and content of material in fact soon became the principal concerns for all of the
teachers. They responded to this felt need in somewhat different ways.
As young teachers, they soon discovered that their role as teacher had to
be established quickly, and that they had to be seen as being in full control of the class. They each attempted to do this in a different way, some
more successfully than others. King Fai quickly sought to establish that
he was strict and that he did not accept or tolerate disruptive or unco-
operative behavior. He intervened frequently to control disruptive students, and was prepared to initiate follow-up actions in extreme cases
(such as sending students to the discipline teacher or contacting parents).
His strictness is evident in the following example:

T: If you keep on talking I will change your seat. Today is quite hot – right? I
don't want to see you er to have a – to have your tie loosely fit here – I
don't want to see you like that again. This the last time – give you – several
times for you you can make improvement – I don't want that anymore.

Wing Yee, on the other hand, sought to win students over by establishing herself as their friend. This involved acting in class like a peer –
at times, even like a playful schoolmate. For example, in the following
exchange, Wing Yee quickly abandons her teacher role in responding to
the students' inappropriate (and indeed rather rude) remarks about her
hair:

T: I give you five minutes – OK? Five minutes and I will collect the papers.
S: *Misi, jouh mat neih go tauh gam sung? Jouh mat mh gel yeh a?* ["Miss,
why is your hair so loose? Why don't you gel it or something?"]
T: Because – last night I washed my hair very late and then just dry – gel used
up already. OK so class – you look at the picture and see what's the type of
the film . . .

Wing Yee's attempt to establish solidarity with her students overrode
other basic teaching principles and caused her to lose her students'
respect for her role as a teacher. As a consequence, her class frequently
deteriorated into disorder, and she usually did not finish what she had
planned. In her lessons, she generally had to spend several minutes at the
beginning of the class period getting the students to calm down and often
had to stop the lesson some time during the period to issue disciplinary
statements or to wake up students who were falling or had fallen asleep.
She frequently showed anger during class and sometimes simply gave up
teaching before the period was over, allowing the students to do nothing
for the last few minutes of class.

As part of her strategy of establishing herself as a friend to the students, Wing Yee spent time with her students in leisure activities outside of school and used casual, conversational Cantonese in class and outside of class with them. She did not make a fine distinction between in-class language/behavior and out-of-class language/behavior, and so lost her authority and control in the classroom. The students were disruptive, making rude remarks and constantly trying to move Wing Yee off the lesson content. She did not resist this pressure successfully.

Teaching the assigned materials was the second overriding issue that shaped the teachers' concerns and efforts throughout the year. Each had been given very specific teaching assignments by their panel chair, and finishing the prescribed amount of work was primary. In the case of one of the teachers (King Fai), his supervisor even made out a schedule of lessons for him to follow. Consequently, the teachers rarely deviated from the syllabus already planned out for them. It seems that the planned syllabus discouraged their initiative. Even when they were being observed, they did little planning beyond mapping out timing for different tasks and reviewing the teacher's manual.

The need to maintain order and follow the set syllabus, in the context of trying to be responsive to classroom context, meant that each of the teachers made allowances, in different ways, for use of the native language in the classroom (Pennington and Lee 1995). Although he adhered to a strict, all-English policy for his own language use and encouraged his students to use English in lesson activities, K. K. allowed his students to respond spontaneously in Cantonese during class time. In similar fashion, Mei Ling maintained an English-only rule for her own classroom language use and encouraged her young students to use the second language, but accepted their responses and questions in Cantonese as well. She also relaxed her English-only rule for teacher-student conferences after class.

Because he was so focused on covering the required material, King Fai often used Cantonese to facilitate the review of grammar rules or exercises previously introduced in English. He felt that use of Cantonese saved time and ensured understanding. Ming likewise employed Cantonese as a strategy for ensuring students' understanding of lesson material. His general approach was to present content first in English and then to explicate this content in Cantonese. The following is an example from a lesson based on a reading passage about McDonald's restaurants:

T: What so impressed Ray Kroc when he visited the hamburger stand – *yat dong yat dong maaih hon bou baau ge dong* – "stand" *haih* – a stand, a stand for selling hamburgers, that "stand" is – hamburger stand – run by – run – *Yih douh mh haih gaai jau, haih gaai ging yihng* – It doesn't mean "rush" here, it means "running business" – run by – run by the McDonald brothers OK.

Wing Yee used Cantonese to an even greater extent in her attempts to ensure student understanding and to keep the lesson on target. In addition, she resorted to the native language to establish rapport as well as discipline with her students. Thus, Wing Yee, like the other four beginning teachers, attempted to implement some of her classroom goals by use of the native language. Such an attempt in each case represented relaxation of the principle of "teaching English through English" and an implicit recognition in the classroom of the bilingual nature of Hong Kong society (Pennington and Lee 1995).

Discussion

Rather than focusing on the principles they were taught in the BA TESL course, the five beginning teachers quickly centered in their first year of teaching on two main themes: (1) establishing their role and relationship with the students and (2) covering required material and preparing for examinations. Their orientation can therefore be summarized as a response to the following two maxims of teaching:

1. Establish and maintain your teacher role and relationship with students in terms of an appropriate degree of authority and distance.
2. Cover the assigned material efficiently and thoroughly.

Their strong orientation to these two personal maxims represented a narrowing of their classroom focus, which caused the teachers for the most part to ignore or abandon many of the principles regarded as central to second language teaching. In particular, they moved away from the principles and practices of communicative language teaching and toward a conception of language as the learning of content, with a focus on lexis and grammar rules. The strong emphasis on covering material pressured them to stay close to their textbooks and to adopt a teacher-centered approach in which the students made minimal use of English and participated only in restricted ways. In the vast majority of the classes observed, the dominant speaker was the teacher, who employed the native language to facilitate rapid coverage of the lesson material, to ensure students' understanding, and to maintain rapport and control.

What caused these teachers to abandon so readily the principles and practices to which they were most centrally exposed in their teacher education course? One reason may be the nature of the course. The instructors have varied cultural backgrounds and experience: Some are expatriates from different countries with varied international experience; most have not taught in Hong Kong secondary schools; and some are Hong Kong Chinese with overseas and local experience, including in some cases experience in Hong Kong secondary schools. Thus a consistent teaching philosophy cannot easily be maintained in the course. It is therefore likely that these first-year teachers, when they were students in the BA TESL course, were exposed to a variety of (overt and covert) teaching philosophies and practices. Perhaps the emphasis on communicative language teaching was not strong enough or pervasive enough to impact their beliefs and practices at a deep enough level to sustain this philosophy in the face of other influences.

Another factor is no doubt the teachers' prior experience as students in the Hong Kong school system. As Lortie (1975) has demonstrated, teachers' models of teaching are strongly affected by their own experience as students. In Hong Kong, this generally means a heavy emphasis on textbooks and examination preparation, an expectation of teacher control, and an acceptance of the need for Cantonese to supplement English instruction. Thus, the teachers' behavior in this study can be seen as simply carrying on a Hong Kong classroom cultural tradition. Again, this suggests that the teacher preparation course was not able to make changes in the teachers' schema that were substantial enough to direct their behavior in the classroom.

The traditional Hong Kong teaching culture was also reinforced for these teachers by several types of "significant others" in their teaching context. One important influence was the panel chair, who closely guided and monitored the new teachers' performance. In most cases, the panel chair, who is responsible for ensuring that the official syllabus is covered in each class in his or her area (e.g., English), represents a conservative influence on teaching that discourages teachers from departing from "tried and true" techniques. The influence of other teachers is also considerable, as the experienced teachers in a school exert influence on the new teachers to conform to the set routines and practices. The students likewise have a strong preference for familiar routines and practices, and they are not reluctant to complain when teachers depart from these. Thus, the teacher who tries to break with tradition and implement new and unfamiliar practices such as communicative language teaching or a strict English-only mode of interaction risks criticism, unpopularity, and sanctions of various kinds. In this respect, as well, the teacher education course seems to have been inadequate in providing a foundation of values and practices that could successfully challenge the overwhelming influence of the status quo of the teaching context.

In addition, these first-year English teachers, like other teachers in Hong Kong, experienced the constraints of their teaching context, including the heavy teaching and nonteaching workload, large class size, and the students' low English proficiency and general lack of discipline. Such factors discourage experimentation and innovation, and encourage a "safe" strategy of sticking close to prescribed materials and familiar teaching approaches. Without any relief from these factors and without any reward for innovating in the face of them, the teachers would naturally be led back toward a conservative teaching approach to align themselves with the characteristics of the existing teaching context. They would therefore be likely to base their teaching more on their previous experience, which they have in common with other teachers and students in Hong Kong, than on their teacher education course.

The fact that these teachers were young and relatively close to the age of their students is no doubt another significant factor in their behavior. They were only a few years out of secondary school themselves, and their recent experience as students in the BA TESL course may have made them able to understand and perhaps personally identify with their students' problems. Thus, for example, they may have been especially sensitive to their students' language problems and accepting of their desire for native language support. At the same time, the relatively small age gap no doubt influenced their perception of the appropriate role for them in relation to their students, such as a strong authority figure (i.e., emphasizing the distance from the students) or a peer (i.e., emphasizing their closeness to the students).

Another important factor affecting these teachers' approach is their inexperience. All of them can be described as operating within the "survival stage" described by Fuller (1969; cited in Arias 1994) of striving to attain control of their classrooms and to attain instructional mastery. The relatively brief real teaching experiences provided in the BA TESL program were clearly insufficient in duration to enable them to develop confidence in managing large classes of young people. Each of the teachers struggled to develop classroom routines and ways of managing the complexity of their teaching contexts in order to achieve consistency in their lessons, their own behavior, and the behavior of students. The teachers' desire to achieve stability perhaps drove them to closure too soon – that is, to stop experimenting too early and to stabilize their teaching prematurely.

As a consequence of this desire for stability, the teachers developed a classroom "ecology" (Doyle and Ponder 1977) that did not take account of enough factors and so was not in full balance – in other words, it was not really an ecology. Their model of the teaching context was too simple, showing the teachers' lack of experience and skill in considering and handling all the relevant factors that affect classroom events. Such an oversimplified model of the teaching context would only be enriched by additional teaching experience. However, given the probability of similar teaching experiences in the coming years, changing and elaborating or rebuilding these teachers' models of teaching is not likely to be highly motivated and, if motivated, will no doubt be a slow and piecemeal affair. It would therefore seem that a more proactive attack on the problem, one involving changes to the teacher education course, is required.

Such changes might profitably expand the course from three to four years, giving more time for practice teaching. However, additional teaching experience will not in and of itself solve the problem, since the increased contact with the Hong Kong teaching context will serve to reinforce the local educational values and traditional practices. What is needed is more teaching practice combined with strong guidance and reflection on the relationship of the elements of the teacher education course to the teacher's classroom experience. By explicitly and consciously relating the classroom experience to the theories and approaches learned in the teacher education course, the teacher will not simply reproduce the existing context but rather will bring new ideas to bear on that context. In this way, the teacher will be able to develop practice that is feasible in the local context while also making a new and unique contribution that is grounded on principles of effective language teaching practice.

Conclusion

This study shows how five graduates of a BA TESL course in Hong Kong survived their first year of teaching by developing a simplified working model of teaching consistent with their classroom and the larger educational context. This model centered on just two areas, the teacher's role relationship with the students and the need to cover a prescribed amount and type of content. It was therefore inadequate to represent the full complexity of the teaching environment and so caused certain problems for these teachers. The emphasis on these two areas also caused the teachers in their first few months of teaching to abandon much of what they had been taught in the BA course.

The teachers' youth and inexperience might have led them to focus on establishing a definite and consistent teacher role and relationship with their students that was relatively inflexible and not sufficiently responsive to circumstances and student needs. This orientation was also doubtless influenced by the overall teaching culture of Hong Kong, which values authority and well-defined roles and relationships. The teachers' felt need to cover the maximum amount of content was strongly influenced as well by the teaching context, its traditions and constraints, and by other participants in that context, including the panel chair, the other teachers in the school, and the students.

This investigation demonstrates the difficulty of influencing teaching practices set by a given culture and background of experience. In relation to the particular course offered to the teachers and studied here, it suggests the potential ineffectiveness of teacher preparation in the light of strong countervailing cultural pressures and minimal preservice classroom experience. The findings reported here therefore strongly imply the need to design teacher education to either explicitly align itself with local practices or to explicitly work to change those practices.

For the latter purpose, instruction alone – even instruction that espouses or demonstrates new philosophies or innovative techniques – will not be sufficient to impact teachers' practices substantially and for the long term. What would perhaps be more effective is an extended period of classroom experience combined with repeated cycles of guided reflection. This suggests a model of teacher preparation using mentors in the university sector who work closely with individual teachers to help them adapt their teaching to the realities of their teaching contexts, while developing their value system and practices in a way that incorporates the knowledge gained in their education courses. Such a course of action requires a commitment to teacher development as a long-term, evolutionary, gradual process facilitated by others not only inside but outside the teaching context. It therefore implies the need for a closer relationship between university education programs and schools, and a more gradual, staged process of teacher development in which professional skills and independence are achieved on the basis of a long apprenticeship.

References

Acheson, K. A., and Gall, M. D. 1987. *Techniques in the Clinical Supervision of Teachers.* New York: Longman.

ACTFL Proficiency Guidelines. 1986. New York: American Council on the Teaching of Foreign Languages.

Allwright, D. 1984. Why don't learners learn what we teach? In D. M. Singleton and D. G. Little (eds.), *Language Learning in Formal and Informal Contexts.* Dublin: IRAAL.

Allwright, R. 1979. Language learning through communication practice. In C. J. Brumfit and K. Johnson (eds.), *The Communicative Approach to Language Teaching.* Oxford: Oxford University Press. 183–91.

Allwright, R. L. 1981. What do we want teaching materials for? *ELT Journal* 36(1): 5–19.

Almarza, G. 1996. Student foreign language teachers' knowledge growth. In D. Freeman and J. C. Richards (eds.), *Teacher Learning in Language Teaching.* New York: Cambridge University Press, 50–78.

Anderson, L. W. (ed.). 1995. *International Encyclopedia of Teaching and Teacher Education,* 2nd ed. New York: Pergamon.

Anderson, R. C. 1984. Some reflections on the acquisition of knowledge. *Educational Researcher* 13(10): 5–10.

Apple, M. 1986. *Teachers and Texts.* New York: Routledge & Kegan Paul.

Apple, M., and Jungck, S. 1990. "You don't have to be a teacher to teach this unit." Teaching, technology, and gender in the classroom. *American Educational Research Journal* 27(2): 227–51.

Arias, R. 1994. Towards a conceptualization of ESL teacher development: The interteaching development hypothesis. Unpublished manuscript. Teachers College, Columbia University, New York.

Ariew, R. 1982. The textbook as curriculum. In T. Higgs (ed.), *Curriculum, Competence and the Foreign Language Teacher.* Lincolnwood, IL: National Textbook Co. 11–34.

Ashworth, M. 1985. *Beyond Methodology.* New York: Cambridge University Press.

Bailey, F. 1996. The role of collaborative dialog in teacher education. In D. Freeman and J. C. Richards (eds.), *Teacher Learning in Language Teaching.* New York: Cambridge University Press. 260–80.

Bailey, K. M. 1990. The use of diary studies in teacher education programs. In J. C. Richards and D. Nunan (eds.), *Second Language Teacher Education.* New York: Cambridge University Press. 215–26.

Bailey, K. M. 1996. The best laid plans: Teachers' in-class decisions to depart from their lesson plans. In K. Bailey and D. Nunan (eds.), *Voices from the Language Classroom.* New York: Cambridge University Press. 15–40.

References

Bailey, K. M., and Nunan, D. (eds.). 1995. *Voices from the Language Classroom.* New York: Cambridge University Press.

Ball, D., and Feiman-Nemser, S. N. 1988. Using textbooks and teachers' guides: A dilemma for beginning teachers and teacher educators. *Curriculum Inquiry* 18(4): 401–23.

Barkhuizen, G. 1995. Dialog journals in teacher education revisited. *College ESL* 5(1): 22–35.

Barrett, T. C. 1968. What is reading? In T. Clymer (ed.), *Innovation and Change in Reading Instruction.* Sixty-seventh Year Book of the National Society for Study of Education. Chicago: University of Chicago Press.

Bartlett, L. 1990. Teacher development through reflective teaching. In J. C. Richards and D. Nunan (eds.), *Second Language Teacher Education.* New York: Cambridge University Press. 202–14.

Berliner, D. C. 1987. Ways of thinking about students and classrooms by more and less experienced teachers. In J. Calderhead (ed.), *Exploring Teachers' Thinking.* London: Cassell. 60–83.

Berliner, D. C. 1990. Implications of studies of expertise in pedagogy for teacher education and evaluation. In *New Directions for Teacher Education and Evaluation: Proceedings of the 1988 ETS Invitational Conference.* Princeton, NJ: Educational Testing Service. 39–67.

Birch, G. 1992. Language learning case study approach to second language teacher education. In J. Flowerdew, M. Brock, and S. Hsia (eds.), *Perspectives on Second Language Teacher Education.* Hong Kong: City University of Hong Kong. 283–94.

Block, D. 1996. A window on the classroom: Classroom events viewed from different angles. In K. Bailey and D. Nunan (eds.), *Voices from the Language Classroom.* New York: Cambridge University Press. 168–94.

Blum, R. E. 1984. *Effective Schooling Practices: A Research Synthesis.* Portland, OR: Northwest Regional Educational Laboratory.

Boud, D.; Keogh, R.; and Walker, D. 1985. Promoting reflection in learning: A model. In D. Boud, R. Keogh, and D. Walker (eds.), *Reflection: Turning Experience into Learning.* New York: Nichols Publishing. 18–40.

Breen, M. P. 1991. Understanding the language teacher. In R. Phillipson, E. Kellerman, L. Selinker, M. Sharwood-Smith, and M. Swain (eds.), *Foreign/Second Language Pedagogy Research.* Clevedon: Multilingual Matters. 213–33.

Brindley, G. 1984. *Needs Analysis and Objective Setting in the Adult Migrant Education Program.* Australia: AMES.

Britzman, D. P. 1991. *Practice Makes Perfect: A Critical Study of Learning to Teach.* New York City: State University of New York Press.

Brock, M.; Yu, B.; and Wong, M. 1992. 'Journaling' together: Collaborative diary-keeping and teacher development. In J. Flowerdew, M. Brock, and S. Hsia (eds.), *Second Language Teacher Education.* Hong Kong: City Polytechnic of Hong Kong. 295–307.

Bullough, R. V., Jr. 1989. *First-Year Teacher: A Case Study.* New York: Teachers College.

Bullough, R. V., Jr., and K. Baughman. 1993. Continuity and change in teacher development: First year teacher after five years. *Journal of Teacher Education* 44(2): 86–95.

Burns, A. 1992. Teacher beliefs and their influence on classroom practice. *Prospect* 7(3): 56–66.

Burns, A. 1995. Teacher researchers: Perspectives on teacher action research and curriculum renewal. In A. Burns and S. Hood (eds.), *Teacher's Voices: Exploring Course Design in a Changing Curriculum.* Sydney: National Centre for English Language Teaching and Research. 3–20.

Burns, A., and Hood, S. (eds.). 1995. *Teachers' Voices: Exploring Course Design in a Changing Curriculum.* Sydney: National Centre for English Language Teaching and Research.

Byrd, P. (ed.). 1995a. *Material Writer's Guide.* Boston: Heinle & Heinle.

Byrd, P. 1995b. Writing and publishing textbooks. In P. Byrd (ed.), *Material Writer's Guide.* Boston: Heinle & Heinle. 3–9.

Calderhead, J. (ed.). 1987. *Exploring Teachers' Thinking.* London: Cassell.

Calderhead, J. 1989. Reflective teaching and teacher education. *Teaching and Teacher Education* 5(1): 43–51.

Calderhead, J., and Robson, M. 1991. Images of teaching: Student teachers' early conceptions of classroom practice. *Teaching and Teacher Education* 7: 8.

Cambridge University. 1991. *Diploma in the Teaching of English as a Foreign Language to Adults—Practical Assessment: Notes for the Guidance of Assessors and Centres.* University of Cambridge Local Examinations Syndicate.

Carnegie Task Force on Teaching as a Profession. 1986. *A Nation Prepared: Teachers for the 21st Century.* Carnegie Forum on Education and the Economy. New York: Carnegie Corporation.

Chaudron, Craig. 1988. *Second Language Classrooms.* New York: Cambridge University Press.

Clandinin, D. J. 1985. Personal practical knowledge: A study of teachers' classroom images. *Curriculum Inquiry* 15(4): 361–85.

Clandinin, D. J. 1986. *Classroom Practice: Teacher Images in Action.* London: Falmer Press.

Clark, C. M., and Peterson, P. 1986. Teachers' thought processes. In M. Wittrock (ed.), *Handbook of Research on Teaching,* 3rd ed. New York: Macmillan. 255–96.

Clark, C. M., and Yinger, R. J. 1979. Teacher thinking. In P. L. Peterson and H. J. Walberg (eds.), *Research on Teaching.* New York: Macmillan. 231–63.

Clark, C. M., and Yinger, R. J. 1987. Teacher planning. In J. Calderhead (ed.), *Exploring Teachers' Thinking.* London: Cassell.

Clift, R. 1991. Learning to teach English—maybe: A study of knowledge development. *Journal of Teacher Education* 42(5): 357–72.

Cochran, F. K.; DeRuiter, J. A.; and King, R. 1993. Pedagogical content knowing: An integrative model for teacher preparation. *Journal of Teacher Education* 44(4): 263–72.

Cochran-Smith, M., and Lytle, S. 1990. Research on teaching and teacher research: The issues that divide. *Educational Researcher* 19(2): 2–11.

Conners, R. D. 1978. An analysis of teacher thought processes, beliefs, and principles during instruction. Doctoral dissertation, University of Alberta, Edmonton, Canada.

Cooper, P. J. 1993. Oral communication training for teachers. In N. Bird, J. Harris, and M. Ingham (eds.), *Language and Content.* Hong Kong: Institute of Language in Education. 433–80.

References

Cortazzi, M. 1991. *Primary Teaching How It Is: A Narrative Account*. London: David Foulton.

Crawford, J. 1995. The role of materials in the language classroom: Finding the balance. *TESOL in Context* 5(1): 25–33.

Cruikshank, D. T.; Holton, J. F.; Williams, D.; Myers, J.; and Hough, J. 1981. *Reflective Teaching*. Bloomington, IN: Phi Delta Kappa.

Cummings, A. 1989. Student teachers' conceptions of curriculum: Towards an understanding of language teacher development. *TESL Canada Journal* 7(1): 33–51.

Daoud, A., and Celce-Murcia, M. 1979. Selecting and evaluating a textbook. In M. Celce-Murcia and L. McIntosh (eds.), *Teaching English as a Second Language*. Rowley, MA: Newbury House. 302–7.

Darling-Hammond, L.; Wise, A.; and Pease, S. 1983. Teacher evaluation in the organizational context: A review of the literature. *Review of Educational Research* 53(3): 285–328.

Day, R. 1990. Teacher observation in second language teacher education. In J. Richards and D. Nunan (eds.), *Second Language Teacher Education*. New York: Cambridge University Press. 43–61.

Delamont, S. 1995. Teachers as artists. In L. Anderson (ed.), *International Encyclopedia of Teaching and Teacher Education*, 2nd ed. New York: Pergamon. 6–9.

Dewey, J. 1904. The relation of theory to practice in education. In C. A. Murry (ed.), *The Relation of Theory to Practice in the Education of Teachers*. Third Yearbook of the National Society for the Scientific Study of Education, Part 1. Chicago: University of Chicago Press. 9–30.

Dewey, J. 1933. How we think. Reprinted in W. B. Kolesnick (ed.), *Mental Discipline in Modern Education*. Madison: University of Wisconsin Press, 1958.

Diller, K. C. 1971. *Generative Grammar, Structural Linguistics, and Language Teaching*. Rowley, MA: Newbury House.

Donovan, M. 1928. Use of research in teaching reading. *Elementary English Review* 5: 104–7.

Doyle, W. 1983. Academic work. *Review of Educational Research* 52(2): 159–99.

Doyle, W., and Ponder, G. A. 1977. The practicality ethic in teacher decision-making. *Interchange* 8(3): 1–12.

Dubin, F. 1995. The craft of materials writing. In P. Byrd (ed.), *Material Writer's Guide*. Boston: Heinle & Heinle. 13–22.

Duffy, G., and Anderson, L. 1986. Teachers' theoretical orientations and the real classroom. *Reading Psychology* 5: 97–104.

Dunkin, M. J., and Biddle, B. J. 1974. *The Study of Teaching*. New York: Holt, Rinehart & Winston.

Elbaz, F. 1981. The teacher's "practical knowledge": Report of a case study. *Curriculum Inquiry* 11: 43–71.

English Language Services. 1964. *English 900*. New York: Collier Macmillan.

Fanselow, J. 1977. Beyond Rashomon: Conceptualizing and observing the teaching act. *TESOL Quarterly* 11(1): 17–41.

Fanselow, J. 1987. *Breaking Rules*. New York: Longman.

Feiman-Nemser, S., and Parker, M. B. 1990. Making subject matter part of the conversation in learning to teach. *Journal of Teacher Education* 41(3): 32–43.

Finocchiaro, M., and Brumfit, C. 1983. *The Functional-Notional Approach: From Theory to Practice.* New York: Oxford University Press.

Fogerty, J. L.; Wang, M. C.; and Creek, R. 1983. A descriptive study of experienced and novice teachers' interactive thoughts and actions. *Journal of Educational Research* 77: 22–32.

Freeman, D. 1982. Observing teachers: Three approaches to in-service training and development. *TESOL Quarterly* 16(1).

Freeman, D. 1989. Teacher training, development, and decision making: A model of teaching and related strategies for teacher education. *TESOL Quarterly* 23(1): 27–46.

Freeman, D. 1995. Educational linguistics and the knowledge-base of second language teaching. In J. Alatis (ed.). *Georgetown University Roundtable on Languages and Linguistics.* Washington, D.C.: Georgetown University Press.

Freeman, D. 1996a. The unstudied problem: Research on learning to teach second languages. In D. Freeman and J. Richards (eds.), *Teacher Learning in Language Teaching.* New York: Cambridge University Press. 351–78.

Freeman, D. 1996b. Renaming experience/reconstructing practice: Developing new understandings of teaching. In D. Freeman and J. Richards (eds.), *Teacher Learning in Language Teaching.* New York: Cambridge University Press. 221–41.

Freeman, D. 1996c. Redefining research and what teachers know. In K. Bailey and D. Nunan (eds.), *Voices from the Language Classroom.* New York: Cambridge University Press. 88–115.

Freeman, D. 1996d. 'To take them at their word': Language data in the study of teachers' knowledge. *Harvard Educational Review* 66(4): 732–61.

Freeman, D., and Cazden, C. 1991. Learning to talk like a professional: Some pragmatics of foreign language teacher training. In L. Bouton and Y. Kachru (eds.), *Pragmatics and Language Learning.* Monograph Series No. 2. Champaign-Urbana: University of Illinois. 225–45.

Freeman, D., and Richards, J. C. 1993. Conceptions of teaching and the education of second language teachers. *TESOL Quarterly* 27(2): 193–216.

Freeman, D., and Richards, J. C. (eds.). 1996. *Teacher Learning in Language Teaching.* New York: Cambridge University Press.

Fujiwara, B. 1996. Planning an advanced listening comprehension elective for Japanese college students. In K. Graves (ed.), *Teachers as Course Developers.* New York: Cambridge University Press. 151–75.

Fuller, F. F. 1969. Concerns of teachers: A developmental conceptualization. *American Educational Research Journal* 6: 207–26.

Gage, N. L. 1978. *The Scientific Basis of the Art of Teaching.* New York: Teachers College Press.

Good, T., and Brophy, F. 1987. *Looking in Classrooms.* New York: Harper & Row.

Gray, W. (ed.). 1936. *The Teaching of Reading.* Thirty-sixth Yearbook of the National Society for the Study of Education, Part 1. Chicago: University of Chicago Press.

Haines, D. 1966. Survival of the fittest. *The Bookseller* (Feb.): 26–34.

Halkes, R., and Deijkers, R. 1984. Teachers' thinking criteria. In R. Halkes and J. Olson (eds.), *Teacher Thinking: A New Perspective on Persisting Problems in Education.* Lisse: Swets & Zeitlinger.

References

Harmer, J. 1991. *The Practice of English Language Teaching*. London: Longman.

Heaton, J. B. 1981. *Using English in the Classroom*. Singapore: Longman.

Hoffman, J. V., and Kugle, C. L. 1982. A study of the theoretical orientation to reading and its relationship to teacher verbal feedback during reading instruction. *Journal of Classroom Interaction* 18: 2–7.

Holliday, A. 1994. *Appropriate Methodology and Social Context*. Cambridge: Cambridge University Press.

Hosenfeld, C. 1984. Case studies of 9th grade readers. In J. C. Alderson and A. S. Urquhart (eds.), *Reading in a Foreign Language*. Harlow: Longman. 231–44.

Hubbard, P.; Jones, H.; Thornton, B.; and Wheeler, R. 1983. *A Training Course for TEFL*. Oxford: Oxford University Press.

Hutchinson, T., and Torres, E. 1994. The textbook as agent of change. *ELT Journal* 48(4): 315–28.

Jarvis, J. 1992. Using diaries for teacher reflection on in-service courses. *ELT Journal* 46(2): 133–43.

Johnson, K. E. 1992a. The relationship between teachers' beliefs and practices during literacy instruction for non-native speakers of English. *Journal of Reading Behavior* 24: 83–108.

Johnson, K. E. 1992b. The instructional decisions of pre-service English as a second language teachers: New directions for teacher preparation programs. In J. Flowerdew, M. Brock, and S. Hsia (eds.), *Perspectives on Second Language Teacher Education*. Hong Kong: City Polytechnic of Hong Kong. 115–34.

Johnson, K. E. 1996. The vision versus the reality: The tensions of the TESOL practicum. In D. Freeman and J. Richards (eds.), *Teacher Learning in Language Teaching*. New York: Cambridge University Press. 30–49.

Johnson, R. K. 1990. Developing teachers' language resources. In J. C. Richards and D. Nunan (eds.), *Second Language Teacher Education*. New York: Cambridge University Press. 269–81.

Johnston, S. 1990. Understanding curriculum decision-making through teacher images. *Journal of Curriculum Studies* 22(5): 463–71.

Johnston, S. 1992. Images: A way of understanding the practical knowledge of student teachers. *Teaching and Teacher Education* 18(2): 128–36.

Kaplan, R. B. (ed.). 1980. *On the Scope of Applied Linguistics*. Rowley, MA: Newbury House.

Kemmis, S., and McTaggart, R. 1981. *The Action Research Planner*. Victoria: Deakin University.

Kleinfeld, J. 1992. Learning to think like a teacher. In J. Shulman (ed.), *Case Methods in Teacher Education*. New York: Teachers College Press. 33–49.

Kornblueth, I., and Schoenberg, S. 1990. Through the looking glass: Reflective methods in teacher training. *TESOL Newsletter* 24(5): 17–18.

Lange, D. 1990. A blueprint for a teacher development program. In J. C. Richards and D. Nunan (eds.), *Second Language Teacher Education*. New York: Cambridge University Press. 245–68.

Larsen-Freeman, D. 1983. Training teachers or educating a teacher? In J. Alatis, H. H. Stern, and P. Strevens (eds.). *Georgetown University Roundtable on Languages and Linguistics,* Washington, D.C.: Georgetown University Press.

Larsen-Freeman, D. 1990. Towards a theory of second language teaching. In J.

Alatis (ed.). *Georgetown University Roundtable on Languages and Linguistics*. Washington, D.C.: Georgetown University Press.

Liskin-Gasparro, J. 1984. The ACTFL proficiency guidelines: A historical perspective. In T. Higgs (ed.), *Teaching for Proficiency: The Organizing Principle*. Lincolnwood, IL: National Textbook Co. 11–42.

Livingston, C., and Borko, H. 1989. Expert-novice differences in teaching: A cognitive analysis and implications. *Journal of Teacher Education* 40(4): 36–42.

Long, M. H. 1984. The effect of teachers' questioning patterns and wait-times. Dept. of ESL, University of Hawaii.

Long, M. H., and Crookes, G. 1992. Three approaches to task-based syllabus design. *TESOL Quarterly* 26(1): 27–56.

Lortie, D. 1975. *School Teacher: A Sociological Study*. Chicago: University of Chicago Press.

Mackinnon, A. 1987. Detecting reflection-in-action among pre-service teachers. *Teacher and Teacher Education* 3(2): 135–45.

Marland, P. W. 1987. Response to Clandinin and Connelly. *Journal of Curriculum Studies* 19(6): 507–9.

Marland, P. W. 1995. Implicit theories of teaching. In L. W. Anderson (ed.), *International Encyclopedia of Teaching and Teacher Education*, 2nd ed. New York: Pergamon. 131–6.

McGraw-Hill. 1993. *Reflecting Diversity: Multicultural Guidelines for Educational Publishing Professionals*. New York: Macmillan.

Medley, D. M. 1979. The effectiveness of teachers. In P. L. Peterson and H. J. Walberg (eds.), *Research on Teaching: Concepts, Findings and Implications*. Berkeley, CA: McCutchan.

Moran, P. R. 1996. "I'm not typical": Stories of becoming a Spanish teacher. In D. Freeman and J. C. Richards (eds.), *Teacher Learning in Language Teaching*. New York: Cambridge University Press. 125–53.

Morris, I. 1954. *The Art of Teaching English as a Living Language*. London: Macmillan.

Murphy-O'Dwyer, L. M. 1985. Diary studies as a method for evaluating teacher training. In J. C. Alderson (ed.), *Evaluation*. Oxford: Pergamon Press. 97–128.

Naiman, N.; Frohlich, M.; Stern, H. H.; and Todesco, A. 1978. *The Good Language Learner*. Toronto: Ontario Institute for Studies in Education.

Nunan, D. 1989. *Understanding Language Classrooms*. Hertfordshire: Prentice Hall.

Nunan, D. 1992. The teacher as decision-maker. In J. Flowerdew, M. Brock, and S. Hsia (eds.), *Perspectives on Second Language Teacher Education*. Hong Kong: City University of Hong Kong. 135–65.

Omaggio-Hadley, A. 1993. *Teaching Language in Context*, 2nd ed. Boston: Heinle & Heinle.

Oxford, R. 1990. *Learning Strategies: What Every Teacher Should Know*. New York: Newbury House.

Pak, J. 1986. *Find Out How You Teach*. Adelaide: National Curriculum Resource Centre.

Pang, K. C. 1992. *Lesson Planning*. Hong Kong: Longman.

Parker, W. C. 1984. Developing teachers' decision making. *Journal of Experimental Education* 52(4): 220–6.

197

References

Pennington, M. C. 1990. A professional development focus for the language teaching practicum. In J. C. Richards and D. Nunan (eds.), *Second Language Teacher Education*. New York: Cambridge University Press. 132–52.

Pennington, M. C., and Lee, Y. P. 1995. *Communicating in the Hong Kong Secondary English Classroom: The Evolution of Second Language Discourses*. Research Monograph No. 7. Department of English, City University of Hong Kong.

Pennycook, A. 1996. Review of pedagogy of multi-literacies: Designing social futures. *TESOL Quarterly* 30(1): 163–71.

Posner, G. 1985. *Field Experience: A Guide to Reflective Practice*. New York: Longman.

Powell, J. P. 1985. Autobiographical learning. In D. Boud, R. Keogh, and D. Walker (eds.), *Reflection: Turning Experience into Learning*. New York: Nichols Publishing. 41–51.

Prahbu, N. S. 1984. Procedural syllabuses. In J. E. Read (ed.), *Trends in Language Syllabus Design*. Singapore: Singapore University Press/RELC. 272–80.

Putorak, E. G. 1993. Facilitating reflective thought in novice teachers. *Journal of Teacher Education* 44(4): 288–95.

Rees-Miller, J. 1993. A critical appraisal of learner training: Theoretical bases and teaching implications. *TESOL Quarterly* 27(4): 679–90.

Richards, J. C. 1984. The secret life of methods. *TESOL Quarterly* 18(1): 7–24.

Richards, J. C. 1991. Content knowledge and instructional practice in second language teacher education. In J. Alatis (ed.), *Georgetown University Round Table on Languages and Linguistics*. Washington, D.C.: Georgetown University Press. 76–99.

Richards, J. C. (ed.). In press. *Teaching in Action: Case Studies from Second Language Classrooms*. Alexandria, VA: TESOL.

Richards, J. C., and Hino, N. 1983. Training ESOL teachers: The need for needs assessment. In J. E. Alatis, H. H. Stern, and P. Strevens (eds.), *Georgetown University Round Table on Languages and Linguistics*. Washington, D.C.: Georgetown University Press. 312–26.

Richards, J. C.; Ho, B.; and Giblin, K. 1996. Learning how to teach in the RSA Cert. In D. Freeman and J. C. Richards (eds.), *Teacher Learning in Language Teaching*. New York: Cambridge University Press. 242–59.

Richards, J. C., and Lockhart, C. 1991. Teacher development through peer observation. *TESOL Journal* 1(2): 7–11.

Richards, J. C., and Lockhart, C. 1994. *Reflective Teaching in Second Language Classrooms*. New York: Cambridge University Press.

Richards, J. C., and Nunan, D. (eds.). 1990. *Second Language Teacher Education*. New York: Cambridge University Press.

Richards, J. C., and Rodgers, T. 1984. *Approaches and Methods in Language Teaching*. New York: Cambridge University Press.

Richards, J. C.; Tung, P.; and Ng, P. 1992. The culture of the English language teacher: A Hong Kong example. *RELC Journal* 23(1): 81–103.

Rivers, W. 1964. *The Psychologist and the Foreign Language Teacher*. Chicago: University of Chicago Press.

Rivers, W. 1981. *Teaching Foreign Language Skills*. Chicago: University of Chicago Press.

Roderick, J. A. 1986. Dialogue writing: Context for reflecting on self as teacher and researcher. *Journal of Curriculum and Supervision* 1(4): 305–15.

Schon, D. A. 1983. *The Reflective Practitioner.* London: Temple Smith.

Schon, D. A. 1987. *Educating the Reflective Practitioner.* New York: Basic Books.

Senior, R. 1995. Teachers' craft knowledge: The importance of developing a positive group feeling in language classrooms. Paper presented at the third International Conference on Teacher Education in Language Teaching, Hong Kong, March 1995.

Shannon, P. 1987. Commercial reading materials, a technological ideology, and the deskilling of teachers. *The Elementary School Journal* 87(3): 307–29.

Shavelson, R. J., and Stern, P. 1981. Research on teachers' pedagogical thoughts, judgments, decisions, and behavior. *Review of Educational Research* 51: 455–98.

Shulman, L. S. 1986. Those who understand: Knowledge growth in teaching. *Educational Researcher* 15(2): 4–14.

Shulman, L. S. 1987. Knowledge and teaching: Foundations of the new reform. *Harvard Education Review* 57(1): 1–22.

Shulman, J. H. (ed.) 1992. *Case Methods in Teacher Education.* New York: Teachers College Press.

Skehan, P. 1996. A framework for the implementation of task-based instruction. *Applied Linguistics* 17(1): 38–62.

Smith, D. 1996. Teacher decision-making in the adult ESL classroom. In D. Freeman and J. Richards (eds.), *Teacher Learning in Language Teaching.* New York: Cambridge University Press. 197–216.

Spolsky, B. 1978. *Educational Linguistics: An Introduction.* Rowley, MA: Newbury House.

Spratt, M. 1994. *English for the Teacher.* Cambridge: Cambridge University Press.

Stern, H. H. 1983. *Fundamental Concepts of Language Teaching.* Oxford: Oxford Unversity Press.

Stevick, E. 1980. *Teaching Language: A Way and Ways.* Rowley, MA: Newbury House.

Strevens, P. D. 1976. A theoretical model of the language learning/teaching process. *Working Papers on Bilingualism.* 11: 129–52.

Studolsky, S. 1989. Is teaching really by the book? In P. W. Jackson and S. Haroutunian-Gordon (eds.), *From Socrates to Software: The Teacher as Text and the Text as Teacher.* Eighty-ninth Yearbook of the National Society for the Study of Education, Part 1. Chicago: University of Chicago Press. 159–84.

Swan, M. 1992. The textbook: Bridge or wall? *Applied Linguistics and Language Teaching* 2(1): 32–5.

Syllabus for Secondary Schools English. 1983. Hong Kong: Government Printer.

Tay, W. 1986. Teaching students how to plan: The dominant model and alternatives. *Journal of Teacher Education* 37(6): 6–12.

Tedick, D., and Walker, C. 1994. Second language teacher education: The problems that plague us. *Modern Language Journal* 78(3): 300–12.

Tetenbaum, T. J., and Mulkeen, T. A. 1986. Designing teacher education for the twenty-first century. *Journal of Higher Education* 57: 621–36.

Thornbury, S. 1991. Watching the whites of their eyes: The use of teaching-practice logs. *ELT Journal* 45(2): 140–6.

Tikunoff, W. S. 1985. *Developing Student Functional Proficiency for LEP Students.* Portland, OR: Northwest Regional Educational Laboratory.

References

Tsui, A. B. M. 1995. Exploring collaborative supervision in inservice teacher education. *Journal of Curriculum Supervision* 10(4): 346–71.

Tyler, R. 1949. *Basic Principles of Curriculum and Instruction.* Chicago: University of Chicago Press.

Ulichny, P. 1996. What's in a methodology? In D. Freeman and J. C. Richards (eds.), *Teacher Learning in Language Teaching.* New York: Cambridge University Press. 178–96.

Wajnryb, R. 1992. *Classroom Observation Tasks.* Cambridge: Cambridge University Press.

Walberg, H. 1977. Decisions and perceptions: New constructs for research on teaching effects. *Cambridge (UK) Journal of Education* 7(1): 12–20.

Werner, P. K., et al. 1995. Working with publishers. In P. Byrd (ed.), *Material Writer's Guide.* Boston: Heinle & Heinle. 173–214.

Willis, J. 1981. *Teaching English through English.* London: Longman.

Wong-Fillmore, L. 1985. When does teacher talk work as input? In S. Gass and C. Madden (eds.), *Input in Second Language Acquisition.* Rowley, MA: Newbury House. 17–50.

Woods, D. 1991. Teachers' interpretations of second language teaching curricula. *RELC Journal* 22(2): 1–19.

Woods, D. 1996. *Teacher Cognition in Language Teaching.* Cambridge: Cambridge University Press.

Woodward, A. 1993. Introduction: Learning from textbooks. In B. K. Britton, A. Woodward, and M. Binkley (eds.), *Learning from Textbooks: Theory and Practice.* Hillsdale, NJ: Erlbaum.

Woodward, T. 1992. *Ways of Training.* Harlow: Longman.

Yim, L. W. 1993. Relating teachers' perceptions of the place of grammar to their teaching practices. Master's thesis, National University of Singapore.

Yinger, R. J. 1987. Learning the language of practice. *Curriculum Inquiry* 17(3): 293–318.

Zahorik, J. A. 1986. Acquiring teaching skills. *Journal of Teacher Education* (March-April): 21–5.

Zeichner, K. M. 1987. Preparing reflective teachers: An overview of instructional strategies which have been employed in pre-service teacher education. *International Journal of Educational Research* 11: 565–75.

Zeichner, K. M., and Liston, D. 1987. Teaching student teachers to reflect. *Harvard Educational Review* 57(1): 23–48.

Zeichner, K., and Liston, D. 1996. *Reflective Teaching: An Introduction.* Mahwah, NJ: Lawrence Erlbaum.

Zeichner, K.; Tabachnik, B. R.; and Densmore, K. 1987. Individual, institutional and cultural influences on the development of teachers' craft knowledge. In J. Calderhead (ed.), *Exploring Teachers' Thinking.* London: Cassell. 21–59.

Author index

Subject index

accuracy, 58
ACTFL Proficiency Guidelines, 40–1
acting, 146, 162
action research, 28, 42, 153
active teaching, 38
adaptability, 118
affective factors, 115
American Council on the Teaching of Foreign Languages, 40–1
appraisal, 146, 162
Appropriate Methodology and Social Context, 12
Art of Teaching English as a Living Language, The, 43
artist metaphor, 43
Asian cultural background, 68
audio recording, 23, 24, 43
audiolingualism, 2, 5, 34
audiovisual aids, 96
Australia, 76
authenticity, 51
autobiography, 22

BA TESL degree, 87, 173, 176, 177–80
Barrett's taxonomy, 137
Basic Principles of Curriculum and Instruction, 104
behavior, student, 143
behavioral objectives model, 103–4
behaviorism, 35, 65
belief systems. *See* teacher beliefs
Breaking Rules, 33
British Council, 52, 108

Canada, 69, 70
case studies, 25, 79–80, 81–5, 119, 153
certification, 5

checking concepts, 75
China, 83–5. *See also* Hong Kong
choral repetition, 5
City University of Hong Kong, 176, 177
classroom dynamics, 68
classroom management, 76
classroom observation. *See* observation
coding forms, 145
cognitive processes, 14, 80–1, 132
cognitive psychology, 50, 66, 75
communication skills, 1, 6–8, 15, 18
communicative language teaching, 2, 5, 39–40, 45–7, 59, 107, 128, 178–80, 181, 186–7
Community Language Learning, 42
conceptual organization, 49–50
conditioning, 35
conformity, 58
content domains, 1–14
contesting, 146, 147, 162
contextual knowledge, 1, 12–13, 15
craft metaphor, 44
critical reflection. *See* reflection
critical thinking, 21, 144
culture of teaching, 51–3
Curran-style lecture, 18
curriculum-centered perspective, 69, 72–3

decision making, 1, 10–12, 15, 43, 44; and belief systems, 51, 55; and improvisational performance, 114–19; interactive, 24, 73–8, 118; and lesson plans, 58–60, 106–7; and planning, 24; preactive, 117–18
deconstruction, 25, 79, 118, 135